SMA

Necrology

Nécrologe

25 Oct 2023

Society of African Missions
Société des Missions Africaines

Via della Nocetta, 111, 00164 ROMA

© 2023 SMA publications

ISBN : 9798862753776

Available on all Amazon websites / Pour toute commande s'adresser aux sites amazon.

Cover image: Courtesy Level_Up_Filming, pixabay.com

Cover design: Brice Afferi SMA

The butterfly represents transformation and the resurrection.

Le papillon représente la transformation et la résurrection.

Table of Contents

Table des matières

Country codes

Codes de pays

AT	AUSTRIA	AUTRICHE
B	BELGIUM	BELGIQUE
BEN	BENIN	BENIN
CD	D.R. CONGO	R.D CONGO
CDN	CANADA	CANADA
CHE	SWITZERLAND	SUISSE
CIV	IVORY COAST	COTE D'IVOIRE
D	GERMANY	ALLEMAGNE
DZ	ALGERIA	ALGERIE
E	SPAIN	ESPAGNE
ET	EGYPT	EGYPTE
ETH	ETHIOPIA	ETIOPIE
F	FRANCE	FRANCE
GB	GREAT BRITAIN	GRANDE BRETAGNE
I	ITALY	ITALIE
IND	INDIA	INDE
IRL	IRELAND	IRLANDE
LB	LEBANON	LIBAN
LU	LUXEMBOURG	LUXEMBOURG
NL	NETHERLANDS	PAYS-BAS
PHL	PHILIPPINES	PHILIPPINES
PL	POLAND	POLOGNE
RCA	CENTRAL AFRICAN REPUBLIC	REPUBLIQUE CENTRAFRICAINE
TG	TOGO	TOGO
USA	UNITED STATES OF AMERICA	ETATS UNIS D'AMERIQUE

Lecture du Nécrologe

January - Janvier

1

1939 Cork (Ireland)   James McNICHOLAS, Achonry (IRL), 44

… is read as follows:

On the first of January 1939 at Cork, Ireland
Father James McNicholas,
of the diocese of Achonry, in Ireland,
died at the age of 44 years.

… se lit ainsi :

Le 1er janvier 1939, à Cork en Irlande,
est mort le Père James McNicholas,
du diocèse d'Achonry, en Irlande,
à l'âge de 44 ans.

Daily Necrology

Nécrologe journalier

January/ Janvier

1

1939	Cork (Ireland)	James McNICHOLAS, Achonry (IRL), 44
1974	Cork (Ireland)	Michael CAVANAGH, Clonfert (IRL), 55
1996	Maastricht (Netherlands)	Pierre CRUTS, Roermond (NL), 83
2020	Nantes (France)	Bernard GUILLARD, Nantes (F), 81

2

1912	Bordeaux (France)	Joseph LANG, Strasbourg (F), 43, Vicaire Apostolique de la Côte du Bénin.
1942	Kumasi (Ghana)	Gerard REIMERT, Utrecht (NL), 38
1970	La Croix-Valmer (France)	François LE PORT, Vannes (F), 80
1990	Castlebar (Ireland)	Francis CONVEY, Tuam (IRL), 77
2003	Dublin (Ireland)	Michael A HIGGINS, Tuam (IRL), 72
2012	Montferrier (France)	Denys BELLUT, Nanterre (F), 86
2014	Cadier en Keer (Netherlands)	Wilhelmus van FRANKENHUIJSEN, Utrecht (NL), 85
2018	Maastricht (Netherlands)	Jan DEKKER, Haarlem-Amsterdam (NL), 94

3

1949	Warri (Nigeria)	John HEALY, Ferns (IRL), 62
1985	Barr (France)	Joseph ZIELIŃSKI, Kraków (PL), 79
1986	Montferrier (France)	Louis MARCHANT, Angers (F), 75, frère Etienne.
2013	Jersey City (U.S.A.)	Clark YATES, Saint Augustine (USA), 87

4

1972	Saint-Pierre (France)	Alphonse STECK, Strasbourg (F), 79
1973	Abidjan (Côte d'Ivoire)	André LOMBARDET, Besançon (F), 54
1978	Cork (Ireland)	Daniel O'CONNELL, Kerry (IRL), 82
1989	Galway (Ireland)	Richard FINN, Tuam (IRL), 76, former Bishop of Ibadan, Nigeria.
2006	Saint-Pierre (France)	Pierre FRITSCH, Strasbourg (F), 84, frère.
2012	Montferrier (France)	Pierre BONNET, Nantes (F), 91

5

1974	Paris (France)	Roger COLLIN, Saint-Brieuc (F), 56
1987	Arnhem (Netherlands)	Adriaan JUYN, Rotterdam (NL), 74
1990	Cork (Ireland)	Luke CARNEY, Tuam (IRL), 74
2012	Paris (France)	Francis HÉRY, Saint-Brieuc (F), 87

6

1953	Ossés (France)	Joseph HÉGUY, Bayonne (F), 47
1958	Echt (Netherlands)	Jacques van LEUVEN, Roermond (NL), 69
2002	Galway (Ireland)	Patrick GANTLY, Galway (IRL), 83
2007	Colmar (France)	Georges ERHARD, Strasbourg (F), 91
2022	Cadier en Keer (Netherland)	Koos JANSSEN, Rotterdam (NL), 85

7

1908	Lagos (Nigeria)	Emile MUNCH, Strasbourg (F), 29
1942	La Croix-Valmer (France)	Simeon ALBENIZ, Calahorra (E), 67
1961	Mulhouse (France)	Auguste BAUMANN, Strasbourg (F), 71
1965	Lyon (France)	Claudius ROUSSEL, Clermont-Ferrand (F), 57
1970	Nantes (France)	André HUCHET, Rennes (F), 46
1971	Chaponost (France)	Claude BALLIGAND, Autun (F), 70, frère Antonin.
1985	Ballymoney (Ireland)	James A McAFEE, Down & Connor (IRL), 75
1989	Uromi (Nigeria)	Michael GRACE, Killaloe (IRL), 70

8

1933	Rezé (France)	Victor MOISON, Rennes (F), 80
1967	Cork (Ireland)	Andrew O'ROURKE, Killaloe (IRL), 54
1970	Lyon (France)	Benoît DESSARCE, Saint-Étienne (F), 68
1973	Heemstede (Netherlands)	Kees TUKKER, Haarlem (NL), 59
1994	Melbourne (U.S.A.)	Cyril J DONNELLY, Middlesbrough (GB), 83
2002	Sélestat (France)	Henri BANNWARTH, Strasbourg (F), 82
2017	Montferrier (France)	Jean-Paul GOURNAY, Bayeux (F), 74

9

1902	Lagos (Nigeria)	Charles SPIESER, Strasbourg (F), 36
1949	Marseille (France)	Alfred LAURENT, Le Puy (F), 68
1964	Waterford (Ireland)	Thomas HURST, Cork (IRL), 86
1999	St Brieuc (France)	Michel KERDERRIEN, St Brieuc (F), 66
2009	Montréal (Canada)	Mme Anne-Marie LOUBIER, Montréal (CDN), 30, laïque associée.

10

1923	Lyon (France)	Georges OLLIER, Le Puy (F), 72, frère.
1931	Paris (France)	Charles GOFFINET, Dijon (F), 60, frère.
1933	La Croix-Valmer (France)	Jules POIRIER, Angers (F), 88
1934	Chanly (Belgique)	Alphonse FURODET, Le Puy (F), 67
1982	Teaneck (U.S.A.)	Albert TURCOTTE, Boston (USA), 62
1987	Montauban (France)	Léon TAVERNIER, Lille (F), 76
2004	Cork (Ireland)	Matthew GILMORE, Tuam (IRL), 88

11

1967	Kumasi (Ghana)	Piet van STRIEN, s'Hertogenbosch (NL), 45
1982	Arnhem (Netherlands)	Gerard POT, Utrecht (NL), 82
2004	Montpellier (France)	Gabriel CHOTARD, Nantes (F), 80
2008	Montferrier (France)	Roger ERHEL, Saint-Brieuc (F), 87
2018	Montferrier (France)	Marcel DUSSUD, Lyon (F), 83

12

1925	Betu (Liberia)	John BARRY, Kerry (IRL), 24
1948	Nantes (France)	Léon HÉRITEAU, Luçon (F), 29
1992	Cork (Ireland)	John G LEE, Cashel & Emly (IRL), 86
1993	Ibadan (Nigeria)	Kevin CARROLL, Liverpool (GB), 72
2008	Bari (Italie)	Mme Tina STEFANACHI, (I), Membre Honoraire.

13

1959	Heerlen (Netherlands)	Gerard ELBERS, s'Hertogenbosch (NL), 49
1960	Englewood (U.S.A.)	Robert STITT, Derry (IRL), 62
1961	Ueberstrass (France)	Antoine BRUNGARD, Strasbourg (F), 64
1982	Bondoukou (Côte d'Ivoire)	Angelo BIANCO, Albenga (I), 38, prêtre associé.
1982	Saint-Pierre (France)	Robert KREMSER, Strasbourg (F), 75, frère.
1985	Oosterbeek (Netherlands)	Wout SAMUELS, Rotterdam (NL), 77
1989	Cork (Ireland)	John HORAN, Glasgow (GB), 67
1993	Obernai (France)	Joseph NONNENMACHER, Strasbourg (F), 85
2007	Cork (Ireland)	David HUGHES, Dublin (IRL), 89

14

1885	Zagazig (Égypte)	Cyprien MALEN, Vannes (F), 38
1998	Eindhoven (Netherlands)	Gerard van de WEIJDEN, s'Hertogenbosch (NL), 87
2017	Heerlen (Netherlands)	Joseph van UUM, Utrecht (NL), 87
2020	Kilnadeema (Ireland)	Patrick J. M. KELLY, Clonfert (IRL), 66
2022	Haute Goulaine (France)	Jean THÉBAULT, Rennes (F), 90

15

1891	Saltpond (Ghana)	Josef GROEBLI, Saint-Gall (CHE), 26
1909	Tanta (Égypte)	Claude CADOR, Lyon (F), 64
1950	Baden (Suisse)	Peter FUST, Saint-Gall (CHE), 57
1991	Cork (Ireland)	Patrick J MURPHY, Ferns (IRL), 78
1993	Cork (Ireland)	Bernard DERVIN, Elphin (IRL), 76

16

1929	La Croix-Valmer (France)	Édouard ZIMMERMANN, Strasbourg (F), 66
1941	Savannah (USA)	Célestin MONPOINT, Strasbourg (F), 57
1964	Cork (Ireland)	James HOLLAND, Ross (IRL), 47
1980	Sommerville (USA)	Thomas O'DONNELL, Boston (USA), 47
1983	Muron (France)	Henri THOMAS, Nantes (F), 59

17

1894	Lyon (France)	Jean-Baptiste CHAUSSE, Saint-Étienne (F), 48, Vicaire Apostolique de la Côte du Bénin.
1932	Cork (Ireland)	Francis YOUNG, Killaloe (IRL), 36
1975	Maroué (France)	Joseph BOULAIRE, Saint-Brieuc (F), 51
1984	Naples (U.S.A.)	Peter J O'CONNELL, Killala (IRL), 48
1984	Newcastle (Ireland)	Philip O'SHEA, Kildare (IRL), 72
2006	Ndola (Zambia)	Fergus CONLAN, Dromore (IRL), 66
2009	Montferrier (France)	Alexandre COLSON, Namur (B), 85
2020	Troyes (France)	Max VIVIER, Lyon (F), 78

18

1979	Le Caire (Égypte)	Jean-Paul NÉDÉLEC, Quimper (F), 57
2006	Morteau (France)	Joseph CHOPARD, Besançon (F), 83
2010	Montferrier (France)	Joseph LASKA, Chetmno (PL), 94, frère.
2013	Prinquiau (France)	Guy OLLIVAUD, Nantes (F), 74

19

1958	Le Caire (Égypte)	Alexandre PAGÉS, Le Puy (F), 81
1995	Kimbongo (R D Congo)	Edouard GRAAS, Liège (B), 66
1999	Cadier en Keer (Netherlands)	Huub LEMMERLING, Roermond (NL), 83
1999	Cork (Ireland)	Fintan P NELLY, Galway (IRL), 79
2013	Cadier en Keer (Netherlands)	Cornelis Z PRIEMS, 's-Hertogenbosch (NL), 92

20

1883	Lagos (Nigeria)	Jean-Paul POURET, Bayonne (F), 36
1892	Obermorschwihr (France)	Paul BREY, Strasbourg (F), 24
1920	Andlau (France)	Casimir SCHIMPFF, Strasbourg (F), 82
1943	Haguenau (France)	Edmond MUTSCHLER, Strasbourg (F), 65
1944	Saint-Pierre (France)	Joseph WERLÉ, Strasbourg (F), 61
1945	(France)	Mme Françoise Marguerite LAURENS, (F), Membre Honoraire.
1973	Georgetown (U.S.A.)	Anthony McANDREW, Killala (IRL), 73
1989	Cadier en Keer (Netherlands)	Louis MOONEN, Roermond (NL), 83
2000	Cadier en Keer (Netherlands)	Nico PRONK, Haarlem (NL), 79
2005	Cork (Ireland)	Laurence SKELLY, Dublin (IRL), 79
2005	Montferrier (France)	Michel DURAND, Nantes (F), 85
2010	Dublin (Ireland)	John MOORE, Dublin (IRL), 68, Evêque de Bauchi (Nigeria).
2010	Bruyères (Belgique)	Georges LEJEUNE, Malines-Bruxelles (B), 88

21

1947	Lyon (France)	Firmin LOISEAU, Poitiers (F), 23, séminariste.
1978	Nijmegen (Netherlands)	Arie de KOK DE, Rotterdam (NL), 70
1986	Oosterbeek (Netherlands)	Henk SOUTBERG, Haarlem (NL), 74
1988	Montferrier (France)	Pierre PETITJEAN, Besançon (F), 76
2003	Montferrier (France)	Yves CALVEZ, Quimper (F), 79
2016	Sarrebourg (France)	M. Antoine THOMAS, Metz (F), 92, Membre Honoraire.
2023	Montferrier (France)	Michel DUJARIER, Tours (F), 91, Membre honoraire.

22

1879	Nice (France)	François CLOUD, Périgueux (F), 43
2011	Strasbourg (France)	Gilbert ANTHONY, Belfort (F), 78
2017	Montferrier (France)	Rene GROSSEAU, Nantes (F), 85

23

1956	Browntown (Ireland)	Thomas BARTLEY, Tuam (IRL), 58
1982	Cotonou (Bénin)	Mgr Moïse DURAND, Cotonou (BEN), 86, Membre Honoraire.
1983	Erstein (France)	Jean JACOBY, Metz (F), 73
1994	Cork (Ireland)	Anthony McDONAGH, Tuam (IRL), 76
1995	Weitbruch (France)	Marcel LICKEL, Strasbourg (F), 76
1997	Coutances (France)	Georges CADEL, Coutances (F), 85, prêtre associé.
2012	Makalondi (Niger)	Yves PELLETIER, Saint-Claude (F), 62
2017	Madurai (India)	Peter Pandi NAYAGAM, Madurai (IND), 52
2017	Cork (Ireland)	James F KIRSTEIN, Cork & Ross (IRL), 82
2018	Montferrier (France)	Louis JACQUOT, Saint-Dié (F), 105

24

1940	Heerlen (Netherlands)	Alfons HAKENS, Roermond (NL), 25, seminarian.
1941	Lyon (France)	Charles LAROCHE, Nancy (F), 81
1977	Rezé (France)	Victor CHOIMET, Nantes (F), 91
1991	Tenafly (U.S.A.)	Adolph GALL, Sioux City (USA), 93
1994	Sélestat (France)	Gustave KLERLEIN, Strasbourg (F), 76
2014	Montferrier (France)	Paul GOTTE, Lyon (F), 87

25

1945	Cork (Ireland)	Patrick O'HERLIHY, Cork (IRL), 53
1974	Tanguieta (Benin)	Raymond MALO, Nantes (F), 69
1979	Rosmalen (Netherlands)	Franz GEIER, Linz (AT), 82, brother.
2001	Edinburgh (Scotland)	Mlle Margaret ASPINALL, Salford (GB), lay associate.
2002	Strasbourg (France)	Gérard ALTHUSER, Strasbourg (F), 69

26

1943	Le Caire (Égypte)	Ambroise LE CORRE, Vannes (F), 58
1959	Cork (Ireland)	Francis McNAMARA, Cork (IRL), 65
1966	Abidjan (Côte d'Ivoire)	Clément AUDRAIN, Nantes (F), 58
1966	Cotonou (Dahomey)	Jean-Marie BAUDU, Rennes (F), 71, Frère Benoît.
1986	Montferrier (France)	Henri BOUIX, Vannes (F), 79
1996	Saint-Pierre (France)	Pierre ROMANIAK, Poznań (PL), 78
1998	Montferrier (France)	Jean Baptiste URVOY, Quimper (F), 89

27

1952	Cork (Ireland)	Patrick DEASY, Achonry (IRL), 67, brother.
1961	Apeldoorn (Netherlands)	Julien TILLEMAN, Utrecht (NL), 72, brother Ignatius.
1970	Arnhem (Netherlands)	Laurens VERMULST, 's-Hertogenbosch (NL), 65
1981	Nijmegen (Netherlands)	Piet DERICKX, Rotterdam (NL), 75
1996	Maastricht (Netherlands)	Piet GIEBELS, 's-Hertogenbosch (NL), 81
2014	Ouidah (Bénin)	Théophile VILLAÇA, Cotonou (BEN), 84, Membre Honoraire.
2021	Montferrier (France)	Athanase LE BERRE, Quimper (F), 86

28

1944	Marseille (France)	Jean GRANDO, Vannes (F), 63
1983	Tucson (U.S.A.)	Maurice McCARTHY, Cloyne (IRL), 63
1991	Maastricht (Belgique)	Hubert WIJNANS, Luik (B), 83
2007	Cadier en Keer (Netherlands)	Wim JANSMAN, Utrecht (NL), 77
2009	Cork (Ireland)	Patrick CARROLL, Liverpool (GB), 84
2023	Cadier en Keer (Netherland)	Willy ZIJLSTRA, Groningen-Leeuwarden (NL), 92

29

1955	Marino (Italie)	Louis GIRE, Reims (F), 55
1970	Cork (Ireland)	Stephen HARRINGTON, Ross (IRL), 71, 8ème Supérieur Général.
1975	Oosterbeek (Netherlands)	Joseph MOUREN, Roermond (NL), 93
1984	Cork (Ireland)	Michael J O'SHEA, Kerry (IRL), 63
1999	Newry (Ireland)	Vincent E BOYLE, Derry (IRL), 78
2002	Tchébébé (Togo)	André BOUHELIER, Besançon (F), 60
2003	Cork (Ireland)	Robert V WISEMAN, Cork (IRL), 73
2013	Craigavon (Ireland)	Martin NOLAN, Ferns (IRL), 78
2016	Harper (Liberia)	Beth OTTING, Waukon (USA), 52, lay associate.

30

1904	Rezé (France)	Louis JAMET, Saint-Brieuc (F), 26, frère.
1917	Asaba (Nigeria)	Carlo ZAPPA, Milano (I), 56, préfet apostolique de la Nigeria occidentale.
1923	Cotonou (Dahomey)	Charles VACHERET, Besançon (F), 58
1947	Cork (Ireland)	Stephen KYNE, Tuam (IRL), 75, Prefect Apostolic of Liberia.
1952	Corchiano (Italie)	Giovanni PIERGENTILI, Civita Castellana (I), 70
1981	Montferrier (France)	Édouard BEILLEVAIRE, Nantes (F), 80
2007	Cork (Ireland)	Christopher MURPHY, Kilmore (IRL), 88
2012	Cork (Ireland)	Mary (Sadie) MCDONAGH, (Sadie) (IRL), 87, Honorary Member.
2020	Cork (Ireland)	Francis E FUREY, Derry (IRL), 78

31

1902	La Croix-Valmer (France)	Alexandre GAUZIC, Rennes (F), 38, frère.
1945	Thorenc (France)	Michel HAY, Poitiers (F), 28, séminariste.
1953	Cork (Ireland)	Michael O'FLYNN, Limerick (IRL), 56
1966	Aalbeek (Netherlands)	Cornelius de ROY, Haarlem (NL), 60
1977	Tuam (Ireland)	John HEANEY, Tuam (IRL), 80
1977	Wissembourg (France)	Aloyse KOELTZ, Strasbourg (F), 70
1997	New York (U.S.A.)	Louis NASSER, Héliopolis (ET), 71
2000	Cork (Ireland)	Patrick O'NEILL, Dublin (IRL), 87
2007	Airdrie (Great Britain)	Joseph McANDREW, Glasgow (GB), 79

February / Février

1

1946	Springfield (U.S.A.)	Francis WEISS, Strasbourg (F), 65
1982	Maastricht (Hollande)	Emmanuel KENNIS, 's-Hertogenbosch (NL), 87
1985	Cork (Ireland)	Florence McCARTHY, Ross (IRL), 77
1986	Trimbach (France)	Wendelin HEINRICH, Strasbourg (F), 75
1999	Manchester (Great Britain)	Alfred BICKERTON, Leeds (GB), 85
2005	Cork (Ireland)	Thomas HIGGINS, Elphin (IRL), 86
2010	Cork (Ireland)	Christopher (Christy) O'SULLIVAN, Cork (IRL), 91, Membre Honoraire.
2013	Montferrier (France)	Michel DURIF, Lyon (F), 88
2018	Cork (Ireland)	Thomas FITZGERALD, brother; Kerry (IRL), 99

2

1895	Lagos (Nigeria)	Pierre SÉDANT, Lyon (F), 35
1926	Cork (Ireland)	Desmond RYAN, Cashel (IRL), 30
1929	Anglet (France)	Alfred-Marie-Alexandre DANJOU DE LA GARENNE, Bayonne (F), 80, Membre Honoraire.
1939	Haguenau (France)	Kilien ZERR, Strasbourg (F), 29
1969	Ballinafad (Ireland)	John LEVINS, Armagh (IRL), 78
2003	Cadier en Keer (Netherlands)	Theo GÖRTZ, Roermond (NL), 89
2007	Montferrier (France)	Francis PLUMELET, Nantes (F), 90

3

1951	Duékoué (Côte d'Ivoire)	Eugène THÊTE, Belley (F), 30
1952	Poitiers (France)	Louis CAILLAUD, Poitiers (F), 39
1976	Daloa (Côte d'Ivoire)	Jean ALLOATTI, Grenoble (F), 48
1980	Heerlen (Netherlands)	Antoon BERGERS, Rotterdam (NL), 81
1988	Cork (Ireland)	+William R FIELD, Cork (IRL), 80, Former Bishop of Ondo (Nigeria).

4

1939	Benha (Égypte)	Henri THIBAUD, Nantes (F), 53
1972	Ozoro (Nigeria)	Thomas HASSETT, Dublin (IRL), 35
1979	Rezé (France)	Gabriel VAUTHIER, Nantes (F), 75, frère.
1995	Enniskillen (Ireland)	James WHITTAKER, Clogher (IRL), 80
2004	Cork (Ireland)	James FLANAGAN, Down & Connor (IRL), 84
2012	Montferrier (France)	+Pierre ROUANET, Albi (F), 94, Ancien Evêque de Daloa, Côte d'Ivoire.
2016	Cork (Ireland)	Thomas GORMAN, Kildare & Leighlin (IRL), 94

5

1947	Courpière (France)	Louis PIREYRE, Clermont-Ferrand (F), 68
1958	Sainte-Foy (France)	Célestin PAICHOUX, Rennes (F), 82
1972	Lyon (France)	Pierre BERNARD, Nantes (F), 70
1981	London (Great Britain)	James O'REILLY, Westminster (GB), 39
1984	Portrane (Ireland)	Timothy CADOGAN, Ross (IRL), 87
1989	Sapele (Nigeria)	Joseph STEPHENS, Tuam (IRL), 73
1999	Montferrier (France)	Georges KERLÉVÉO, St Brieuc (F), 86
2001	Helmstedt (Germany)	Cornelius POTTERS, Breda (NL), 91
2011	Nijmegen (Netherlands)	Maarten WESSELING, Rotterdam (NL), 73
2013	Aubenas (France)	Joseph ARSAC, Le Puy (F), 81
2019	Montferrier (France)	François MARGERIT, Le Puy (F), 91

6

1892	Nice (France)	Georges ULRICH, Strasbourg (F), 28
1953	Lomé (Togo)	Jacques HEGGER, Roermond (NL), 34
1961	La Croix-Valmer (France)	Émile BARRIL, Grenoble (F), 87
1969	Cork (Ireland)	Patrick KILLEEN, Killaloe (IRL), 46
2009	Downpatrick (Ireland)	Henry CASEY, Down & Connor (IRL), 67
2017	Montferrier (France)	Louis PERROCHAUD, Nantes (F), 94

7

1945	Sainte-Foy (France)	Ambroise PRIOUL, Rennes (F), 53
1972	Toulon (France)	Joseph MIET, Poitiers (F), 71
2001	La Marne (France)	Joseph MICHAUD, Nantes (F), 77, Membre Honoraire.
2002	Mierlo-Hout (Netherlands)	Frits BOLLEN, 's-Hertogenbosch (NL), 94
2004	Lauzerte (France)	Casimir BADOC, Rodez (F), 86

8

1892	Asaba (Nigeria)	Josué CRÉTAZ, Aosta (I), 34
1946	Le Caire (Egypte)	Patrick LYNN, Limerick (IRL), 33
1949	Ho (Ghana)	Bertus BERNTS, 's-Hertogenbosch (NL), 46
1951	Zinswald (France)	Louis BRUGGER, Strasbourg (F), 61
1951	Issele-Uku (Nigeria)	Charles BURR, Strasbourg (F), 69
1969	La Croix-Valmer (France)	Pierre BRÉTÉCHÉ, Nantes (F), 82, Frère Pierre-Claver.
1970	Cotiakou (Dahomey)	Maxime CHAZAL, Clermont-Ferrand (F), 73
1972	Lyon (France)	Jean POTIRON, Nantes (F), 37, frère.
1979	Clermont-Ferrand (France)	Jean-Marie MAISONNEUVE, Nantes (F), 88, frère.
1992	Lomé (Togo)	Albert REIFF, Strasbourg (F), 72
2020	Parakou (Benin)	Jesús FERNANDEZ DE TROCONIZ, Vitoria (E), 77

9

1979	Cork (Ireland)	Martin KENNY, Tuam (IRL), 71
1980	Rezé (France)	Joseph RAINGEARD, Angers (F), 77

10

1980	Helmond (Netherlands)	Adriaan KEIJSERS, 's-Hertogenbosch (NL), 75
1981	Dublin (Ireland)	Kevin McKEOWN, Armagh (IRL), 73
1988	Cleethorpes (Great Britain)	Patrick M KELLY, Kildare & Leighlin (IRL), 83
2003	Montferrier (France)	Ambroise VEILLARD, Rennes (F), 84
2012	Galway (Ireland)	Patrick WHELAN, Tuam (IRL), 79
2020	Cork (Ireland)	Terence GUNN, Cork & Ross (IRL), 84

11

| 1981 | Ho (Ghana) | Nico STEEMERS, Utrecht (NL), 55 |
| 2004 | Montferrier (France) | Victor MERCIER, Saint-Brieuc (F), 90 |

12

1949	Lyon (France)	Eugène NAEGEL, Strasbourg (F), 76
1963	Bocanda (Côte d'Ivoire)	Jean-Claude DENNIEL, Nantes (F), 36
1987	Lucerne (Suisse)	Jacques FISCHER, Bâle (CHE), 91
1990	Cork (Ireland)	Denis MINIHANE, Ross (IRL), 84

13

1937	Ballinrobe (Ireland)	Eugene WYNNE, Clonfert (IRL), 22, seminarian.
1976	Nijmegen (Netherlands)	Gerard HOMBERGEN, 's-Hertogenbosch (NL), 64
1984	Castlebar (Ireland)	James GARRETT, Cashel (IRL), 71, brother.
1986	Saint-Pierre (France)	Albert DIEBOLD, Strasbourg (F), 75
2009	Haguenau (France)	Gilbert JUNG, Strasbourg (F), 63, Membre Honoraire.

14

1902	Ibadan (Nigeria)	Charles AUGIER, Belley (F), 31
1962	Chanly (Belgique)	Julien LE GLOAHEC, Vannes (F), 88
1980	Montferrier (France)	Jean-Marie SALAÜN, Quimper (F), 76, Frère Yves.
1987	Heerlen (Netherlands)	Chris FILIPPINI, 's-Hertogenbosch (NL), 81, frère.
1999	Sitard (Netherlands)	Gerard van HOUT, 's-Hertogenbosch (NL), 80

15

1866	Ouidah (Dahomey)	Justin BURLATON, Lyon (F), 35
1896	Oyo (Nigeria)	Jean-Marie CROHAS, Clermont-Ferrand (F), 30
1966	Cork (Ireland)	James McGUIRK, Dublin (IRL), 77
1968	Cadier en Keer (Netherlands)	Hubert JANSSEN, Roermond (NL), 67
1993	Barr (France)	Jules KRAUSS, Strasbourg (F), 85
1998	Montpellier (France)	Jean Marie HUET, Rennes (F), 83
2012	Cork (Ireland)	Michael CAHILL, Galway (IRL), 75
2017	Cork (Ireland)	Edward CASEY, Galway (IRL), 89

16

1918	Ouidah (Dahomey)	Camille BEL, Grenoble (F), 68
1942	Cork (Ireland)	Michael McKENNA, Armagh (IRL), 40, brother.
1971	Kumasi (Ghana)	Kees KLAVER, Rotterdam (NL), 57
2006	Montferrier (France)	François-Marie FLOCH, Quimper (F), 91, frère.

17

1928	Tanta (Égypte)	Alphonse BERLIOUX, Grenoble (F), 45
1960	Lyon (France)	Jean-André COLOMBET, Le Puy (F), 58
1973	New Milford (U.S.A.)	Alphonse SITTLER, Strasbourg (F), 79
1986	Strasbourg (France)	Victor HOLLENDER, Strasbourg (F), 78
1996	Magherafelt (Ireland)	John J MACKLE, Derry (IRL), 80
1997	Grenoble (France)	Louis ALLIBE, Grenoble (F), 69
2001	Cork (Ireland)	Edward HARRINGTON, Kerry (IRL), 85
2003	Akwatia (Ghana)	Antonius MANSHANDEN, Haarlem (NL), 69
2008	Bruxelles (Belgique)	Henri THEIZEN, Namur (B), 72
2010	Kumasi (Ghana)	Robertus CLOBUS, Groningen (NL), 72
2012	Montferrier (France)	Raymond PASCAL, Mende (F), 97
2019	Cork (Ireland)	Michael BRADY, Cork (IRL), 77
2021	Warrenpoint (Ireland)	Michael BOYLE, Derry (IRL), 96

18

1966	Strasbourg (France)	Frédéric KURZ, Strasbourg (F), 63
1973	Tanguieta (Dahomey)	Jean CLOUET, Nantes (F), 41
2006	Montferrier (France)	Joseph COLSON, Namur (B), 85
2013	Haguenau (France)	Jacques VAROQUI, Gap (F), 64

19

1915	Cadier en Keer (Netherlands)	Antoine VACHON, Lyon (F), 84, frère.
1941	Saint-Pierre (France)	Ernest ERHART, Strasbourg (F), 56
1942	Axim (Ghana)	Johan HEEMSKERK, Haarlem (NL), 28
1953	Tunis (Tunisie)	Émile MALASSENET, Paris (F), 55
1963	Aalbeek (Netherlands)	Wim van HOUT, 's-Hertogenbosch (NL), 49
2004	Montferrier (France)	Maurice DUQUESNE, Lille (F), 82

20

1947	Strasbourg (France)	Georges BRÉDIGER, Metz (F), 71
1961	Lyon (France)	Antoine CLEYET-MAREL, Lyon (F), 57
2006	Cork (Ireland)	James G LEE, Down & Connor (IRL), 81
2009	Montferrier (France)	Yves LE MIGNON, Quimper (F), 85
2013	Maastricht (Netherlands)	Antonius J HULSHOF, Utrecht (NL), 86

21

1898	Anécho (Togo)	Théodore VIALLE, Le Puy (F), 32
1948	Dinan (France)	Joseph HARTZ, Strasbourg (F), 63

22

1881	Tanta (Égypte)	Michael O'CARROLL, Cashel (IRL), 29
1929	Menton (France)	+Pierre KERNIVINEN, Saint-Brieuc (F), 53, Préfet Apostolique de Korhogo, Côte d'Ivoire.
1947	Lyon (France)	Jean-Baptiste BURGEL, Strasbourg (F), 62, frère.
1953	Vénissieux (France)	Julien PRAUD, Nantes (F), 63
1962	sur mer	Gérard CHAUVINEAU, Luçon (F), 23, séminariste.
1971	Ibadan (Nigeria)	Thomas MURRAY, Down & Connor (IRL), 65
2012	Montferrier (France)	Henri CHALOPIN, Poitiers (F), 91
2014	Cork (Ireland)	Sean RYAN, Armagh (IRL), 80
2020	Cork (Ireland)	Michael M EVANS, Southwark (GB), 89
2023	Cork (Ireland)	Fintan D DALY, Clonfert (IRL), 85

23

1900	Sainte-Anne-d'Évenos (France)	Alexandre DORGÈRE, Nantes (F), 45
1950	Zinswald (France)	Joseph HAGENBACH, Strasbourg (F), 74
1997	Cork (Ireland)	Michael CONWAY, Tuam (IRL), 79
2005	Maastricht (Netherlands)	Jan TILLIE, Roermond (NL), 79
2007	Montferrier (France)	Paul AILLERIE, Nantes (F), 75
2017	Saint Pierre (France)	Albert LIROT, Strasbourg (F), 80

24

1975	Monrovia (Liberia)	Alfred LOVE, Down & Connor (IRL), 63
1976	Sélestat (France)	Théodore KALBERMATTEN, Sion (CHE), 85, frère.
1979	Cork (Ireland)	Thomas DUFFY, Achonry (IRL), 81
1980	Montferrier (France)	Antoine RICHARD, Nantes (F), 80, frère.
2003	Maastricht (Netherlands)	Stef KERSTEN, Utrecht (NL), 82

25

1941	Assinie (Côte d'Ivoire)	Louis PARAGE, Luçon (F), 41
1943	Hasparren (France)	Albert PARTARRIEU, Bayonne (F), 30
1969	Montpellier (France)	Henri BARTHÉLEMY, Rodez (F), 55
1987	Montferrier (France)	Roger JOYEAU, Vannes (F), 72
2003	Sarrebourg (France)	Pascal MARIN, Belfort-Montbéliard (F), 66, frère.
2012	Cork (Ireland)	James REDMOND, Ferns (IRL), 80, brother.

26

1975	Tralee (Ireland)	John G O'NEILL, Kerry (IRL), 67
1979	Dongen (Netherlands)	Jacques VERHEUGD, Haarlem (NL), 79
1991	Nantes (France)	Jean-Louis BRÉHIER, Nantes (F), 88
1999	Cork (Ireland)	Francis P McGOVERN, Dublin (IRL), 78
2001	Rochdale (Great Britain)	Leonard WALKER, Salford (GB), 90, lay associate.
2016	Gênes (Italie)	Giuseppe, CAVALLI, Gênes (I), 87, Membre Honoraire.

27

1924	Grand-Lahou (Côte d'Ivoire)	Auguste GAULÉ, Rennes (F), 37
1947	Janzé (France)	Jules TIGEOT, Rennes (F), 78
2002	Paris (France)	John A FEELEY, Cork (IRL), 82, Membre Honoraire.
2007	Cork (Ireland)	John McCREANOR, Dromore (IRL), 87

28

1867	Porto-Novo (Dahomey)	Alphée JOLANS, Grenoble (F), 26
1974	Saint-Pierre (France)	Emile RIEBSTEIN, Strasbourg (F), 83
1986	Cork (Ireland)	Thomas M GREENE, Tuam (IRL), 83

March/ Mars

1

1899	Keta (Ghana)	Benjamin HAAS, Strasbourg (F), 25
1947	Kilcolgan (Ireland)	Peter ROGERS, Down & Connor (IRL), 38
1954	Abidjan (Côte d'Ivoire)	Jean-Baptiste VEST, Strasbourg (F), 64
1966	Abidjan (Côte d'Ivoire)	Georges MINKER, Metz (F), 38
2003	St-Jérôme (Canada)	Fernand ALAIN, Québec (CDN), 66
2006	Cork (Ireland)	Joseph BRENNAN, Hexham & Newcastle (GB), 80

2

1943	Saint-Pierre (France)	Henri HORN, Strasbourg (F), 68
1945	Tenafly (U.S.A.)	Joseph MARGREITHER, Strasbourg (F), 60
1959	Philadelphia (U.S.A.)	Charles CANAVAN, Down & Connor (IRL), 60
1963	La Croix-Valmer (France)	Joseph VALLÉE, Saint-Brieuc (F), 88
1966	Tenafly (U.S.A.)	Patrick FITZSIMONS, Dublin (IRL), 57
1981	Mittelbergheim (France)	Jean ANGST, Strasbourg (F), 68
1982	Orsett (Great Britain)	Cornelius D MURPHY, Cork (IRL), 60
1982	Huppaye (Belgique)	Jean TOUSSAINT, Namur (B), 60
1990	Montferrier (France)	Jacques BERTHO, Nantes (F), 87
1993	Ibadan (Nigeria)	Maurice MAGUIRE, Down & Connor (IRL), 75
1993	Arnhem (Netherlands)	Cor van OERS, 's-Hertogenbosch (NL), 79
1994	Montferrier (France)	Joseph LEMARIÉ, Nantes (F), 89
2002	Cotonou (Bénin)	René FAURITE, Viviers (F), 61
2011	Carcassonne (France)	Jean BIAU, Carcassonne (F), 95, Membre Honoraire.
2015	Cork (Ireland)	John CASEY, Cork (IRL), 84

3

1945	Lomé (Togo)	+Jean-Marie CESSOU, Quimper (F), 61, Vicaire apostolique de Lomé, Togo.
1961	Monrovia (Liberia)	+John M COLLINS, Ross (IRL), 72, Apostolic Vicar of Monrovia, Liberia.
1963	Lyon (France)	Henri MOUËZY, Rennes (F), 64
1969	Cork (Ireland)	John CONNOLLY, Cork (IRL), 58
1986	Cork (Ireland)	Thomas O'CONNOR, Cashel & Emly (IRL), 62
1992	Maastricht (Netherlands)	Harrie PORTIER, 's-Hertogenbosch (NL), 76

4

1867	Naufragé (Naufragé)	Joachim HALGAN, Nantes (F), 32
1867	Naufragé (Naufragé)	Barthélemy PUECH, Albi (F), 57
1934	Marseille (France)	Adrien BAUZIN, Saint-Etienne (F), 59
1956	La Croix-Valmer (France)	François LEBERT, Nantes (F), 76
1991	Frelinghien (France)	Jean-Marie FÉRA, Lille (F), 59
2004	Ingwiller (France)	André DEUTSCH, Strasbourg (F), 70

5

1904	Anécho (Togo)	Auguste CHOISNET, Laval (F), 29
1942	Toulouse (France)	Michel BOILLON, Besançon (F), 23, novice.
1960	Clonakilty (Ireland)	Henry BAKER, Dublin (IRL), 70
1981	Montferrier (France)	Joseph HUCHET, Luçon (F), 80

6

1871	Lagos (Nigeria)	Gonzague THOLLON, Grenoble (F), 32
1940	Dakar (Sénégal)	Jean FUCHS, Strasbourg (F), 41
1963	Saint-Pierre (France)	Camille RIEDLIN, Strasbourg (F), 57
1985	Winneba (Ghana)	Hans van de VEN, 's-Hertogenbosch (NL), 37
1993	Oosterbeek (Netherlands)	Jan BOVENMARS, Utrecht (NL), 75, brother.
2010	Montferrier (France)	Ange MABON, Vannes (F), 86
2015	Abidjan (Cote d'Ivoire)	Francesco ARNOLFO, Cuneo (I), 69
2020	Besançon (France)	Jean-Baptiste ZANCHI, Bergamo (I), 83, Membre honoraire.

7

1906	Porto-Novo (Dahomey)	Clément LAUBIAC, Nantes (F), 25
1922	Rezé (France)	Auguste LEBOUVIER, Angers (F), 75
1978	Mallow (Ireland)	James SAUL, Dublin (IRL), 80
1996	Ndola (Zambia)	Brendan MURRAY, Dublin (IRL), 58, brother.

8

1969	Oosterbeek (Netherlands)	Johannes ROTHOFF, Breda (NL), 72
1981	Corby (Great Britain)	John DESMOND, Cork (IRL), 72
1991	Barr (France)	Martin BATO, Strasbourg (F), 79, frère.
2008	Cadier en Keer (Netherlands)	Chris DOUMA, Utrecht (NL), 83

9

| 1902 | Zagnanado (Dahomey) | Pierre PICHAUD, Nantes (F), 32 |
| 1998 | Limerick (Ireland) | Terence BERMINGHAM, Meath (IRL), 65 |

10

1886	Porto-Novo (Dahomey)	Hippolyte BOZON, Tarentaise (F), 28
1954	Saint-Pierre (France)	Georges BADER, Strasbourg (F), 65
1963	Sainte-Foy (France)	Jean LECORNO, Vannes (F), 69, Frère Vincent.
2000	Norwood (U.S.A.)	Francis HYNES, Elphin (IRL), 81
2004	Notre-Dame des Landes (France)	Jean-Paul GUILLARD, Nantes (F), 66
2012	Abidjan (Côte d'Ivoire)	Gérard BARBIER, Grenoble (F), 73
2023	Cadier en Keer (Netherland)	Gé BUURMAN, Utrecht (NL), 85

11

1885	Abeokuta (Nigeria)	Antonio TETTAMANTI, Como (I), 32
1914	Lyon (France)	+Paul PELLET, Grenoble (F), 54, 3ème Supérieur général, ancien Vicaire Apostolique de la Côte du Bénin.
1959	at sea (Naufragé)	Philip CORISH, Ferns (IRL), 56
1970	Cork (Ireland)	Francis O'SHEA, Cork (IRL), 60
1977	Passaic (U.S.A.)	Louis IMBACH, Strasbourg (F), 85
1998	Metz (France)	Gilbert BREM, Strasbourg (F), 66
1998	Montferrier (France)	Paul GACHET, Fribourg (CHE), 94
2001	Montferrier (France)	André CASSARD, Nantes (F), 88
2020	Madrid (Espagne)	María Auxiliadora FERNÁNDEZ GARCÍA, Siguenza (E), 66, Membre honoraire.

12

1888	Nice (France)	Eugene COMBY, Lyon (F), 21, séminariste.
1921	La Croix-Valmer (France)	Armand PERRAUD, Nantes (F), 36
1965	La Croix-Valmer (France)	Armand BOURASSEAU, Luçon (F), 71
1972	Cork (Ireland)	Robert O'LEARY, Cork (IRL), 72
1976	Cork (Ireland)	Florence O'RIORDAN, Cork (IRL), 56
1978	Geest-Gerompont (Belgique)	Jean BRUGGEMANS, Malines-Bruxelles (B), 82
1984	Saint-Pierre (France)	+Joseph STREBLER, Strasbourg (F), 91, Ancien Archevêque de Lomé, Togo.
1984	Saint-Pierre (France)	Rémi BRUNGARD, Strasbourg (F), 95
1991	Montferrier (France)	Camille CHIROL, Grenoble (F), 85
1992	Lomé (Togo)	Guy KRAEMER, Paris (F), 58
1994	Barr (France)	+Émile DURRHEIMER, Strasbourg (F), 84, Ancien Evêque de Katiola, Côte d'Ivoire.

13

1909	Ibadan (Nigeria)	Pierre FOURAGE, Nantes (F), 33
1924	Cape Coast (Ghana)	+Ignace HUMMEL, Strasbourg (F), 54, Vicaire Apostolique de la Côte-de-l'Or.
1962	Arnhem (Netherlands)	Mathieu WOUTERS, Haarlem (NL), 79
1969	Paris (France)	Henri GIRARD, Le Mans (F), 80
1988	Cork (Ireland)	John MOORHEAD, Meath (IRL), 69
2003	Cork (Ireland)	William POWER, Cloyne (IRL), 79

14

1906	Axim (Ghana)	Nicolas SCHEIER, Metz (F), 24
1978	Liège (Belgique)	Joseph AALBERS, Utrecht (NL), 78
1992	Abidjan (Côte d'Ivoire)	Joseph PFISTER, Strasbourg (F), 81
1994	Dublin (Ireland)	Gerard FERGUS, Clonfert (IRL), 70
1995	Montferrier (France)	Albert CHAIZE, Lyon (F), 82
2002	Cork (Ireland)	John J BROWNE, Kerry (IRL), 86

15

1893	Elmina (Ghana)	Émile BURGEAT, Strasbourg (F), 25
1915	Strasbourg (France)	Alphonse GRASS, Strasbourg (F), 27
1943	Lyon (France)	Joseph GUÉNO, Nantes (F), 42
1984	Saverne (France)	Charles HAEFFNER, Strasbourg (F), 76
1993	Béoumi (Côte d'Ivoire)	Adrien JEANNE, Coutances (F), 55
2002	Winneba (Ghana)	Frits HEBBEN, Roermond (NL), 69

16

1944	Bitche (France)	Ludan ANTZ, Strasbourg (F), 62
1965	Abidjan (Côte d'Ivoire)	Paul LARVOR, Quimper (F), 47
1975	Parakou (Bénin)	Jean PRIGENT, Quimper (F), 50
1979	La Croix-Valmer (France)	Raymond GAVILLET, Annecy (F), 74, frère.
1985	Bouaké (Côte d'Ivoire)	Jean GRETER, Strasbourg (F), 47
2015	Cadier en Keer (Pays Bas)	Johannes Th WAGEMAKERS, Rotterdam (NL), 98

17

1962	Horn (Netherlands)	Antoon MEEUWSEN, 's-Hertogenbosch (NL), 68
1964	Brownshill (Great Britain)	John WOOD, Birmingham (GB), 61
1983	München-Gladbach (Germany)	Theo VENHOVENS, Munster (D), 73
1989	Strasbourg (France)	Czesław SWIERKOWSKI, Poznań (PL), 71
1993	Schiltigheim (France)	Antoine JUNG, Strasbourg (F), 75
2005	Montferrier (France)	François Marie ABGUILLERM, Quimper (F), 97, frère.
2020	Cork (Ireland)	James O'HEA, Cork & Ross (IRL), 93

18

1958	Le Caire (Égypte)	Claude FAILLANT, Lyon (F), 85
1972	Galway (Ireland)	Peter GILROY, Armagh (IRL), 62
1975	Belfast (Ireland)	Denis MAGUIRE, Down & Connor (IRL), 55
1979	Dundee (Scotland)	Denis HORGAN, Cork (IRL), 83
1982	Cadier en Keer (Netherlands)	Hendrik RUBIE, Roermond (NL), 88, frère Nicolas.
2017	Montferrier (France)	Hubert DAUDE, Nimes (F), 83

19

1975	Cork (Ireland)	Maurice B KELLY, Ross (IRL), 70
1978	Strasbourg (France)	Louis NOËL, Strasbourg (F), 65
1997	Castelbar (Ireland)	James HEALY, Killala (IRL), 83
2004	Amsterdam (Netherlands)	Tamis WEVER, Haarlem (NL), 67
2007	Bouaké (Côte d'Ivoire)	René HOC, Lille (F), 67

20

1936	East Saint-Louis (U.S.A.)	Joseph CRAWFORD, Liverpool (GB), 49
1937	Cotonou (Dahomey)	Toussaint JOLIF, Rennes (F), 64
1973	La Croix-Valmer (France)	Jean-Marie COSSET, Nantes (F), 83, Frère Gérard.
2000	Montferrier (France)	Georges GROS, Saint Claude (F), 86
2018	Bagamoyo (Tanzania)	Adam BARTKOWICZ, Tarnów (PL), 35
2020	Boves (Italie)	Dario FALCONE, Fossano (I), 82

21

1886	sur mer (Naufragé)	Auguste MOREAU, Lyon (F), 39
1955	Cork (Ireland)	Nicholas HEFFERNAN, Cloyne (IRL), 79
1963	Zeddam (Netherlands)	Anno REEKERS, Groningen (NL), 64

22

1900	Cape Coast (Ghana)	Ernst SULTZBERGER, Saint-Gall (CHE), 28
1924	Agenebode (Nigeria)	Pierre PIOTIN, Grenoble (F), 57
1970	Cork (Ireland)	John O'DOHERTY, Derry (IRL), 70
1999	Mulhouse (France)	Henri KUENEMANN, Strasbourg (F), 74
2009	Maastricht (Netherlands)	Dionysius van de LAAK, 's-Hertogenbosch (NL), 72
2009	Montpellier (France)	Louis GONON, Saint-Étienne (F), 78
2012	Montréal (Canada)	Jean-Paul PARISEAU, Québec (CDN), 81

23

1950	Héliopolis (Égypte)	+Jules GIRARD, Le Puy (F), 87, Vicaire Apostolique du Delta du Nil.
1952	Cotonou (Dahomey)	Paul FERLANDIN, Saint-Brieuc (F), 41
1977	Malo-les-Bains (France)	Charles WOISSELIN, Lille (F), 74, Frère Marie-Bernard.
1992	Hornerheide (Netherlands)	Piet FEIJEN, Roermond (NL), 57
2003	Montpellier (France)	Joseph MITTAINE, Saint-Claude (F), 78
2007	Newry (Ireland)	Peter DEVINE, Armagh (IRL), 73

24

1903	Impérié (Côte d'Ivoire)	Pierre RÉGUILLON, Grenoble (F), 23
1904	Illah (Nigeria)	Joseph STUDER, Strasbourg (F), 28
1909	Shendam (Nigeria)	Charles SCHUMACHER, Strasbourg (F), 25
1966	Cork (Ireland)	Thomas J HUGHES, Tuam (IRL), 67
1998	Montferrier (France)	Jacques DALBIN, Rodez (F), 84
2020	Cork (Ireland)	John Mc CORMACK, Tuam (IRL), 76

25

1933	Lyon (France)	Jean-Marie CHABERT, Lyon (F), 59, 5ème Supérieur général.
1955	Daloa (Cote d'Ivoire)	+Alphonse KIRMANN, Strasbourg (F), 68, Vicaire apostolique de Sassandra.
1969	Lyon (France)	Mélaine ROUGER, Rennes (F), 69
2013	Cork (Ireland)	Billy O'SULLIVAN, Cork (IRL), 79

26

1938	Abeokuta (Nigeria)	Thomas ROLT, Down & Connor (IRL), 26
1944	Sluis (Netherlands)	Rudolf HOEPPNER, Metz (F), 59
1973	Arnhem (Netherlands)	Jan van den BROEK, Roermond (NL), 64
1982	Cadier en Keer (Netherlands)	Cornelius COMMANDEUR, Haarlem (NL), 98, brother Joannes Berchmans.
1989	Arnhem (Netherlands)	Piet MEEUWENOORD, Rotterdam (NL), 81
2007	Cork (Ireland)	Michael KENNEDY, Kerry (IRL), 80

27

1878	Zagazig (Egypte)	Auguste MANSOUR, Oran (DZ), 1878, frère.
1946	Donaueschingen (Allemagne)	Jean GOASDUFF, Quimper (F), 23, séminariste.
1972	Cork (Ireland)	William FEGAN, Down & Connor (IRL), 75
1983	Soyaux (France)	Jacques MARSTEAU, Poitiers (F), 59
1984	Cork (Ireland)	James V YOUNG, Killaloe (IRL), 80
2010	London (Great Britain)	Richard Douglas BLUETT, Dublin (IRL), 75

28

1893	Cape Coast (Ghana)	Philippe HEILIGENSTEIN, Strasbourg (F), 24
1924	Abomey (Dahomey)	Henri VERMULST, 's-Hertogenbosch (NL), 30, frère.
1938	Sainte-Foy (France)	Antonin BRESSOL, Le Puy (F), 71
1950	La Croix-Valmer (France)	Jean VINSONNEAU, Toulouse (F), 79, frère.
1964	Abidjan (Côte d'Ivoire)	Alfred LEICHTNAM, Metz (F), 46
1980	Cadier en Keer (Netherlands)	Joannes BRANTJES, Haarlem (NL), 84, brother Odulphus.
2018	Montferrier (France)	Paul BRION, Angers (F), 85
2018	Ibadan (Nigeria)	Sylvester OGBOGU, Lagos (NGA), 46
2023	Montpellier (France)	Jean-Pierre MICHAUD, Nantes (F), 91

29

1900	Lyon (France)	Joseph LATARD, Chambéry (F), 29
1903	Grand-Bassam (Côte d'Ivoire)	Louis RAUSCHER, Strasbourg (F), 29
1935	Agnat (France)	+Jules MOURY, Le Puy (F), 62, Vicaire Apostolique de la Côte d'Ivoire.
1952	Ouidah (Dahomey)	+François STEINMETZ, Strasbourg (F), 84, Vicaire Apostolique du Dahomey.
1979	Agroyesum (Ghana)	Thijs WESTENBROEK, Groningen (NL), 59
1985	Cork (Ireland)	Stephen MURPHY, Cork (IRL), 73
1990	Montferrier (France)	Pierre LE GUEN, Quimper (F), 82

30

1893	Lyon (France)	Michael O'DONNELL, Tuam (IRL), 22, seminarian.
1904	Moossou (Côte d'Ivoire)	Joseph WOERTH, Strasbourg (F), 25
1922	Betu (Liberia)	Francis J McGOVERN, Ardagh (IRL), 24
1955	La Croix-Valmer (France)	Auguste BONNET, Le Puy (F), 71
1972	Héliopolis (Égypte)	Alexandre GAIGNOUX, Rennes (F), 70
1992	Albuquerque (U.S.A.)	Henry P J RUSSELL, Down & Connor (IRL), 79
1996	Saint-Chaffrey (France)	Bernard CHAPEAU, Nantes (F), 68
2012	Cork (Ireland)	Dermot HEALY, Kerry (IRL), 86
2013	Montferrier (France)	Clément CADIEU, Rennes (F), 98
2016	Chaponost (France)	Mme Dominique PILLARD, Lyon (F), 64, Membre Honoraire.

31

1957	Abidjan (Côte d'Ivoire)	André CARRÉ, Soissons (F), 32
2011	Cork (Ireland)	Gerard HACKETT, Ardagh (IRL), 80
2013	Castelnau (France)	Jaël Joseph ISOLÉRI, Lyon (F), 84
2021	Cork (Ireland)	Daniel BURKE, Waterford & Lismore (IRL), 88

April/ Avril

1

1945	Cork (Ireland)	Martin LAVELLE, Tuam (IRL), 53
1948	La Croix-Valmer (France)	Aimé POUPLIN, Nantes (F), 68, frère.
1956	La Croix-Valmer (France)	Théophile BOULANGER, Laval (F), 72
1964	Lyon (France)	Guy RABILLAT, Clermont-Ferrand (F), 43
1967	Tenafly (U.S.A.)	Pierre HESS, Strasbourg (F), 95

2

1942	Natchez (U.S.A.)	Denis O'SULLIVAN, Kerry (IRL), 65
1957	Dimbokro (Côte d'Ivoire)	Gaston TEILLET, Luçon (F), 36
1997	Cadier en Keer (Netherlands)	Jan MEULEPAS, 's-Hertogenbosch (NL), 78
1999	Cork (Ireland)	Anthony L MURPHY, Elphin (IRL), 84
2007	Heerlen (Netherlands)	Jacques van den BRONK, Haarlem (NL), 88
2008	Gênes (Italie)	Giacomo UBBIALI, Bergamo (I), 75
2020	Brest (France)	Roger LE ROCH, Quimper (F), 93

3

1895	Cape Coast (Ghana)	Emile MOSSER, Strasbourg (F), 25
1895	Tanta (Egypte)	Jean-Baptiste RIBAUD, Bale (CHE), 61, frère.
1905	Ouidah (Dahomey)	+Louis DARTOIS, Lille (F), 44, Vicaire Apostolique du Dahomey.
1972	Colchester (Great Britain)	Patrick McKAY, Down & Connor (IRL), 61
1986	New York (U.S.A.)	Philip C BAGNASCO, Brooklyn (USA), 59
2007	Cadier en Keer (Netherlands)	Herman van de LAAR, Roermond (NL), 88
2011	Cork (Ireland)	James CONLON, Cork (IRL), 83
2016	Cork (Ireland)	James J HIGGINS, Achonry (IRL), 92

4

1925	Lagos (Nigeria)	Joseph GEELS, Haarlem (NL), 30
1944	Toulon (France)	Aristide BLAIN, Rennes (F), 72
1945	Tenafly (U.S.A.)	John PRENDERGAST, Ossory (IRL), 67
1983	Cork (Ireland)	Michael CAROLAN, Kildare (IRL), 70
1992	Sarreguemines (France)	Pie SEILER, Metz (F), 73
1999	Madurai (India)	SAHAYARAJ, Madurai (IND), 25, seminarian.
2012	Montferrier (France)	André GUILLARD, Nantes (F), 84

5

1952	Lyon (France)	Lucien ARIAL, Nantes (F), 75
1956	Ballinamore (Ireland)	Patrick McHUGH, Achonry (IRL), 62
1987	Cork (Ireland)	Patrick Joseph KETT, Limerick (IRL), 79
1999	Katiola (Côte d'Ivoire)	François HUMBERT, Strasbourg (F), 64
2004	Maastricht (Netherlands)	André STOFFELS, Roermond (NL), 93
2014	Cork (Ireland)	Liam O'CALLAGHAN, Cork (IRL), 95
2016	Bayonne (U.S.A.)	Daniel CULLEN, Down & Connor (IRL), 96
2016	Cambo-les-Bains (France)	Michel IRIQUIN, Bayonne (F), 66
2016	Sélestat (France)	Joseph FOLMER, Metz (F), 91
2020	Cork (Ireland)	Patrick JENNINGS, Down & Connor (IRL), 95

6

1888	Agoué (Dahomey)	Jean-Marie JACQUET, Lyon (F), 29
1916	Verdun (France)	François MOLLIER, Tarentaise (F), 34
1943	Lyon (France)	Maurice FABLET, Vannes (F), 70, frère.
1977	Belfast (Ireland)	Patrick KERR, Down & Connor (IRL), 65
1989	Teaneck (USA)	Daniel LOONEY, Cork (IRL), 58
2005	Cork (Ireland)	Oliver SMITH, Kerry (IRL), 84
2017	London (Great Britain)	Michael McPARTLAND, Middlesbrough (GB), 78, Former Prefect Apostolic Falkland Islands.
2017	Madrid (Espagne)	José PÉREZ GÓMEZ, Toledo (E), 73, Membre honoraire.

7

1888	Elmina (Ghana)	Alexis FAGA, Chambéry (F), 25
1928	Incino-Erba (Italie)	Giovanni Battista FRIGERIO, Como (I), 59
1951	Aalbeek (Netherlands)	Harrie HOUSMANS, Roermond (NL), 75
1976	Colmar (France)	Xavier WELTERLIN, Strasbourg (F), 86, frère.
1992	Montferrier (France)	Joseph LABROSSE, Lyon (F), 84
1993	Cork (Ireland)	Jeremiah COAKLEY, Cork (IRL), 80
1997	Cork (Ireland)	Anthony J FOLEY, Ossory (IRL), 80
2008	Cork (Ireland)	Dominic KEARNS, Achonry (IRL), 83
2020	Cork (Ireland)	Daniel J O'BRIEN, Cork & Ross (IRL), 75

8

1893	Abeokuta (Nigeria)	Pierre BALLAC, Nantes (F), 27
1908	Porto-Novo (Dahomey)	Jules NOUVEL, Rennes (F), 44
1939	Cork (Ireland)	Michael ROWAN, Meath (IRL), 62
1945	Lomé (Togo)	+Auguste HERMAN, Strasbourg (F), 65, Vicaire Apostolique de la Basse Volta.
1946	Iteuil (France)	Ernest COMPAGNON, Poitiers (F), 58
1952	Zinswald (France)	Joseph WINGERTSZAHN, Strasbourg (F), 71
1958	East Saint-Louis (U.S.A.)	Claude TAYLOR, Leeds (GB), 63
1969	Cork (Ireland)	Michael CUMMINS, Clonfert (IRL), 71
1986	Den Hague (Netherlands)	Henk SMEELE, Rotterdam (NL), 76
1997	Montpellier (France)	Pierre BONY, Clermont-Ferrand (F), 66
2005	Cork (Ireland)	Robert J MOLLOY, Tuam (IRL), 92
2005	Saint-Aubin des Châteaux (France)	Julien GAILLARD, Rennes (F), 90

9

1861	Freetown (Sierra Leone)	Louis EDDE, Chartres (F), 24
1895	Cape Coast (Ghana)	Joseph KAPFER, Strasbourg (F), 25
1901	Bordères (France)	Irénée LAFITTE, Aire et Dax (F), 64
1912	Ibonwon (Nigeria)	Henri VANLEKE, Bruges (B), 35
1926	Grand-Bassam (Côte d'Ivoire)	Joseph REYMANN, Strasbourg (F), 54
1945	Anécho (Togo)	Aloïse BALTZ, Strasbourg (F), 38
1983	Reinhardsmunster (France)	+Louis WACH, Strasbourg (F), 75, Ancien Préfet Apostolique de Korhogo, Côte d'Ivoire.
1987	Englewood Cliffs (U.S.A.)	Patrick O'DONOGHUE, Kildare (IRL), 78
1994	Cadier en Keer (Netherlands)	Harry van NULAND, 's-Hertogenbosch (NL), 88

10

1884	Nice (France)	Gustave BOUVET, Annecy (F), 26
1896	Oyo (Nigeria)	Émile VERMOREL, Lyon (F), 31
1956	Cork (Ireland)	Joseph McCABE, Dublin (IRL), 78, brother.
1978	Strasbourg (France)	Eugène SIRLINGER, Strasbourg (F), 91
1993	Thurles (Ireland)	Thomas KENNEDY, Kerry (IRL), 65
1998	Kandi (Bénin)	Joseph NEYME, Lyon (F), 64
2022	Montferrier (France)	Andre GUERET, Nantes (F), 91

11

1974	Cork (Ireland)	Malachy MORRIS, Derry (IRL), 66
1978	Oosterbeek (Netherlands)	Jan OOSTENBACH, Roermond (NL), 58
1989	Saint-Pierre (France)	Antoine HICKENBICK, Strasbourg (F), 90
2011	Montferrier (France)	Marcel MAHY, Namur (B), 85

12

1977	Paris (France)	Désiré CUQ, Albi (F), 63
1999	M'bingué (Côte d'Ivoire)	Léopold LACROIX, Québec (CDN), 53
2007	Kilteevan (Ireland)	Bernard HORAN, Achonry (IRL), 71

13

1887	Lagos (Nigeria)	William CONNAUGHTON, Meath (IRL), 34
1946	Sainte-Foy (France)	Eustache CHENU, Tarentaise (F), 81
1958	Paris (France)	Louis RAST, Strasbourg (F), 64
1973	Lyon (France)	Ernest DESSEILLE, Namur (B), 53
2019	Colmar (France)	Antoine BRUNGARD, Strasbourg (F), Frère, 79
2020	Longford (Ireland)	Brendan DUNNING, Elphin (IRL), 77

14

1885	Lagos (Nigeria)	Théodore HOLLEY, Coutances (F), 33
1958	Zinswald (France)	Armand GUTKNECHT, Strasbourg (F), 64
1967	Blienschwiller (France)	Raymond ESCHENBRENNER, Metz (F), 44
1972	Liverpool (Great Britain)	+Joseph Gerald HOLLAND, Liverpool (GB), 67, Former Bishop of Keta, Ghana.
1995	Cadier en Keer (Netherlands)	Toon DOMENSINO, 's-Hertogenbosch (NL), 98
2001	Teaneck (USA)	Kevin SCANLAN, Killaloe (IRL), 70
2023	Cork (Ireland)	John DUNLEAVY, Tuam (IRL), 87

15

1898	Saltpond (Ghana)	Michael WADE, Dublin (IRL), 36
1923	La Croix-Valmer (France)	André GEX, Chambéry (F), 59
1948	Zinswald (France)	Léon BURG, Strasbourg (F), 65
1976	Abeokuta (Nigeria)	Richard FITZGERALD, Kerry (IRL), 69
1980	Heerlen (Netherlands)	Gerard van de PASCH, Utrecht (NL), 60, brother.
1997	Saint-Pierre (France)	Konrad WALKOWIAK, Poznań (PL), 79
1998	Dublin (Ireland)	Maurice BURKE, Waterford & Lismore (IRL), 70
2021	Berkhout (Netherland)	Herman BOMMER, Haarlem (NL), 84

16

1940	Jos (Nigeria)	Andrew GERAGHTY, Meath (IRL), 29
1950	Gagnoa (Côte d'Ivoire)	Henri BIGORGNE, Saint-Brieuc (F), 31
1956	Rome (Italie)	Jacob MUYSER, Rotterdam (NL), 60
1958	La Croix-Valmer (France)	Louis VOUILLON, Lyon (F), 85
1998	Ouidah (Bénin)	Gabriel HOUÉZÉ, Cotonou (BEN), 105, frère, Membre Honoraire.
2021	Cork (Ireland)	Leo E SILKE, Kildare & Leighlin (IRL), 93

17

1891	Topo (Nigeria)	Aimé BEAUQUIS, Annecy (F), 40
1930	Lyon (France)	François DEVOUCOUX, Nevers (F), 84
1945	Wolfach (Allemagne)	Joseph STAMM, Strasbourg (F), 63
1957	Cork (Ireland)	+Thomas P HUGHES, Tuam (IRL), 66, Bishop of Ondo-Ilorin, Nigeria.
1970	London (Great Britain)	Martin NADORP, Rotterdam (NL), 64
1971	La Croix-Valmer (France)	Jean ALLEZARD, Le Puy (F), 78
1981	Dublin (Ireland)	James MURPHY, Ross (IRL), 62
1989	Sainte-Sigolène (France)	Jean DRIOT, Le Puy (F), 60
2013	Castelnau (France)	Louis BOIRON, Saint-Étienne (F), 86
2019	Cork (Ireland)	Alberto OLIVONI, Torino (I), 82

18

1896	at sea (Naufragé)	John GARVEY, Tuam (IRL), 25
1936	Colmar (France)	Eugène KELLER, Strasbourg (F), 54
1952	Laval (France)	Clovis OLIVE, Coutances (F), 76
2003	Saint-Pierre (France)	Pierre SCHMITT, Strasbourg (F), 89
2009	Tuticorin (India)	Anthony RAJAREEGAM, Tuticorin (IND), 73, Associate Priest.
2020	Cork (Ireland)	John CLANCY, Killaloe (IRL), 89

19

1915	La Croix Valmer (France)	Eugène CHAUTARD, Clermont-Ferrand (F), 64
1949	Sokodé (Togo)	Louis FREYBURGER, Strasbourg (F), 74
1949	Lyon (France)	Prosper CARTAL, Le Puy (F), 69
1955	Zinswald (France)	Louis FUCHS, Strasbourg (F), 82
1971	Resteigne (Belgique)	Albert FRANÇOIS, Namur (B), 67, curé de Chanly, Membre Honoraire.
1991	Ferkessédougou (Côte d'Ivoire)	Richard BROWN, Philadelphia (USA), 45
1994	Mechernich (Germany)	Theo MAESSEN, Roermond (NL), 75
2003	Saint-Pierre (France)	Joseph GASS, Strasbourg (F), 90
2016	Besançon (France)	Jean BOUHELIER, Besançon (F), 79, Membre Honoraire.

20

1869	Lagos (Nigeria)	Claude VERMOREL, Lyon (F), 45
1942	Cotonou (Dahomey)	Firmin COLINEAUX, Vannes (F), 67
1968	La Croix-Valmer (France)	Louis JOLIF, Rennes (F), 86
1990	Kano (Nigeria)	Martin McDONNELL, Elphin (IRL), 80
1997	près Marsa-Matrouh (Égypte)	René SAGNI, Atakpamé (TG), 31, séminariste.

21

1939	Lomé (Togo)	Georges HARTMANN, Strasbourg (F), 29
1960	Ouidah (Benin)	+Louis PARISOT, Dijon (F), 75, Archevêque de Cotonou.
1974	Teaneck (U.S.A.)	Thomas LARKIN, Tuam (IRL), 57
1979	Manchester (Great Britain)	Patrick GUINAN, Ardagh (IRL), 62
2019	Wellington (Great Britain)	Peter B HERSEY, Clifton (GB), 78
2022	Manchester (Great Britain)	Gerald A J TONER, Northampton (GB), 79

22

1927	Ettendorf (France)	Louis FRIESS, Strasbourg (F), 50
1942	Cork (Ireland)	Edward WARD, Clogher (IRL), 37
1944	Laura (Allemagne)	Maurice COUTIN, Nantes (F), 24, séminariste.
1969	Toulon (France)	Alexandre DESBOIS, Rennes (F), 74
1974	Roermond (Netherlands)	Jan VAES, Roermond (NL), 70
1976	Alegria (Espagne)	Zacharias REMIRO, Vitoria (E), 63
1998	Saint Pierre (France)	Gabriel EUVRARD, Strasbourg (F), 63
2006	Cork (Ireland)	John BREHENY, Achonry (IRL), 74

23

1873	Porto-Novo (Dahomey)	Pierre VACHER, Tulle (F), 29
1944	Cairo (Égypte)	Joseph DONAGHY, Down & Connor (IRL), 45
1969	Cork (Ireland)	John LUPTON, Dromore (IRL), 81
1980	Oosterbeek (Netherlands)	Jan van der KOOY, Rotterdam (NL), 73
1981	Oosterbeek (Netherlands)	Frits KOOLEN, 's-Hertogenbosch (NL), 92
1984	Poznań; (Pologne)	Bolesław SZMANIA, Poznań (PL), 76
2017	Montferrier (France)	Yves BERGERON, Lyon (F), 76
2019	Cork (Ireland)	Margaret McMAHON, Cork & Ross (IRL), 93, Honorary Member.
2020	Uromi (Nigeria)	Robert OBRO, Warri (NGA), 58

24

1895	Cape Coast (Ghana)	+Jean-Marie MICHON, Autun (F), 43, Préfet apostolique de la Côte-de-l'Or.
1970	Créhen (France)	+Jean-Baptiste BOIVIN, Saint-Brieuc (F), 72, Archevêque d'Abidjan.
1977	Kano (Nigeria)	John M MURPHY, Toronto (CDN), 47
2005	Lecarrow (Ireland)	John J (Sean) KELLY, Elphin (IRL), 70

25

1954	Zinswald (France)	Joseph FREYBURGER, Strasbourg (F), 78
1969	Joure (Netherlands)	Rudolf ZIJLSTRA, Groningen (NL), 74
1993	Belfast (Ireland)	Martin CONBOY, Down & Connor (IRL), 72
2017	Gênes (Italie)	Carmine CARMINATI, Crema (I), 87

26

1872	Lagos (Nigeria)	Giovanni Battista ARTERO, Torino (I), 34
1889	Lyon (France)	Pierre BLANCHON, Viviers (F), 23, séminariste.
1916	Lyon (France)	Edouard RANCHIN, Viviers (F), 45
1952	Cork (Ireland)	William HOLLAND, Cork (IRL), 41
1962	Vlodrop (Netherlands)	Joseph MULDERS, Roermond (NL), 55
1966	Saint-Truiden (Belgique)	Bernard van den BERG, 's-Hertogenbosch (NL), 57
1968	Chamalières (France)	Louis ROMAGON, Le Puy (F), 82
1975	Cork (Ireland)	Michael DRUMMOND, Cork (IRL), 70
1982	Nijmegen (Netherlands)	Kees van GENNIP, 's-Hertogenbosch (NL), 76, brother.
1986	Vitoria (Espagne)	Candido TROCONIZ, Vitoria (E), 76
1999	Montferrier (France)	Victor LERDOU, Bayonne (F), 85
2008	Virginia Beach (U.S.A.)	Edward RICHARDSON, Philadelphia (USA), 89
2010	Heitenried (Suisse)	Pierre Canisius ZOSSO, Fribourg (CHE), 97
2020	Lusaka (Zambia)	Brian KATUNANSA, Solwezi (ZMB), 44

27

1898	Lyon (France)	Philibert COURDIOUX, Autun (F), 60
1911	Asaba (Nigeria)	Joseph FERRIEUX, Grenoble (F), 30
1912	Memni (Côte d'Ivoire)	Casimir AMALRIC, Albi (F), 26
1965	Strasbourg (France)	Joseph FURST, Strasbourg (F), 54
1971	Bélesta (France)	André GUILLO, Saint-Brieuc (F), 53
1989	Strasbourg (France)	Jean-Paul SCHUR, Strasbourg (F), 53
1992	Sheffield (Great Britain)	Martin O'MEARA, Killaloe (IRL), 80
2010	Cork (Ireland)	Paul D'ARCY, Tuam (IRL), 65
2012	Sélestat (France)	Aloyse RAUNER, Strasbourg (F), 94

28

1903	Cape Coast (Ghana)	Eugène-Bernard RAESS, Strasbourg (F), 34
1955	Saginaw (U.S.A.)	James RAFFERTY, Down & Connor (IRL), 49
1964	Agbor (Nigeria)	John LYONS, Motherwell (GB), 52
1975	Arnhem (Netherlands)	Rudolf van OOIJEN, 's-Hertogenbosch (NL), 83
1989	Tenafly (U.S.A.)	Eugène GEISSER, Strasbourg (F), 84
1993	Saint Pierre (France)	Henri GRUNENWALD, Strasbourg (F), 69
2004	Cork (Ireland)	Eugene CASEY, Kerry (IRL), 75
2011	Cork (Ireland)	Eugene CONNOLLY, Achonry (IRL), 87

29

1869	Lyon (France)	Jean VERDELET, Saint-Etienne (F), 32
1899	Elmina (Ghana)	Jean LANG, Strasbourg (F), 26
1987	Lomé (Togo)	André WIDLOECHER, Strasbourg (F), 67
2018	Montferrier (France)	Andre ANDRE, Quimper (F), 88, frère.

30

1883	Nice (France)	Arsène DARDENNE, Rennes (F), 30
1895	Saltpond (Ghana)	Alexandre RICHE, Lyon (F), 27
1901	Lagos (Nigeria)	Jean DEMERLÉ, Metz (F), 32
1936	Southampton (Great Britain)	Stephen WOODLEY, Shrewsbury (GB), 49
1968	Heerlen (Netherlands)	Harrie SEVRIENS, Roermond (NL), 62
1981	Montferrier (France)	Germain BOUCHEIX, Clermont-Ferrand (F), 70
1990	Manchester (Great Britain)	Joseph G CONBOY, Kilmore (IRL), 75
2000	Dunblane (Scotland)	Michael J WALSH, Waterford (IRL), 85
2019	Lyon (France)	Joseph MOULIAN, Aire/Dax (F), 71

May/ Mai

1

1968	Abidjan (Côte d'Ivoire)	Charles VANDAELE, Lille (F), 42
1983	Brest (France)	Joseph Le ROCH, Quimper (F), 54
1999	Sittard (Netherlands)	Cor BEURSKENS, Roermond (NL), 74
2003	Saint Pierre (France)	Bernard KLAMBER, Strasbourg (F), 77
2003	Sélestat (France)	Joseph SPEITEL, Strasbourg (F), 82
2023	Pilaszkow (Pologne)	Władysław PENKALA, Wrocław (PL), 76

2

1915	Les Dardanelles (Turquie)	Marcel BUGNON, Grenoble (F), 27, séminariste.
1959	Sur mer (Naufragé)	Justin ADRIAN, Strasbourg (F), 63
1998	Cork (Ireland)	Anthony JENNINGS, Killala (IRL), 75
2005	Mulhouse (France)	Albert HAAS, Strasbourg (F), 71
2021	Gênes (Italie)	Gerardo BOTTARLINI, Bergamo (I), 87
2022	Cork (Ireland)	Owen MCKENNA, Cork & Ross (IRL), 87

3

1941	Munster (France)	Robert FLESCH, Strasbourg (F), 51
1947	Saint-Tropez (France)	Joseph GAGNAIRE, Le Puy (F), 71
1968	Tel Aviv (Israël)	Robert SIMON, Strasbourg (F), 59
1978	Blackburn (Great Britain)	William BRESLIN, Dublin (IRL), 54
1978	Maastricht (Netherlands)	Frits van TRIGT, 's-Hertogenbosch (NL), 68
1983	Kérou (Bénin)	Daniel VERHILLE, Lille (F), 57
1985	Sarrebourg (France)	+Jérôme LINGENHEIM, Strasbourg (F), 78, Ancien Evêque de Sokodé, Togo.
1986	Obernai (France)	Joseph FEDERSPIEL, Strasbourg (F), 89, frère.
1991	Strasbourg (France)	François-Xavier RASSER, Strasbourg (F), 55
1992	Hoenheim (France)	Joseph FUCHS, Strasbourg (F), 59
2006	Cork (Ireland)	Thomas EGAN, Achonry (IRL), 80
2015	Maastricht (Netherlands)	Hubertus VERREUSSEL, Roermond (NL), 93, brother.
2020	Cork (Ireland)	John (Seán) KILBANE, Tuam (IRL), 88

4

1971	Allauch (France)	Alfred COLIN, Nantes (F), 72
1995	Cork (Ireland)	Francis O'MAHONY, Cork (IRL), 78
2006	Douamenez (France)	Yves GUILLOU, Quimper (F), 83
2019	Cork (Ireland)	William CUSACK, Waterford & Lismore (IRL), 79

5

1898	Saltpond (Ghana)	Joseph GUMY, Lausanne (CHE), 27
1916	Avaucourt (France)	Ernest GUILLEMIN, Dijon (F), 28
1934	Lyon (France)	Alphonse MATHIVET, Le Puy (F), 68
1997	Saint-Pierre (France)	Joseph BOHN, Strasbourg (F), 86, frère.

6

1877	Nice (France)	Adolphe PAPETARD, Châlons-sur-Marne (F), 69
1981	Mallow (Ireland)	John McGUINNESS, Kilmore (IRL), 53
1991	Tenafly (U.S.A.)	Aloysius RAMSTEIN, Strasbourg (F), 90
1993	Zanesville (U.S.A.)	John Vincent MULVEY, Columbus (USA), 94
2020	Montferrier (France)	Jean CHENEVIER, Valence (F), 98

7

1870	Lyon (France)	Santiago BEAUVERT, Mallorca (E), 39, frère.
1898	Saltpond (Ghana)	Ernest STEBER, Strasbourg (F), 25
1940	Abidjan (Côte d'Ivoire)	Henri LACROIX, Saint-Brieuc (F), 37
1962	Lorquin (France)	Nicolas MULLER, Metz (F), 71, frère.
1985	Montferrier (France)	+ Noël BOUCHEIX, Clermont-Ferrand (F), 84, Ancien Evêque de Porto-Novo, Bénin.

8

1943	Athiémé (Dahomey)	Joseph PROU, Nantes (F), 33
1990	Nantes (France)	Mme Georgette LEFEUVRE, Nantes (F), 1990, Membre Honoraire.
1997	Moncontour-de-Bretagne (France)	François PRUAL, Saint-Brieuc (F), 83
2011	Enschede (Netherlands)	Johannes SMITS, Utrecht (NL), 76

9

1914	Sasstown (Liberia)	William SHINE, Elphin (IRL), 26
1977	Paris (France)	Jacques MONTAGUT, Bayonne (F), 54
2003	Brest (France)	Roger STÉPHAN, Quimper (F), 77
2014	Glen Ellyn (USA)	John GUINEY, Cashel & Emly (IRL), 81

10

1920	Macon (U.S.A.)	Joseph DAHLENT, Strasbourg (F), 44
1959	Abidjan (Côte d'Ivoire)	Alphonse BERNUIZET, Lyon (F), 54
1989	Montferrier (France)	Basilio SEGUROLA, Vitoria (E), 77
2013	Cork (Ireland)	Michael DARCY, Kilmore (IRL), 78

11

1878	Lagos (Nigeria)	Alphonse POUSSIN, Le Mans (F), 24
1957	Tralee (Ireland)	Maurice SLATTERY, Kerry (IRL), 83, 7ème Supérieur Général.
1971	Cork (Ireland)	John O'SHEA, Cork (IRL), 69
1987	Kumasi (Ghana)	Leo BEKEMA, Groningen (NL), 69
1990	Cork (Ireland)	William SHEEHAN, Cloyne (IRL), 62
1991	Cadier en Keer (Netherlands)	+Antoon KONINGS, Roermond (NL), 81, Former Bishop of Keta-Ho, Ghana.
1993	Hersbach (France)	Frédéric STEINER, Strasbourg (F), 81
2003	Montpellier (France)	Pierre LAMANDÉ, Saint-Brieuc (F), 81

12

| 1980 | Chaponost (France) | Claude DAUVERGNE, Autun (F), 70 |
| 1995 | Lagos (Nigeria) | John GUBBINS, Cloyne (IRL), 63 |

13

1899	sur mer (Naufragé)	Joseph PIED, Nantes (F), 51
1899	Grand-Bassam (Côte d'Ivoire)	+Matthieu RAY, Clermont-Ferrand (F), 51, Préfet Apostolique de Côte d'Ivoire.
1905	Zifta (Égypte)	Jean MÉNAGER, Nantes (F), 25
1959	Ballinamore (Ireland)	Michael SCULLY, Clonfert (IRL), 59
1968	Strasbourg (France)	Alfred LEGRAND, Strasbourg (F), 73
1976	Rezé (France)	Jean LE GOFF, Quimper (F), 69
1997	Cadier en Keer (Netherlands)	+André van de BRONK, Haarlem (NL), 90, vicaire apostolique du delta du Nil; évêque de Kumasi, Ghana. Evêque de Parakou, Bénin.
2008	Paris (France)	+Bernardin GANTIN, Cotonou (BEN), 86, Cardinal Membre Honoraire.
2013	Cork (Ireland)	Hugh McLAUGHLIN, Cork (IRL), 82
2013	Montferrier (France)	Jean-Marie SÉBILO, Vannes (F), 88

14

1965	Kumasi (Ghana)	Gerrit van der LEEUW, Rotterdam (NL), 62
1979	Cadier en Keer (Netherlands)	Joseph BASTIAENS, Roermond (NL), 74
2008	Obernai (France)	Charles CUENIN, Besançon (F), 73

15

1950	Nice (France)	Mlle Germaine GUTHMANN, Lyon (F), Membre Honoraire.
1980	Carcassonne (France)	Paul BRUNET, Lyon (F), 64
2022	Haguenau (France)	Marcel SCHNEIDER, Strasbourg (F), 79

16

1908	Axim (Ghana)	Kees MOLENAARS, Breda (NL), 30
1976	Saint-Jacut-les-Pins (France)	+Jean-Marie ÉTRILLARD, Vannes (F), 76, Evêque de Daloa puis de Gagnoa, Côte d'Ivoire.
1979	Toulouse (France)	Joseph DUBOIS, Lille (F), 78

17

1884	Lagos (Nigeria)	Sébastien ANDRÉ, Valence (F), 31
1891	Nice (France)	Vincenzo ROMEO, Gênes (I), 23
1899	Grand-Bassam (Côte d'Ivoire)	Albert VIGNA, Besançon (F), 26
1924	Ouidah (Dahomey)	Emmanuel SERENNE, Nantes (F), 36, frère.
1928	La Croix-Valmer (France)	Celso SIRONI, Milano (I), 66
1955	Kolowaré (Togo)	Georges FISCHER, Strasbourg (F), 70
1971	Tuam (Ireland)	Bernard CUNNINGHAM, Philadelphia (USA), 54
1976	Teaneck (U.S.A.)	Alphonse BARTHLEN, Strasbourg (F), 95
1980	Luc (France)	Joseph SPAMPINATI, Beyrouth (LB), 72
1996	Englewood (U.S.A.)	Sylvester John MURRAY, Boston (USA), 67
1997	Glasgow (Scotland)	Thomas Anthony DUKE, Middlesbrough (GB), 68

18

1899	Moossou (Côte d'Ivoire)	Louis TEYSSIER, Saint-Étienne (F), 33
1911	Magny-Court (France)	Georges KOCH, Strasbourg (F), 33
1936	Tunis (Tunisie)	Adolphe ROUSSELET, Saint-Claude (F), 68
1945	New York (USA)	Patrick MOYLAN, Limerick (IRL), 56
1983	Haguenau (France)	Eugène GESTER, Strasbourg (F), 73
1995	Montferrier (France)	Germain FLOURET, Mende (F), 62
2011	Sélestat (France)	Marcel HUNTZINGER, Strasbourg (F), 89
2015	Cork (Ireland)	William KENNEDY, Elphin (IRL), 88

19

1915	Ségou (Mali)	Louis TRANCHANT, Nantes (F), 27
1924	Bingerville (Côte d'Ivoire)	Joseph GORJU, Rennes (F), 51
1952	Anvers (Belgique)	François BACKER de, Malines-Bruxelles (B), 68
1992	Amsterdam (Netherlands)	Johan MENSINK, Groningen (NL), 66
1995	Kikwit (R D Congo)	Faustin MANZANZA, Kikwit (CD), 40
2005	Montferrier-sur-Lez (France)	Robert LANOË, Vannes (F), 80
2008	Saint-Pierre (France)	Ugo BOSETTI, Saint-Boniface (CDN), 93
2014	Montréal (Canada)	Raymond LORTIE, Québec (CDN), 89

20

1917	Kriegstetten (Suisse)	Joseph BURGER, Strasbourg (F), 45
1936	Villebois-Lavalette (France)	Joseph DEFOIN, Namur (B), 70
1946	Half Assini (Ghana)	Servaas KERKHOFFS, Roermond (NL), 35
1957	Chicago (U.S.A.)	Denis O'CONNOR, Achonry (IRL), 63
1961	Cape Coast (Ghana)	Patrick O'LEARY, Cork (IRL), 38
1989	Arnhem (Netherlands)	Jan DOESWIJK, Haarlem (NL), 85
2012	Montferrier (France)	André MARTIN, Gap (F), 89
2021	Montferrier (France)	Pierre BROSSAUD, Nantes (F), 94

21

1914	Lyon (France)	Paul ROUFFIAC, Albi (F), 26, séminariste.
1952	Grand-Bassam (Côte d'Ivoire)	Pierre PORTE, Le Puy (F), 68
1962	Derby (Great Britain)	James B McCARTHY, Cloyne (IRL), 59
1969	Dutton Manor (Great Britain)	Maurice WALSH, Ossory (IRL), 60
1988	Saint-Pierre (France)	Lucien REIBEL, Strasbourg (F), 79
2003	Rotterdam (Netherlands)	Theodorus VELDBOER, Rotterdam (NL), 95
2020	Francheville (France)	Jean COMBY, Lyon (F), 89, Membre honoraire.

22

1886	Oyo (Nigeria)	Benoît VENESSY, Grenoble (F), 26
1899	Zagnanado (Dahomey)	Louis MOLLIER, Tarentaise (F), 25
1911	Agoué (Dahomey)	Camille MALGOIRE, Mende (F), 27
2005	Montpellier (France)	Maurice PAVAGEAU, Nantes (F), 82

23

1881	Agoué (Dahomey)	Auguste TULASNE, Angers (F), 32
1887	Elmina (Ghana)	Ange GAUDEUL, Rennes (F), 39
1953	Lyon (France)	Joseph WOLFF, Strasbourg (F), 62

24

1897	Marseille (France)	Peter SCHENKEL, Indianapolis (USA), 32
1899	Grand-Bassam (Côte d'Ivoire)	Étienne PELLET, Grenoble (F), 43
1913	Ouidah (Dahomey)	Jean-Marie GUÉGUEN, Quimper (F), 35
1916	Rennes (France)	Pierre BERTHELOT, Rennes (F), 38
1946	Cork (Ireland)	Martin John WALSH, Waterford (IRL), 42
1971	Vescheim (France)	Joseph FRANCK, Strasbourg (F), 58
1980	Bangor (Ireland)	Daniel CANNON, Down & Connor (IRL), 64
2006	Saint-Pierre (France)	Antoine BRUNNER, Metz (F), 71

25

| 1973 | Abeokuta (Nigeria) | Joseph CAREW, Waterford (IRL), 60 |

26

1895	Newport (Great Britain)	Charles DRISCOLL, Newport (GB), 29, seminarian.
1944	Lyon (France)	Justin STEINMETZ, Strasbourg (F), 38
1953	Zinswald (France)	Pierre GOELLER, Metz (F), 73
1971	Abeokuta (Nigeria)	Patrick CULLIGAN, Killaloe (IRL), 64
1978	Cork (Ireland)	Jeremiah HIGGINS, Limerick (IRL), 70
1981	Montferrier (France)	Albert MEY, Saint-Étienne (F), 80
1990	Cadier en Keer (Netherlands)	James TRIEPELS, Roermond (NL), 98, brother.

27

1886	sur mer (Naufragé)	Pierre PIOLAT, Grenoble (F), 28
1925	sur mer (Naufragé)	Xavier KUHN, Strasbourg (F), 36
1939	Kandi (Dahomey)	Jean-Baptiste TRUHAND, Rennes (F), 41
1940	Saint-Pierre (France)	Michel SCHERRER, Strasbourg (F), 71
1970	Jefferson City (U.S.A.)	James STANLEY, Kildare (IRL), 80
1970	Jatxou (France)	Jean-Baptiste CASTANCHOA, Bayonne (F), 60
2003	Cadier en Keer (Netherlands)	Cornelius SCHELTINGA, Haarlem (NL), 89

28

1895	Lagos (Nigeria)	Justin FRANÇOIS, Verdun (F), 33
1902	Moossou (Côte d'Ivoire)	Pierre MOLLIER, Tarentaise (F), 24
1926	Asaba (Nigeria)	Philip CASSIDY, Achonry (IRL), 38
1926	Cadier en Keer (Netherlands)	Antoine BURG, Strasbourg (F), 53
1972	Newry (Ireland)	Patrick McKENNA, Armagh (IRL), 79
1977	Lampaul Guimilliau (France)	François PELTIER, Rennes (F), 69
1986	Montpellier (France)	Jean-Baptiste BAUWENS, Liège (B), 63
1994	Englewood (U.S.A.)	William J ELLIOTT, Tuam (IRL), 67
1996	Saint-Pierre (France)	Alphonse HAEUSSLER, Strasbourg (F), 89
2020	Montferrier (France)	Gabriel MOUESCA, Bayonne (F), 91

29

1928	Monza (Italie)	Natale RADAELLI, Milano (I), 65
1941	Colmar (France)	Alphonse RIBER, Strasbourg (F), 65
2012	Montpellier (France)	Paul GAUTRET, Nantes (F), 86

30

1901	Cadier en Keer (Netherlands)	Auguste VONVILLE, Strasbourg (F), 31
1987	Heerlen (Netherlands)	Jacques GEURTS, Roermond (NL), 90
1989	Bicton (Australia)	Donal CONNOLLY, Dublin (IRL), 48

31

1934	La Croix-Valmer (France)	Charles LISSNER, Strasbourg (F), 82, frère.
1967	Dublin (Ireland)	Michael FOLEY, Tuam (IRL), 54
1978	Monrovia (Liberia)	Edward McCROREY, Boston (USA), 31
1984	Englewood (U.S.A.)	Patrick FLEMING, Tuam (IRL), 80
2013	Cork (Ireland)	Donal Michael O'CONNOR, Kerry (IRL), 80

June/ Juin

1

1940	Seclin (France)	Maurice PARIS, Angers (F), 27
1950	Doué-la-Fontaine (France)	Séraphin MORON, Angers (F), 72
1984	Saint-Vincent (France)	Louis AGUILHON, Le Puy (F), 64
1996	Cork (Ireland)	Francis HUGHES, Glasgow (GB), 82
1997	Cork (Ireland)	John CANTILLON, Cork (IRL), 75
2007	Haguenau (France)	Gilbert WILHELM, Metz (F), 73
2013	Alma (Canada)	Benoît BOUCHARD, Chicoutimi (CDN), 83

2

1859	Freetown (Sierra Leone)	Louis RIOCREUX, Saint-Étienne (F), 27
1876	Porto-Novo (Dahomey)	Édouard RUAULT, Coutances (F), 31
1944	Haguenau (France)	Michel SCHUH, Strasbourg (F), 76
1961	Roermond (Netherlands)	Piet MAASSEN, Haarlem (NL), 59
1973	Manchester (Great Britain)	John DUFFY, Glasgow (GB), 67
1974	Waterford (Ireland)	William DEELEY, Clonfert (IRL), 67
1978	Strasbourg (France)	Joseph DASTILLUNG, Metz (F), 58
1980	Lurgan (Ireland)	John MURTAGH, Dromore (IRL), 67
1994	Portaferry (Ireland)	Michael TONER, Down & Connor (IRL), 74
1997	Colmar (France)	Pierre LÉVÊQUE, Strasbourg (F), 73, Membre honoraire.
2011	Cork (Ireland)	Christopher McKEOGH, Meath (IRL), 76

3

1924	Lomé (Togo)	Charles HERVOUET, Nantes (F), 34
1976	Newry (Ireland)	Ambrose O'HAIRE, Clonfert (IRL), 76
1990	Needham (U.S.A.)	Owen O'SULLIVAN, Dublin (IRL), 60
2008	Echirolles (France)	Maurice ACHARD, Grenoble (F), 84
2022	Montferrier (France)	Jean PAUGAM, Quimper (F), 97

4

1928	Rezé (France)	Joseph HAUTBOIS, Rennes (F), 73, frère.
1932	Lyon (France)	Victor RAVOUX, Monaco (F), 61
1979	Cork (Ireland)	John J COLLINS, Cork (IRL), 71
1997	Cork (Ireland)	John B DONNELLY, Down & Connor (IRL), 82
2001	Cork (Ireland)	Peter HOULIHAN, Kerry (IRL), 86, brother.
2015	Cork (Ireland)	Patrick McGOVERN, Kilmore (IRL), 85
2020	Bischwiller (France)	Louis KUNTZ, Strasbourg (F), 90

5

1859	Freetown (Sierra Leone)	Jean-Baptiste BRESSON, Autun (F), 47
2006	Tenafly (U.S.A.)	Francis Thomas GILFETHER, Cleveland (USA), 82
2020	Sokodé (Togo)	Bernard BARDOUILLET, Saint-Claude (F), 83
2022	Gênes (Italie)	Giovanni AIMETTA, Fossano (I), 84
2023	Gênes (Italie)	Marco PRADA, Milano (I), 64

6

1973	La Croix-Valmer (France)	Henri POIDEVINEAU, Poitiers (F), 69
1986	Creggs (Ireland)	John J KEAVENEY, Elphin (IRL), 74
1987	Oloron (France)	Jean PALLARÈS, Bayonne (F), 59
1996	Cork (Ireland)	Vincent O'NEILL, Derry (IRL), 52

7

1966	Heerlen (Netherlands)	Joseph COUENBERG, Haarlem (NL), 64
1993	Salin de Giraud (France)	+Patient REDOIS, Nantes (F), 68, Evêque de Natitingou.
2000	Nantes (France)	Paul CORBINEAU, Nantes (F), 70, frère.

8

1945	Dzelukope (Ghana)	Willem HENDRIX, Roermond (NL), 33
1961	Haguenau (France)	Xavier RASSER, Strasbourg (F), 71
1976	Lyon (France)	Pierre CHIPOT, Saint-Dié (F), 55
2019	Montpellier (France)	Ernest MOULIN, Luçon (F), 77

9

1946	Vienne (France)	Ferdinand FER, Nantes (F), 71
1975	Rezé (France)	Claude MORISSEAU, Poitiers (F), 75
1995	Skerries (Ireland)	+Nicholas GRIMLEY, Dublin (IRL), 77, former Vicar Apostolic of Cape Palmas, Liberia.
1997	Clermont-Ferrand (France)	André ROUX, Clermont-Ferrand (F), 69
2003	Manchester (Great Britain)	Jeremiah CROWE, Dublin (IRL), 76
2021	Plymouth (Great Britain)	Darryl Peter BURROWS, Los Angeles (USA), 81, Honarary Member.

10

1883	Elmina (Ghana)	Peter MIESSEN, Trier (D), 30
1893	Elmina (Ghana)	Pierre DANIEL, Vannes (F), 27
1909	Keku (Liberia)	David FAESSLER, Chur (CHE), 32
1918	La Ferté-sous-Jouarre (France)	Émile GAUDEUL, Rennes (F), 30
1934	Toulon (France)	Eugène RICHARD, Saint-Dié (F), 59
1984	Benin City (Nigeria)	John Henry JONES, Down & Connor (IRL), 61
1996	Arnhem (Netherlands)	Jan BERGERVOET, Utrecht (NL), 86
2000	Montferrier (France)	Joseph PARRIAUX, Besançon (F), 75
2002	Sélestat (France)	Hubert GRIENEISEN, Strasbourg (F), 91
2018	Joliette (Canada)	Léo LATENDRESSE, Joliette (CDN), 86

11

1952	Cork (Ireland)	Philip MAHON, Ossory (IRL), 45
1975	Cork (Ireland)	+John McCARTHY, Ross (IRL), 73, former Archbishop of Kaduna, Nigeria.
1992	Cork (Ireland)	Joseph DONNELLY, Elphin (IRL), 75
2002	Montferrier (France)	Joseph DANIEL, Nantes (F), 96
2003	Saint-Pierre (France)	Charles LOTZ, Strasbourg (F), 74
2005	Cork (Ireland)	Richard DEVINE, Achonry (IRL), 73

12

1873	Lyon (France)	Etienne ARNAL, Carcassonne (F), 72
1900	Ibadan (Nigeria)	Jacques WERLY, Strasbourg (F), 27
1958	La Croix-Valmer (France)	Théodore TRANCHANT, Saint-Brieuc (F), 72
2021	Teillé (France)	Alphonse RAPION, Nantes (F), 86

13

1859	Freetown (Sierra Leone)	Gratien MONNOYEUR, Saint-Claude (F), 29, frère.
1960	Belfast (Ireland)	Gerald COLLINS, Down & Connor (IRL), 58, brother.
1984	Dromantine (Ireland)	Gerard A McGAHAN, Armagh (IRL), 61
1995	Montferrier (France)	Paul RIVAL, Vannes (F), 67
2019	Portglenone (Ireland)	T Patrick MACKLE, Derry (IRL), 94

14

1901	Ibadan (Nigeria)	Alphonse VONAU, Strasbourg (F), 25
1912	Notre-Dame-du-Laus (France)	Charles BONAPFEL, Strasbourg (F), 35
1925	Elmina (Ghana)	Henry de JONG, Utrecht (NL), 27
1934	Lyon (France)	Jean-Baptiste DOURIS, Clermont-Ferrand (F), 64
1940	Ante (France)	Henry PASQUERON DE FOMMERVAULT, Poitiers (F), 23, séminariste.
1984	Zinswald (France)	Paul FRÉRING, Strasbourg (F), 68
2006	Cadier en Keer (Netherlands)	Frans SPRONCK, Roermond (NL), 84
2006	Montferrier (France)	Albert MATHIEU, Saint-Dié (F), 91

15

1928	Grand-Popo (Dahomey)	Alexandre DURAFOUR, Belley (F), 42
1969	Akoupé (Côte d'Ivoire)	Bernard REVEL, Lyon (F), 39
1973	Trieste (Italie)	Michael DREW, Meath (IRL), 52
1987	Saint-Pierre (France)	Louis GESTER, Strasbourg (F), 78
1997	Cork (Ireland)	Laurence DOLAN, Tuam (IRL), 89
1997	Le Pin (France)	Joseph PUAUT, Poitiers (F), 71

16

1907	Asaba (Nigeria)	Paolo FERRERO, Ivrea (I), 31
1966	Dutton Manor (Great Britain)	+William PORTER, Liverpool (GB), 79, former Prefect Apostolic of Northern Nigeria and former Archbishop of Cape Coast, Ghana.
1967	La Croix-Valmer (France)	Marius MICOUD, Grenoble (F), 75
1969	Mommenheim (France)	Joseph LEIBENGUTH, Strasbourg (F), 60
2014	Montferrier (France)	Marcel RANCHIN, Viviers (F), 88

17

1992	Cork (Ireland)	Richard O KELLEHER, Cloyne (IRL), 43
2000	Cork (Ireland)	Bartholomew McCARTHY, Cork (IRL), 76
2022	Montpellier (France)	Paul CHATAIGNE, Nantes (F), 81

18

1983	Paris (France)	Paul BAUDU, Rennes (F), 68
2000	Cork (Ireland)	Thomas LENNON, Kildare & Leighlin (IRL), 79
2014	Cork (Ireland)	Michael McEGAN, Kerry (IRL), 80

19

1923	Cork (Ireland)	Richard O'SULLIVAN, Killaloe (IRL), 26
1964	Boston (Great Britain)	Patrick O'CONNELL, Limerick (IRL), 71
1965	Eustis (U.S.A.)	George McCORMACK, Tuam (IRL), 64
1982	Montréal (Canada)	Gabriel HADDAD, Héliopolis (ET), 59
1992	Newry (Ireland)	Thomas O'SHAUGHNESSY, Galway (IRL), 81
2013	Montferrier (France)	Jean-Baptiste LEBRUN, Angers (F), 83

20

1922	Anécho (Togo)	Alphonse LEDIS, Blois (F), 33
1931	Chanly (France)	Yves L'ANTHOËN, Saint-Brieuc (F), 64
1963	Paris (France)	Bernard GUILLIEN, Paris (F), 39
1981	Beaulieu (France)	Jean-Marie FAVIER, Le Puy (F), 75
1984	Bladel (Netherlands)	Henk SMETS, 's-Hertogenbosch (NL), 81
1997	Cork (Ireland)	Benedict NOLAN, Kildare & Leighlin (IRL), 82
2000	Montferrier (France)	Joseph MALVAL, Rennes (F), 84
2009	Englewood Cliffs (U.S.A.)	Claire TYNAN, Kildare & Leighlin (IRL), 78, (Sister), Honorary member.

21

1935	Atlanta (U.S.A.)	Alphonse WOLFF, Strasbourg (F), 57
1969	Schweyen (France)	Jean-Pierre SPRUNCK, Metz (F), 50
1973	Arnhem (Netherlands)	Jacques ten HAVE, Utrecht (NL), 78
1989	Cork (Ireland)	Martin WHYTE, Achonry (IRL), 70
1995	Heerlen (Netherlands)	Antoon van HOUT, 's-Hertogenbosch (NL), 83
2022	Cork (Ireland)	John FLYNN, Ardagh (IRL), 91
2023	Montferrier (France)	Georges LABORDE-BARBANEGRE, Bayonne (F), 91

22

1895	Ouidah (Dahomey)	+Joseph LECRON, Nantes (F), 40, Préfet Apostolique du Dahomey.
1927	Plessé (France)	Emile VALLÉE, Nantes (F), 26
1964	La Croix-Valmer (France)	Michel COUSTEIX, Tulle (F), 70
2003	Montferrier (France)	Yves ROCHER, Rennes (F), 85
2022	Cork (Ireland)	John FLYNN, Ardagh (IRL), 92

23

1894	Tanta (Egypte)	Louis DEVAUD, Chur (CHE), 1894, frère.
1944	Kaduna (Nigeria)	Patrick LEE, Galway (IRL), 41
1976	Warrenpoint (Ireland)	Peter MOORE, Down & Connor (IRL), 65
1978	Saint-Pierre (France)	Eugène WICKY, Strasbourg (F), 82
1982	Nijmegen (Netherlands)	Theo SLOOTS, 's-Hertogenbosch (NL), 84
1992	Montournais (France)	Bernard FORTIN, Luçon (F), 71

24

1963	Cork (Ireland)	Patrick Joseph DUFFY, Glasgow (GB), 54
1965	Mulhouse (France)	Joseph FISCHER, Strasbourg (F), 66
1967	Tenafly (U.S.A.)	John CORCORAN, Ossory (IRL), 85
1971	Dublin (Ireland)	Joseph HILLIARD, Kildare (IRL), 57
1971	Vitré (France)	Joseph BONNANT, Rennes (F), 66, Frere Victor.
1981	Jos (Nigeria)	Michael Anthony GLYNN, Clonfert (IRL), 66
1983	Paris (France)	Raymond COTTEZ, Saint-Claude (F), 83
1983	Mulhouse (France)	René MOCKERS, Strasbourg (F), 73
1989	Montferrier (France)	Jean-François MARTEL, Rennes (F), 76
2014	Montferrier (France)	Louis ROLLAND, Nantes (F), 88

25

1859	Freetown (Sierra Leon)	+Melchior Marie Joseph de MARION BRÉSILLAC, Carcassonne (F), 46, Fondateur et 1er Supérieur général de la Société des Missions Africaines. Vicaire apostolique de Coimbatore, Vicaire apostolique de Sierra Leone.
1906	Ouidah (Dahomey)	Aristide MÉNAGER, Nantes (F), 24
1936	Haguenau (France)	Jean-Baptiste THUET, Strasbourg (F), 76
1968	Lomé (Togo)	Edmond GASSER, Strasbourg (F), 54
1984	Lomé (Togo)	Ernest KRAUTH, Strasbourg (F), 63
1998	Cork (Ireland)	John V O'BRIEN, Ross (IRL), 78
1998	Egmond aan Zee (Netherlands)	Wim van LEEUWEN, Haarlem (NL), 90, brother.
2017	Cork (Ireland)	Vincent GLENNON, Clonfert (IRL), 70
2021	Montpellier (France)	Bernard RAYMOND, Saint-Etienne (F), 88

26

1891	Elmina (Ghana)	Ernest GRANIER, Tarentaise (F), 32
1965	La Croix-Valmer (France)	Joseph HERVOUET, Nantes (F), 86
1974	Roubaix (France)	Théophile BLIN, Lille (F), 76
1976	Southwark (Great Britain)	John COLEMAN, Achonory (IRL), 80
2003	Montpellier (France)	Raymond BINOCHE, Paris (F), 79

27

1910	Cork (Ireland)	John Baptist BARRETT, Tuam (IRL), 66
1933	Abeokuta (Nigeria)	Jean-Marie COQUARD, Nantes (F), 74
1975	Maastricht (Netherlands)	Theo HOLLANDER, Utrecht (NL), 61, brother.
1981	Eschweiler (Allemagne)	Jan ENGELEN, Roermond (NL), 65
1992	Cork (Ireland)	John POWER, Waterford & Lismore (IRL), 64
2005	Saint-Pierre (France)	André NETH, Strasbourg (F), 89
2008	Cadier en Keer (Netherlands)	Jaap BAKKER, Haarlem (NL), 86
2010	Cadier en Keer (Netherlands)	Theodorus BROCKHOFF, Amsterdam (NL), 94

28

1859	Freetown (Sierra Leone)	Louis REYMOND, Besançon (F), 36
1973	Haguenau (France)	Jean-Pierre BITTMANN, Strasbourg (F), 37
1974	Jos (Nigeria)	Michael HARRISON, Elphin (IRL), 70
1988	Maastricht (Netherlands)	Theo BLOM, Rotterdam (NL), 67
2001	Manchester (Great Britain)	Mlle Anne TIMOTHY, Salford (GB), lay associate.
2021	Montferrier (France)	Bernard GUICHARD, Saint-Etienne (F), 95

29

1938	Kouto (Côte d'Ivoire)	Étienne VION, Poitiers (F), 52
1988	Montferrier (France)	Yves PIRIOU, Quimper (F), 80, frère Michel.
1995	Cadier en Keer (Netherlands)	Sjeng JACOBS, Roermond (NL), 73
2001	Manchester (Great Britain)	Patrick McANALLY, Down & Connor (IRL), 92
2001	Rochefort (France)	Jean-Luc GUILBAUD, Nantes (F), 62
2010	Montferrier (France)	Gérard VOLARD, Nantes (F), 75
2019	Sélestat (France)	Roger MORITZ, Strasbourg (F), 87

30

1889	Agoué (Dahomey)	Jacques PASQUEREAU, Angers (F), 42
1982	Sélestat (France)	Aloyse BISCHOFBERGER, Saint-Gall (CHE), 85
1992	Montferrier (France)	Joseph ROUX, Autun (F), 71, prêtre associé.
2001	Cadier en Keer (Netherlands)	Kees KONIJN, Haarlem (NL), 77
2004	Montpellier (France)	Jean-Baptiste ROSIER, Le Puy (F), 82
2017	Montferrier (France)	Paul LE GOFF, Saint-Brieuc (F), 91

July/ Juillet

1

1864	Porto-Novo (Dahomey)	Hector NOCHÉ, Grenoble (F), 30
1871	Lagos (Nigeria)	Denis MEYRANX, Aire et Dax (F), 26
1968	Lyon (France)	Désiré LIENHARDT, Strasbourg (F), 79, frère.
1970	La Croix-Valmer (France)	Pierre GAUTRAIS, Rennes (F), 71, Frère Bernard.
1972	Oosterbeek (Netherlands)	Wim van LIESHOUT, 's-Hertogenbosch (NL), 76
1994	Paris (France)	Maurice GRENOT, Dijon (F), 78
1997	Teaneck (USA)	Ernest MAGEE, Down & Connor (IRL), 74
2006	Villeurbanne (France)	Jean-Baptiste CORBINEAU, Nantes (F), 70
2013	Sierck-les-Bains (France)	Jean-Paul FELDER, Strasbourg (F), 79

2

1964	Galway (Ireland)	Thomas W HUGHES, Ardagh (IRL), 72, brother.
1968	Gironcourt (France)	Pierre ZERRINGER, Saint-Dié (F), 61
1977	Lyon (France)	Jean-Baptiste BRUYAS, Saint-Étienne (F), 66
1981	Montferrier (France)	Paul REY, Grenoble (F), 79
1996	Saint Nicolas de Redon (France)	Clovis NIEL, Nantes (F), 71
1996	Montpellier (France)	Joël ROY, Nantes (F), 69
2000	Marly (Suisse)	Marcel ROULIN, Lausanne (CHE), 90, frère.
2001	Belleville, Illinois (U.S.A.)	Michael MAUGHAN, Tuam (IRL), 83

3

1937	Poznań; (Pologne)	Aloyse KURACZ, Poznań (PL), 22, séminariste.
1938	Sasstown (Liberia)	Matthew McDONNELL, Cork (IRL), 33
1981	Cork (Ireland)	Jerome SHEEHAN, Cork (IRL), 87
2015	Pénestin (France)	Mlle Elise GILROY, Quimper (F), 106, Membre Honoraire.

4

1879	Porto-Novo (Dahomey)	Alphonse LEPOULTEL, Coutances (F), 26
1933	Chamalières (France)	Stanislas DESRIBES, Tarbes (F), 73
1966	Lomé (Togo)	Paul WELSCH, Metz (F), 51
1969	Hamm (Allemagne)	Michael CONVEY, Tuam (IRL), 54
1980	Teaneck (U.S.A.)	John GALVIN, Clonfert (IRL), 75
1990	Montferrier (France)	Joseph AYOUL, Vannes (F), 78
2022	Montferrier (France)	Louis GENEVAUX, Saint-Claude (F), 78

5

1893	Rome (Italie)	Louis BOUTRY, Coutances (F), 43
1945	Quimper (France)	Jean-Marie HÉLIAS, Quimper (F), 38
1972	Meyreuil (France)	André CHASSAIGNON, Lyon (F), 71

6

1899	La Roche (France)	Antoine PROVENCHÈRE, Clermont-Ferrand (F), 41
1939	Mulhouse (France)	+Oswald WALLER, Strasbourg (F), 73, Préfet apostolique du Nigeria orientale.
1942	Kumasi (Ghana)	Joseph VOGEL, Strasbourg (F), 58
1965	Dublin (Ireland)	John SHEEHAN, Ross (IRL), 58
1968	Lyon (France)	François PEYVEL, Le Puy (F), 61
1992	Cork (Ireland)	Denis MANNING, Cork (IRL), 92
2008	Saint-Pierre (France)	Michel WACK, Strasbourg (F), 95
2014	Sélestat (France)	Claude MASSON, Verdun (F), 82

7

1880	Lagos (Nigeria)	Liguori PAGÉS, Cahors (F), 37
1893	Clermont-Ferrand (France)	Claude PAGNON, Belley (F), 39
1916	en Galicie (Pologne)	Isidore CHRIST, Strasbourg (F), 38, frère.
1936	Saltpond (Ghana)	Kees FABRIE, 's-Hertogenbosch (NL), 29
1961	Dublin (Ireland)	Alfred GLYNN, Portsmouth (GB), 50
1982	Vannes (France)	François GALLIOU, Quimper (F), 76
1986	La Rioja (Espagne)	Juan Maria CÁMARA, Calahorra-La Calzada (E), 63
2003	Limerick (Ireland)	James B HILL, Killaloe (IRL), 86
2003	Cork (Ireland)	Denis SLATTERY, Cloyne (IRL), 87
2011	Bacolod City (Philippines)	Bembolio de los SANTOS, Kabankalan (PHL), 37
2011	Chanly (Belgique)	Louis MAHY, Namur (B), 89
2018	Washington (USA)	Donatien DJOHOSSOU, Lokossa (BEN), 54

8

1938	Allada (Dahomey)	Julien GUYOT, Rennes (F), 29
1938	Abidjan (Côte d'Ivoire)	+François PERSON, Vannes (F), 48, Vicaire Apostolique de Côte d'Ivoire.
1940	Kumasi (Ghana)	Theo CUP, Roermond (NL), 34
1962	Lomé (Togo)	Johann Baptist RIMLÉ, Saint-Gall (CHE), 76
1980	Heerlen (Netherlands)	Jan van den HOUT, 's-Hertogenbosch (NL), 83
1997	Cork (Ireland)	Patrick J MURPHY, Cork (IRL), 67
2003	Beaune (France)	René GAUTHIER, Besançon (F), 73
2016	Lyon (France)	Josée POLOCE, Lyon (F), 92, Membre Honoraire.
2019	Cork (Ireland)	Johnie HAVERTY, Galway (IRL), 83

9

1940	Saint-Sulpice (France)	Pierre DOUILLARD, Luçon (F), 21, séminariste.
1959	Saint-Pierre (France)	François-Xavier SITZMANN, Strasbourg (F), 80
2002	Cork (Ireland)	Francis McARDLE, Dublin (IRL), 89
2015	Tenefly (U.S.A.)	John F MURRAY, New York (USA), 92
2016	Colmar (France)	Jean-Paul BAUMANN, Strasbourg (F), 77, frère.
2020	Montferrier (France)	Edmond COLSON, Cambrai (F), 93

10

1988	Man (Côte d'Ivoire)	Octave HOUTMANN, Strasbourg (F), 85, frère.
1992	Sélestat (France)	Philippe NUSS, Strasbourg (F), 74

11

1977	La Croix-Valmer (France)	Simon-Pierre COSSÉ, Nantes (F), 79
1983	Montpellier (France)	Alphonse GUÉRIN, Nantes (F), 78
1999	Venray (Netherlands)	Martin GEELEN, Roermond (NL), 73
2001	Cork (Ireland)	Michael J FEELEY, Cork (IRL), 83

12

1912	Rezé (France)	Auguste-Joseph MOREAU, Nantes (F), 39
1926	La Croix-Valmer (France)	Jean-Baptiste ROUSSEAU, Nantes (F), 70, frère.
1945	Dublin (Ireland)	Patrick CAHILL, Dublin (IRL), 43
1955	Echt (Netherlands)	Albert ROELOFS, Breda (NL), 52
1959	Galway (Ireland)	John O'FLAHERTY, Tuam (IRL), 58
1961	Ambleside (Great Britain)	Michael McENIRY, Elphin (IRL), 65
1980	Cork (Ireland)	John MAHON, Ossory (IRL), 77
1989	Montferrier (France)	Jacques RICARD, Montauban (F), 94, frère.
2005	Cork (Ireland)	Daniel DALY, Limerick (IRL), 95
2021	Sélestat (France)	Materne HUSSHERR, Strasbourg (F), 88

13

1915	Saltpond (Ghana)	Valentin STOLZ, Strasbourg (F), 27
1930	Marseille (France)	Daniel O'SULLIVAN, Cork (IRL), 72
1983	Southfield (U.S.A.)	John HARRINGTON, Philadelphia (USA), 66
1985	Colmar (France)	Joseph PETER, Strasbourg (F), 65
2015	Montréal (Canada)	Jean-Guy MARTEL, Chicoutimi (CDN), 74

14

| 1973 | Paris (France) | Louis ROUÉ, Quimper (F), 61, Frère Roger. |
| 2004 | Montferrier (France) | Joseph DEMEYÈRE, Lille (F), 100 |

15

1903	Le Caire (Egypte)	Victor DROUAULT, Laval (F), 20, séminariste.
1912	Cotonou (Dahomey)	Jules GESLINIER, Sées (F), 38
1939	Le Caire (Egypte)	Jean FRANCIS, Beyrouth (LB), 44
1942	Trégueux (France)	Joseph PHILIPPE, Saint-Brieuc (F), 21, novice.
1962	Belfast (Ireland)	Patrick O'HARA, Dublin (IRL), 51
1974	Dongen (Netherlands)	Franciscus VERHAGEN, Haarlem (NL), 72, brother.
1983	Cork (Ireland)	Timothy O'DRISCOLL, Cork (IRL), 76
2010	Spokane (U.S.A.)	James PERRONE, Hartford (USA), 82
2014	Cork (Ireland)	Sean HAYES, Limerick (IRL), 78
2022	Montferrier (France)	Emile POTTIER, Nantes (F), 93

16

1885	sur mer (Naufragé)	John HENEBERRY, Ossory (IRL), 24
1889	Asaba (Nigeria)	Étienne COCHET, Tarentaise (F), 27
1905	Saint-Aaron (France)	Paul GUINARD, Saint-Brieuc (F), 28
1959	Asaba (Nigeria)	William KEENAN, Ardagh (IRL), 62
2009	Warrenpoint (Ireland)	Seaghan RAFFERTY, Dromore (IRL), 85
2010	Hégeney (France)	Marius KRUTT, Strasbourg (F), 75
2020	Cork (Ireland)	John QUINLAN, Kerry (IRL), 84

17

1921	Lyon (France)	Henri CRESPEL, Rennes (F), 24, séminariste.
1953	Lyon (France)	Jean GOUGEON, Nantes (F), 29
1980	Haguenau (France)	René JUNGMANN, Strasbourg (F), 45
2007	Cadalen (France)	Georges YÈCHE, Albi (F), 91
2016	Cork (Ireland)	Eugene RIORDAN, Cork (IRL), 94

18

1931	Bitschwiller (France)	Joseph MULLER, Strasbourg (F), 53
1940	Warri (Nigeria)	Patrick BERMINGHAM, Kildare (IRL), 44
1963	Cotonou (Dahomey)	Jean-Marie FAVIER, Le Puy (F), 37
1981	Pommiers (France)	Séraphin VINET, Luçon (F), 69
1982	Montferrier (France)	Henri PERNOT, Saint-Claude (F), 78
1985	Montferrier (France)	Jean-Marie ROCHERY, Nantes (F), 79, frère.
1989	Cork (Ireland)	James BYRNE, Meath (IRL), 73

19

1921	Savannah (U.S.A.)	Joseph ZIMMERMANN, Bale (CHE), 72
1926	Benin City (Nigeria)	William BOND, Liverpool (GB), 30
1972	Westcliff-on-sea (Great Britain)	James McEVOY, Down & Connor (IRL), 63
1994	Paris (France)	Dominique MAUGARD, Dijon (F), 49, frère.

20

1918	Plessis-lès-Hurlus (France)	Henri GILOTEAU, Nantes (F), 33, frère.
1923	Madrid (Espagne)	Masimino GARCIA, Burgos (E), 51
1985	Beaune (France)	Alfred DUFOUR, Maurienne (F), 65
1985	Liège (Belgique)	Jean LEJEUNE, Malines (B), 61
1998	Claregalway (Ireland)	Joseph D BARRETT, Tuam (IRL), 87

21

1937	Lyon (France)	André GRANGEON, Le Puy (F), 57
1967	Mulhouse (France)	Arthur HECK, Strasbourg (F), 80
1970	Bayonne (France)	Ignace GOYHENETCHE, Bayonne (F), 59
1973	Les Gras (France)	Robert CHOPARD-LALLIER, Lausanne (CHE), 52, Ancien Préfet Apostolique de Parakou, Dahomey.
1980	Paris (France)	+Amand HUBERT, Nantes (F), 80, Ancien vicaire apostolique d'Héliopolis, Egypte.
1981	Belfast (Ireland)	William McAULEY, Down & Connor (IRL), 71

22

1899	Saltpond (Ghana)	Michel DAHLENT, Strasbourg (F), 26
1966	Camors (France)	René BOTHUA, Vannes (F), 60
1966	Galway (Ireland)	John McELGUNN, Cashel (IRL), 45
1975	Cork (Ireland)	Patrick McCARTHY, Ross (IRL), 78
1992	Ardfert (Ireland)	S Joseph STYLES, Kerry (IRL), 78
1996	Montpellier (France)	Antonin BRUYAS, Lyon (F), 88
1997	Aachen (Germany)	Joseph LOCHTMAN, Roermond (NL), 80
2004	Adelaide (Australia)	Petrus de VRIES, Groningen (NL), 89
2011	Cadier en Keer (Netherlands)	Henricus KONING, Haarlem (NL), 72

23

1950	La Croix-Valmer (France)	Édouard LAQUEYRIE, Cahors (F), 72
1973	Cork (Ireland)	Michael COLLINS, Ross (IRL), 90
1983	Sélestat (France)	Joseph-Arthur ESCHLIMANN, Strasbourg (F), 76

24

1898	Elmina (Ghana)	Othon HILBERER, Freibourg im Breisga (D), 34
1906	Héric (France)	Auguste BRÉJÉ, Nantes (F), 27, frère.
1906	Kilstett (France)	Jean LICHTENAUER, Strasbourg (F), 37
1987	Lyon (France)	Ange BOULO, Vannes (F), 72
1991	Oosterbeek (Netherlands)	Theodorus de ROOY, Haarlem (NL), 76
2001	Herbeumont (Belgique)	Albert Georges LEROY, Namur (B), 75
2008	Montpellier (France)	Gérard VIAUD, Nantes (F), 77

25

1930	Abidjan (Côte d'Ivoire)	Ferdinand ALLAIN, Luçon (F), 43, frère.
1930	Korhogo (Côte d'Ivoire)	Louis SAECKINGER, Strasbourg (F), 37
1968	Belfast (Ireland)	John O'HARA, Down & Connor (IRL), 55
1969	Oosterbeek (Netherlands)	Gerrit van DIJK, 's-Hertogenbosch (NL), 72
2007	Montferrier (France)	René LEMASSON, Nantes (F), 83
2012	Montpellier (France)	Fernand BIORET, Nantes (F), 88
2014	Fécamp (France)	Pierre MORILLON, Le Havre (F), 75
2017	Montferrier (France)	Camille ALLAIN, Nantes (F), 80

26

1929	Lyon (France)	Joseph PLANQUE, Lille (F), 60
1959	Teaneck (U.S.A.)	William DUNNE, Dublin (IRL), 44
1970	Arnhem (Netherlands)	Antoon PEETERS, Roermond (NL), 60
1976	Rennes (France)	Louis BOUVIER, Rennes (F), 76
2012	Ballinasloe (Ireland)	Mrs Ellen GALVIN, Clonfert (IRL), 87, Honorary Member.

27

1942	La Croix-Valmer (France)	Joseph FUGIER, Grenoble (F), 85
1958	Smeermaas (Belgique)	Sjeng LEMMENS, Roermond (NL), 60
1977	Glenay (France)	Élie COUSSEAU, Poitiers (F), 63
2006	Chennai (India)	Joseph RAMESH, Tuticorin (IND), 33
2021	Braamt (Netherland)	Rinke de VREEZE, Groningen-Leeuwarden (NL), 99

28

| 1983 | Abeokouta (Nigeria) | Michael McLOUGHLIN, Tuam (IRL), 78 |
| 1999 | Limerick (Ireland) | James HAYES, Cashel & Emly (IRL), 70 |

29

1914	Lyon (France)	Jean-Baptiste LIBS, Strasbourg (F), 40
1960	Lyon (France)	Louis-Pierre MALLET, Le Puy (F), 79
1976	Cork (Ireland)	Justin McCARTHY, Cork (IRL), 61
1981	Montferrier (France)	Joseph GUÉRIN, Nantes (F), 80
2002	Cork (Ireland)	Patrick J GLYNN, Tuam (IRL), 82
2014	Cork (Ireland)	Martin J WALSH, Liverpool (IRL), 87
2022	Nantes (France)	Charles CHEVALIER, Nantes (F), 83

30

1879	Lagos (Nigeria)	Jean PINEAU, Angers (F), frère.
1976	Goleen (Ireland)	Jeremiah RING, Cork (IRL), 53, brother.
2014	Cork (Ireland)	William FOLEY, Kerry (IRL), 79
2014	Nantes (France)	Claude TEMPLE, Nantes (F), 71
2017	Reichstett (France)	Marie Reine SCHNEIDER, Strasbourg (F), 72, Membre honoraire.
2022	Saint Symphorien sur Coise (France)	Michel CARTERON, Lyon (F), 85

31

1887	Akexandrie (Égypte)	Étienne CARAMBAUD, Moulins (F), 44
1927	Dakar (Sénégal)	Matthieu BERRIÈRE, Roermond (NL), 51, brother.
1991	Avignon (France)	Johannes Mattheus GEUSKENS, Roermond (NL), 53, brother.
2000	Voorburg (Netherlands)	Jacques van VEEN, Rotterdam (NL), 74
2015	Tanguieta (Benin)	Chabi Emile BIAOU, Dassa-Zoumé (BEN), 36

August/ Août

1

| 1974 | Strasbourg (France) | Bruno HAUSHERR, Strasbourg (F), 62 |
| 2000 | Liège (Belgique) | Jacques TOUSSAINT, Namur (B), 73 |

2

1898	Zifta (Égypte)	Charles KIEFFER, Saint-Claude (F), 25
1910	La Croix-Valmer (France)	Jérôme REINHARDT, Strasbourg (F), 36
1942	Cotonou (Dahomey)	Albert FECHTER, Strasbourg (F), 53
1953	Ouidah (Dahomey)	Isidore PÉLOFY, Carcassonne (F), 79
1981	Heerlen (Netherlands)	Bernard GOOTZEN, Roermond (NL), 72
2009	Rennes (France)	Georges LEGRAND, Vannes (F), 89
2014	Dijon (France)	Mme Colette GRIVEL, Paris (F), 83, Membre Honoraire.
2016	Montferrier (France)	Yves BLOT, Amiens (F), 82
2022	Cadier en Keer (Netherland)	Wiel van EIJK, Roermond (NL), 93

3

1929	sur mer (Naufragé)	+Ferdinand TERRIEN, Nantes (F), 52, Vicaire Apostolique de la Côte du Bénin.
1940	Vichy (France)	Alphonse DRÉAN, Vannes (F), 23, novice.
1940	Dublin (Ireland)	Michael McCAFFREY, Dublin (IRL), 64
1969	Forbach (France)	Aloïse BLANCK, Strasbourg (F), 64
1981	Sélestat (France)	Joseph VOGEL, Strasbourg (F), 92
1989	Dublin (Ireland)	Michael O'KEEFFE, Cork (IRL), 66
1999	Le Russey (France)	Modeste BILLOTTE, Besançon (F), 65

4

1913	Sauzon (France)	Léandre Le GALLEN, Vannes (F), 66
1927	Chanly (Belgique)	Xavier KELLER, Strasbourg (F), 20, séminariste.
1938	Dublin (Ireland)	Patrick Joseph KELLY, Dublin (IRL), 42
1939	Abidjan (Côte d'Ivoire)	+Edmond WOLFF, Strasbourg (F), 40, Préfet Apostolique de Korhogo Côte d'Ivoire.
1990	Lyon (France)	François KAPUŚCIK, Czèstochowa (PL), 72
2009	Cork (Ireland)	James O'CONNELL, Dublin (IRL), 72

5

1880	Elmina (Ghana)	Eugène MURAT, Saint-Étienne (F), 31
1957	Kumasi (Ghana)	Joseph-Benoît EVERS, Roermond (NL), 47
1972	Forbach (France)	Jean DAUPHIN, Metz (F), 65
1972	Bangor (Ireland)	Edward RICE, Down & Connor (IRL), 61
1975	Arnhem (Netherlands)	Wim BOND, Haarlem (NL), 74
1979	La Croix-Valmer (France)	Gervais KÉROUANTON, Quimper (F), 72
1982	Carcassonne (France)	Kees LIGTVOET, 's-Hertogenbosch (NL), 67
2008	Cork (Ireland)	Jeremiah DWYER, Cork (IRL), 84

6

1886	Lyon (France)	Louis POLYCARPE, Tarbes (F), 21, séminariste.
1950	Haguenau (France)	Martin PFLEGER, Strasbourg (F), 78
1987	Belmullet (Ireland)	John McANDREW, Killala (IRL), 71
1993	Cork (Ireland)	Bernard DOLAN, Clogher (IRL), 72
2001	Cadier en Keer (Netherlands)	Jan COOLEN, 's-Hertogenbosch (NL), 87

7

1887	Atakpamé (Togo)	Jeremiah MORAN, Killaloe (IRL), 28
1898	La Croix-Valmer (France)	Pierre-Marie BARON, Nantes (F), 40
1944	Lyon (France)	Victor HÉROLD, Strasbourg (F), 72
1948	Teaneck (U.S.A.)	Ignace LISSNER, Strasbourg (F), 81
1963	Takoradi (Ghana)	Denis FLORACK, Roermond (NL), 47
1975	In an aeroplane	Piet FISCHER, Roermond (NL), 71
1980	Les Houches (France)	Paul FALCON, Mende (F), 63
1985	Cork (Ireland)	Thomas J GALVIN, Clonfert (IRL), 83
2001	Cork (Ireland)	Seán O'MAHONY, Cloyne (IRL), 81
2007	Bangui (R Centrafrique)	Paul FLAGEUL, Nantes (F), 62, frère.
2011	Nelling (France)	Paul ROSTOUCHER, Metz (F), 82

8

1927	Obuasi (Ghana)	Philippe MUNTZINGER, Strasbourg (F), 39
1959	Lagos (Nigeria)	John P MOONEY, Dublin (IRL), 49
1974	La Croix-Valmer (France)	Joseph PORCHEROT, Dijon (F), 77
1991	Dunkineely (Ireland)	John James BRESLIN, Raphoe (IRL), 75
1998	Saint-Nazaire (France)	Noël DOUAU, Nantes (F), 75
2001	Cork (Ireland)	John RODGERS, Cork (IRL), 76
2006	Gênes (Italie)	Luigi FINOTTI, Chioggia (I), 73
2006	Montferrier (France)	Antoine VALÉRO, Rodez (F), 80

9

1932	Dromantine (Ireland)	Thomas KELLY, Meath (IRL), 46, brother.
1963	Mulhouse (France)	Auguste GASSER, Strasbourg (F), 53
2001	Lourdes (France)	Noël TEKRY KOKORA, Gagnoa (CIV), 79, Membre Honoraire, Archevêque de Gagnoa, Côte d'Ivoire.

10

1920	Lyon (France)	Ignace MEDER, Strasbourg (F), 51
1922	Lagos (Nigeria)	Victor DELFOSSE, Strasbourg (F), 46
1951	Chemillé (France)	Joseph JOULORD, Angers (F), 80
1960	La Croix-Valmer (France)	André PÉRÉS, Quimper (F), 74
1990	Oosterbeek (Netherlands)	Jo LEFERINK, Roermond (NL), 73
1999	Monrovia (Liberia)	Paul DICKRELL, La Crosse (USA), 37, lay associate.
2019	Montferrier (France)	Andre DESBOIS, Nantes (F), 92
2020	Chazelles-sur-Lyon (France)	Roger VÉRICEL, Saint-Etienne (F), 86
2022	Cork (Ireland)	Maurice KELLEHER, Southwark (GB), 84

11

1942	Lomé (Togo)	Hermann KEIMER, Saint-Gall (CHE), 59
1949	Cork (Ireland)	William COTTER, Cloyne (IRL), 65
1954	Strasbourg (France)	Jules LIEB, Strasbourg (F), 66
1975	Paris (France)	Pierre HÉNAFF, Quimper (F), 73
1975	Kerkrade (Netherlands)	Frans PAS, 's-Hertogenbosch (NL), 61
1976	Ado-Ekiti (Nigeria)	Michael BRENNAN, Cork (IRL), 26
1981	Cork (Ireland)	Francis DOYLE, Cork (IRL), 65
1982	Nantes (France)	Paul LOMELET, Nantes (F), 67

12

1884	Lagos (Nigeria)	Antoine DURIEUX, Saint-Etienne (F), 35
1902	Grand-Bassam (Côte d'Ivoire)	Maurizio GROSJACQUES, Aosta (I), 34
1917	Savannah (USA)	Jean-Louis EHRET, Strasbourg (F), 36
1942	Bouaké (Côte d'Ivoire)	Jean-Paul VOGEL, Strasbourg (F), 29
1966	Cadier en Keer (Hollande)	+HUBERT PAULISSEN, Roermond (NL), 85, Bishop of Kumasi Ghana.
1970	Tenafly (USA)	Georges LAUGEL, Strasbourg (F), 83
1981	Cork (Ireland)	Patrick HURST, Tuam (IRL), 78
1983	Montferrier (France)	Louis GOMMEAUX, Arras (F), 70
2009	Cadier en Keer (Netherlands)	Jan KOENDERS, Utrecht (NL), 92

13

1907	Shendam (Nigeria)	Ernest BELIN, Rennes (F), 26
1948	Sallee-de-Vihiers (France)	Pierre BARON, Nantes (F), 67
1951	Le Caire (Egypte)	Emile SCIAVI, Asmara (ETH), 70
1984	Lyon (France)	René ROBERT, Angers (F), 83
1992	Cork (Ireland)	Michael MOORHEAD, Meath (IRL), 80

14

1896	Saint-Priest (France)	Joseph MORY, Clermont-Ferrand (F), 27
1901	Asaba (Nigeria)	Jean-Baptiste VOIT, Saint-Gall (CHE), 44
1934	East-St-Louis (U.S.A.)	Eugène O'HEA, Ross (IRL), 45
1973	Kaduna (Nigeria)	Eric WHITE, Dublin (IRL), 54
1986	Colmar (France)	Jacques KNAEBEL, Strasbourg (F), 77
2006	Poitiers (France)	Marie-Marthe PORTIER, Laval (F), 83, Soeur, Membre Honoraire.
2021	Montferrier (France)	Jean DHUMEAU, Poitiers (F), 95

15

1953	Tunis (Tunisie)	Joseph SCHMIDT, Strasbourg (F), 76
1966	Strasbourg (France)	Georges KNAEBEL, Strasbourg (F), 50
1987	Montferrier (France)	Pierre GUÉGADEN, Quimper (F), 79
1996	Cork (Ireland)	Benno WOLFF, Aachen (D), 71

16

1944	Maison-Carrée (Algérie)	Jean MICHAŁEK, Chełmno (PL), 32
1964	Arrigas (France)	Gabriel CLAMENS, Nîmes (F), 57
1973	Saint-Pierre (France)	Joseph BARDOL, Strasbourg (F), 73
1973	Nîmes (France)	Marcel CALMET, Nîmes (F), 50
2001	Aix-en-Provence (France)	Michel ROBERT, Mende (F), 87
2014	Lomé (Togo)	Gérard BRETILLOT, Besançon (F), 76
2022	Cadier en Keer (Netherland)	Arjen van BALEN, Groningen-Leeuwarden (NL), 98

17

1886	Lokoja (Nigeria)	Andrew DORNAN, Down & Connor (IRL), 30
1923	Nantes (France)	Émile LEMAIRE, Saint-Dié (F), 77
1977	Nice (France)	François BRÉGAINT, Saint-Brieuc (F), 60
1983	Bersac-sur-Rivaillier (France)	Émile ALLAINMAT, Saint-Brieuc (F), 75
1985	Cesson-Sévigné (France)	Yves DUVAL, Rennes (F), 63
1991	Montferrier (France)	Jacques CLARISSE, Bayeux (F), 73
2016	Cork (Ireland)	Jeremiah P O'CONNELL, Cork & Ross (IRL), 84

18

1891	Cistrères (France)	Eugène ASTIER, Le Puy (F), 28
1911	Grand-Bassam (Côte d'Ivoire)	Jean-Louis MÉHEUST, Saint-Brieuc (F), 44
1991	Cork (Ireland)	Patrick J KELLY, Clonfert (IRL), 96, Former Bishop of Benin City, Nigeria.
1994	Lyon (France)	Jacques DUJARDIN, Nantes (F), 68
2017	Cork (Ireland)	Francis MEEHAN, Tuam (IRL), 88
2020	Siant Pierre (France)	Jean Baptiste FOLMER, Metz (F), 100

19

1939	Kete-Krachi (Ghana)	Leendert de KOK, Rotterdam (NL), 31
1957	Arnhem (Netherlands)	Jan BEENKER, Groningen (NL), 49
1962	La Croix-Valmer (France)	Albert GAYMARD, Grenoble (F), 72
1971	Belfast (Ireland)	Patrick DORR, Achonry (IRL), 64
1972	La Croix-Valmer (France)	Joseph ANGIBAUD, Nantes (F), 75
1993	Cadier en Keer (Netherlands)	Wim RECKMANN, Utrecht (NL), 79
2002	Cork (Ireland)	Francis MURPHY, Dublin (IRL), 86
2014	Cadier en Keer (Netherlands)	Josephus Petrus VALENTIN, Rotterdam (NL), 74

20

1863	Lyon (France)	Laurent MATHON, Gap (F), 29, novice.
1964	Felixtowe (Great Britain)	John P MURPHY, Kerry (IRL), 60
1973	Cork (Ireland)	Patrick HARMON, Kildare (IRL), 87
1977	Barr (France)	Henri BAROTTIN, Nancy (F), 73
2009	Morlaix (France)	Paul-Henri DUPUIS, Arras (F), 83

21

1905	Oyo (Nigeria)	Léon BRAUD, Nantes (F), 25
1907	Lyon (France)	Augustin PLANQUE, Cambrai (F), 81, 2ème Supérieur Général
1972	Torino (Italie)	Giuseppe MONTICONE, Torino (I), 86, Membre Honoraire.
1982	Eindhoven (Netherlands)	John van HEESEWIJK, 's-Hertogenbosch (NL), 85
1982	Heerlen (Netherlands)	Piet WOUTERS, Roermond (NL), 80
1985	Strasbourg (France)	Joseph ROTH, Strasbourg (F), 68
1989	Barr (France)	Jean MAURER, Bâle (CHE), 80, frère.
1998	Dublin (Ireland)	John J DUNNE, Dublin (IRL), 72
2012	Cork (Ireland)	Robert O'REGAN, Cork and Ross (IRL), 97
2023	Montferrier (France)	Jean RASSINOUX, Lucon (F), 90

22

1933	Kete-Krachi (Ghana)	Antoon SMETZERS, 's-Hertogenbosch (NL), 30
1962	Navan (Ireland)	Vincent FINNEGAN, Clogher (IRL), 48
1963	Helden (Netherlands)	Jo BEUMERS, Roermond (NL), 46
1974	Nantes (France)	Joseph ÉVAIN, Nantes (F), 50
1975	Athlone (Ireland)	Patrick SHINE, Elphin (IRL), 75
2011	Gent (Belgique)	Paulus van WINDEN, Rotterdam (NL), 44

23

1912	Metzeral (France)	Paul FRÉRY, Strasbourg (F), 30
1933	Le Caire (Égypte)	Frédéric BRACHET, Lyon (F), 27
1944	Newry (Ireland)	James McDONNELL, Ardagh (IRL), 49
1977	La Croix-Valmer (France)	Prosper MALO, Nantes (F), 69
1984	Montferrier (France)	Louis DELBAERE, Lille (F), 87
1988	Heerlen (Netherlands)	Sjef GIESEN, Roermond (NL), 78
1994	Schiltigheim (France)	Claude SCHNEIDER, Metz (F), 63

24

1963	Belfast (Ireland)	John Patrick GRANT, Down & Connor (IRL), 49
1964	Echt (Netherlands)	Jan SEVRIENS, Roermond (NL), 68
1973	Bobbio (Italie)	+Pietro ZUCCARINO, Gênes (I), 75, Evêque de Bobbio Membre Honoraire
2013	Mirandol (France)	Mlle Philomène CROS, Albi (F), 100, Membre Honoraire.

25

1955	Veghel (Netherlands)	Jan van den DONK, 's-Hertogenbosch (NL), 49
1964	Nantes (France)	Eugène MASSON, Rennes (F), 64
1966	Tchaourou (Dahomey)	Antonin GAUTIER, Nantes (F), 82
2000	Still (France)	Lucien REYSER, Strasbourg (F), 91
2017	Cadier en Keer (Netherlands)	Arjen RIJPKEMA, Groningen-Leeuwarden (NL), 90
2020	Lyon (France)	Jean PICHAT, Lyon (F), 77, Membre honoraire.

26

1992	Eindhoven (Netherlands)	Jan van DEUN, 's-Hertogenbosch (NL), 71
2018	Cork (Ireland)	Cornelius O'LEARY, Cork & Ross (IRL), 88
2020	Montferrier (France)	Claude GAVARD, Montpellier (F), 73

27

1914	Seicheprey (France)	Joseph DESFONTAINES, Nantes (F), 26, séminariste.
1958	Oosterbeek (Netherlands)	Piet MAURIKS, Roermond (NL), 55
1960	Oosterbeek (Netherlands)	Willem MEELBERG, Rotterdam (NL), 65
1995	Nancy (France)	René WACHT, Metz (F), 61, frère.
2016	Cork (Ireland)	Daniel J O'NEILL, Meath (IRL), 79

28

1910	Dolores (Mexique)	Eugène HATTEMER, Strasbourg (F), 31
1911	Einsiedeln (Suisse)	Lucien BREITEL, Strasbourg (F), 59
1928	Sinématiali (Côte d'Ivoire)	Émile BONHOMME, Mende (F), 75
1930	Lokoja (Nigeria)	Walter KEARY, Achonry (IRL), 29
1973	Strasbourg (France)	Jules MEYER, Strasbourg (F), 63
1980	Arnhem (Netherlands)	Frans HERTSIG, 's-Hertogenbosch (NL), 79
1997	Cork (Ireland)	Michael McFADDEN, Tuam (IRL), 81
2002	Cork (Ireland)	Daniel J O'CONNOR, Cork (IRL), 72

29

1920	La Croix-Valmer (France)	+Auguste DURET, Nantes (F), 74, 4ème Supérieur général, ancien Vicaire Apostolique du Delta du Nil.
1938	Mango (Togo)	Georges KRAUTH, Strasbourg (F), 52
1938	Grand-Popo (Dahomey)	Emile GAUDIN, Nantes (F), 37
1997	Buggenum (Netherlands)	Jeu FLORACK, Roermond (NL), 78

30

1955	Zuénoula (Côte d'Ivoire)	Camille CHARRIER, Luçon (F), 34
1969	Cork (Ireland)	Charles WEST, Liverpool (GB), 71, brother.
1978	Dinan (France)	Jules SAVÉAN, Versailles (F), 68
1980	Veenendaal (Netherlands)	Johannes de ROOY, Haarlem (NL), 74
1993	New Milford (U.S.A.)	Freda M WALTER, Vienne (USA), 83, Membre Honoraire.
1994	Los Angeles (U.S.A.)	James MORRISON, Cork (IRL), 71
1996	Saint André Treize Voies (France)	Robert THIBAUD, Nantes (F), 61
2009	Saint-Pierre (France)	Antoine GOETZ, Strasbourg (F), 87
2009	Cork (Ireland)	James HARROLD, Limerick (IRL), 91

31

2014	Tenafly (U.S.A.)	Thomas E HAYDEN, Boston (USA), 82
2022	Nairobi (Kenya)	Lawrence N. ONGOMA, Kakamega (KEN), 42

September/ Septembre

1

1921	Sasstown (Liberia)	Denis O'HARA, Achonry (IRL), 29
1982	Cork (Ireland)	James AHERN, Cloyne (IRL), 69, brother.
1987	Dublin (Ireland)	Thomas O'ROURKE-HUGHES, Down & Connor (IRL), 82

2

1945	Cape Coast (Ghana)	Henri SCHOEN, Strasbourg (F), 64
1970	Kinnegad (Ireland)	Michael WALKER, Achonry (IRL), 29
1990	Dublin (Ireland)	James CARROLL, Cloyne (IRL), 80
2012	Montpellier (France)	Jean-Baptiste DUFFÈS, Viviers (F), 88

3

| 1983 | Montferrier (France) | Eugène OLIVAIN, Le Puy (F), 85 |
| 1994 | Newry (Ireland) | Patrick BRANIFF, Down & Connor (IRL), 89 |

4

1939	Keta (Ghana)	René van GOETHEM, Breda (NL), 31
1942	Warri (Nigeria)	Thomas Sexton CAHILL, Down & Connor (IRL), 35
2002	Blaasveld (Belgique)	Bernard DODENBIER, Utrecht (NL), 98
2007	Cork (Ireland)	Francis McCABE, Elphin (IRL), 89

5

1885	Abeokuta (Nigeria)	Louis BLANC, Albi (F), 30
1963	Sainte-Foy (France)	+François FAROUD, Grenoble (F), 78, Préfet apostolique de Parakou, Dahomey.
1991	Tenafly (U.S.A.)	Laurier W HAINES, Portland (USA), 57
2002	Cardiff (Galles)	P Gerard SCANLAN, Killaloe (IRL), 82
2015	Aabenraa (Denmark)	Theodorus L (Dick) BAKKER, Haarlem-Amsterdam (NL), 83
2016	Cork (Ireland)	T Vincent LAWLESS, Clonfert (IRL), 85

6

1870	Lyon (France)	François LECAER, Saint-Brieuc (F), 26, séminariste.
1914	Marne (France)	Ferdinand PIÉDALOS, Nantes (F), 22, séminariste.
2012	Montpellier (France)	Paul AUBRY, Nantes (F), 79
2015	Montferrier (France)	Jacques LALANDE, Paris (F), 88
2017	Lomé (Togo)	Andre CHAUVIN, Rennes (F), 85

7

1874	Nantes (France)	Léon LEBRUN, Nantes (F), 25, séminariste.
1887	Ouidah (Dahomey)	Pierre SADELER, Luxembourg (LU), 28
1950	Zagnanado (Dahomey)	Joseph BARREAU, Luçon (F), 69
1992	Kumasi (Ghana)	Piet NEEFJES, Haarlem (NL), 58
2020	Dublin (Ireland)	James HICKEY, Dublin (IRL), 97

8

1916	Cloughballymore (Ireland)	Count Llewellyn BLAKE, Tuam (IRL), 77, Honorary Member.
1923	Lagos (Nigeria)	Victor WURTH, Strasbourg (F), 36
1944	Santa-Maria (Italie)	Paul FLEITH, Strasbourg (F), 23, séminariste.
1969	Cork (Ireland)	Paul HURST, Cork (IRL), 75, brother.
1979	Cork (Ireland)	Malachy GATELY, Elphin (IRL), 73

9

1881	Lorient (France)	Jean-Louis GUYOMAR, Vannes (F), 21, séminariste.
1942	Los Angeles (U.S.A.)	Edmond SCHLECHT, Strasbourg (F), 49
1953	Galway (Ireland)	Edward BERMINGHAM, Galway (IRL), 37
2014	Cork (Ireland)	Thomas S DORAN, Down & Connor (IRL), 81

10

1903	Luchon (France)	Pierre-Bertrand BOUCHE, Toulouse (F), 68
1913	La Walk (France)	Charles BALTZ, Strasbourg (F), 36
1914	Tanta (Égypte)	Albert LEGEARD, Le Mans (F), 52
1989	Sélestat (France)	Edouard BLARER, Saint-Gall (CHE), 90, frère.
2015	Montferrier (France)	Jean-Charles RAMIN, Lyon (F), 91
2020	Nantes (France)	Bernard FAVIER, Lyon (F), 86

11

| 1980 | Glasgow (Scotland) | Gerard PHILLIPS, Down & Connor (IRL), 73 |

12

1937	Rome (Italie)	Luigi TACCHINI, Milano (I), 62
1963	Villefort (France)	Georges OLLIER, Mende (F), 80
1971	Drogheda (Ireland)	John LYNOTT, Limerick (IRL), 73
1976	Tenafly (U.S.A.)	Laurence CARR, Dublin (IRL), 56
1992	Sélestat (France)	Eugène WOELFFEL, Strasbourg (F), 82
1996	Montferrier (France)	Bertrand HELLEUX, Rennes (F), 69
2000	Lyon (France)	Jean DURIF, Lyon (F), 78

13

1923	Lyon (France)	Alexandre LECOMTE, Rennes (F), 31, séminariste.
1939	Au front (France)	Jean GILORY, Luçon (F), 24, séminariste.
1966	Largentière (France)	Émile HEBTING, Strasbourg (F), 78
1971	La Croix-Valmer (France)	Paul EZANNO, Vannes (F), 83
1991	Cork (Ireland)	David MULCAHY, Limerick (IRL), 84
1996	Cork (Ireland)	Michael McCOY, Clogher (IRL), 74
1996	Oosterbeek (Netherlands)	Hein VERSPEEK, 's-Hertogenbosch (NL), 69
2016	Nantes (France)	Pierre TRICHET, Chalons (F), 83

14

1946	Hastings (Great Britain)	Jan HOUTMAN, Rotterdam (NL), 79
1949	Lyon (France)	Gustave BONNEFOY, Besançon (F), 74, frère.
1958	Cotonou (Dahomey)	Joseph DOUAUD, Nantes (F), 37
1992	Tenafly (U.S.A.)	Hugh A McLAUGHLIN, Derry (IRL), 88

15

1931	Niamey (Niger)	René GROSSEAU, Nantes (F), 30
1963	Haguenau (France)	+Joseph DISS, Strasbourg (F), 85, Préfet apostolique de Korhogo, Côte d'Ivoire.
2008	Lodi (U.S.A.)	James Harold SULLIVAN, New York (USA), 74

16

1930	La Croix-Valmer (France)	Henri WELLINGER, Paris (F), 83
1932	Asaba (Nigeria)	James McGETTIGAN, Raphoe (IRL), 51
1941	Marseille (France)	Joseph QUICKERT, Strasbourg (F), 30
1943	Nantes (France)	Jean DUHAMEL, Saint-Brieuc (F), 32
1963	La Croix-Valmer (France)	Darius DUHILL, Rennes (F), 72
1968	Gagnoa (Côte d'Ivoire)	Raymond ÉVAIN, Vannes (F), 44
1990	Sittard (Netherlands)	Wim van de LAAR, Roermond (NL), 72
1997	Cork (Ireland)	Thomas DRUMMOND, Kerry (IRL), 75
2014	Bangui (R Centrafique)	Barthélémy NAMDEGANAMNA, Bossangoa (RCA), 49

17

1938	Cadier en Keer (Netherlands)	Georges LANG, Strasbourg (F), 72, frère.
1938	Hastings (Great Britain)	Edward LEGGE, Cardiff (GB), 23, seminarian.
2015	Maastricht (Netherlands)	Petrus G KESSELS, Roermond (NL), 88

18

1951	Abidjan (Côte d'Ivoire)	Laurens DANKERS, 's-Hertogenbosch (NL), 51
1953	La Croix-Valmer (France)	Simon FONTVIEILLE, Clermont-Ferrand (F), 72
2004	Montferrier (France)	Jean-Louis GUÉNOLÉ, Quimper (F), 86

19

1919	Demshi (Nigeria)	Donat SCHELCHER, Strasbourg (F), 31
1973	Romford (Great Britain)	Michael HOLTON, Waterford (IRL), 58
2011	Cork (Ireland)	Bernard RAYMOND, Dublin (IRL), 80
2012	Gulpen (Netherlands)	Johannes Maria KOEK, Haarlem (NL), 67

20

1891	Keta (Ghana)	Cor van de PAVOORDT, Haarlem (NL), 30
1960	Kilcolgan (Ireland)	Thomas DEELEY, Clonfert (IRL), 57
1979	Nantes (France)	Francis VERGER, Nantes (F), 56
1981	Cork (Ireland)	John O'MALLEY, Tuam (IRL), 63
1992	Cadier en Keer (Netherlands)	Jan GOOREN, Roermond (NL), 74
1995	Montferrier (France)	Jean BRIENS, Saint-Brieuc (F), 86
2012	Madurai (India)	Aarokiasamy GNANAPRAGASAM, Tuticorin (IND), 84

21

| 1913 | Athiémé (Dahomey) | Jean-Marie PANNETIER, Rennes (F), 27 |
| 2007 | Cadier en Keer (Netherlands) | James van OUDHEUSDEN, Rotterdam (NL), 92 |

22

1930	Lyon (France)	Barthélemy SABOT, Saint-Étienne (F), 24
1962	Coniston (Great Britain)	+William LUMLEY, Meath (IRL), 64, Prefect Apostolic of Jos, Nigeria.
1966	Brooklyn (U.S.A.)	John SHEEHY, Brooklyn (USA), 66
1977	Abeokuta (Nigeria)	John KILBEY, Dublin (IRL), 85
1990	Cadier en Keer (Netherlands)	Hubert LEHAEN, Luik (B), 85
2001	Cadier en Keer (Netherlands)	Wynand RUYLING, Roermond (NL), 74
2010	Mulranny (Ireland)	Martin MCNEELY, Tuam (IRL), 77

23

1903	Topo (Nigeria)	Victorin GALLAUD, Valence (F), 49
1950	Antony (France)	Louis COMBAT, Paris (F), 44
1968	Toulon (France)	Joseph LEGRAND, Paris (F), 84
1990	Obernai (France)	Nicolas WEBER, Strasbourg (F), 79
2001	Cadier en Keer (Netherlands)	Sjef LENNERTZ, Roermond (NL), 84
2012	Montferrier (France)	Petrus REYNARD, Saint-Etienne (F), 83
2014	Montferrier (France)	Elie COCHO, Le Puy (F), 82

24

1892	Lyon (France)	Patrick DOWNEY, Ossory (IRL), 31
1900	Abeokuta (Nigeria)	Alois SCHROD, Mainz (D), 25
1931	Bouaké (Côte d'Ivoire)	Alphonse LEBUS, Strasbourg (F), 33
1939	Dublin (Ireland)	Nicholas CLERY, Dublin (IRL), 54
1943	Atlanta (U.S.A.)	Victor BAECHTEL, Strasbourg (F), 36
1988	Montferrier (France)	Frédéric MÉNARD, Saint-Brieuc (F), 71
1990	Montferrier (France)	François NOËL, Vannes (F), 79, frère.
1993	Cork (Ireland)	Edward F COLEMAN, Cloyne (IRL), 78
2013	Cadier en Keer (Netherlands)	Willebrordus HUISMAN, Groningen (NL), 92

25

1893	Kerbach (France)	Pierre KLAM, Metz (F), 24, séminariste.
1915	Mesnil-les-Hurlus (France)	Alexis SÉCHER, Nantes (F), 30, frère.
1925	Bagneux (France)	Jean PAY, Angers (F), 48
1942	Morestel (France)	Adolphe IMOBERDORF, Sion (CHE), 71
1970	Pau (France)	Bernard SOULÉ, Bayonne (F), 40

26

1947	Chicago (U.S.A.)	Valentine BARNICLE, Tuam (IRL), 46
1968	La Croix-Valmer (France)	Gabriel LELIÈVRE, Nantes (F), 87
2014	Lyon (France)	Michel LOIRET, Nantes (F), 77
2022	Montferrier (France)	Jacques SICARD, Le Puy (F), 86

27

1895	Lyon (France)	Michel KIEFFER, Strasbourg (F), 20, séminariste.
1947	Lyon (France)	Joseph MONNEY, Lausanne (CHE), 54
1949	Teaneck (USA)	Alfred LAUBÉ, Strasbourg (F), 69
1974	Lolobi (Ghana)	Jan BACKES, Roermond (NL), 54
1974	Essen (Germany)	Adrie SUIJKERBUIJK, Breda (NL), 62
2008	Corcoué-sur-Logne (France)	Michel DENIAUD, Nantes (F), 73
2022	Cork (Ireland)	Michael NOHILLY, Tuam (IRL), 76

28

| 1937 | Kwande (Nigeria) | John MARREN, Achonry (IRL), 29 |
| 1995 | Montferrier (France) | Maxime GAUME, Besançon (F), 84 |

29

1886	Nice (France)	Clément GUILLON, Nantes (F), 41
1887	Lyon (France)	Noël BAUDIN, Nevers (F), 43
1963	Belfast (Ireland)	John O'NEILL, Down & Connor (IRL), 53
1974	Cork (Ireland)	John MORAN, Tuam (IRL), 68
1997	Montpellier (France)	Louis PANIS, Albi (F), 79

30

1884	Tanta (Egypte)	Victor MANDONNET, Lausanne (CHE), 24, frère.
1912	Mouscron (Belgique)	+Ernest-Marie MÉNAGER, Rennes (F), 64, Préfet Apostolique du Dahomey.
1940	Cork (Ireland)	William BUTLER, Ossory (IRL), 59
2016	Montferrier (France)	Louis-Marie MOREAU, Lucon (F), 85
2017	Andlau (France)	Francis KUNTZ, Strasbourg (F), 87

October/ Octobre

1

1951	Savannah (USA)	Gustave OBRECHT, Strasbourg (F), 76
1954	Savannah (U.S.A.)	Alphonse KOCH, Strasbourg (F), 54
1957	Agboville (Côte d'Ivoire)	Martin FÈVRE, Langres (F), 45
1992	Giens (France)	Jean-Dominique CHATTOT, Lyon (F), 49
2017	Montferrier (France)	Charles SANDERS, Liège (F), 87

2

1979	Colmar (France)	Eugene CHRIST, Strasbourg (F), 67
1980	Wavrin (France)	Ignace DELANNOY, Lille (F), 54
1983	Cork (Ireland)	Richard BEAUSANG, Cork (IRL), 61
2010	Chanly (Belgique)	Jean-Marie LAMOTTE, Namur (B), 78
2017	Cork (Ireland)	John A TRAVERS, Armagh (IRL), 92

3

1858	Lyon (France)	Pierre GUILLET, Autun (F), 24, frère.
1951	Strasbourg (France)	François-Xavier HIRSCH, Strasbourg (F), 60
1964	Cork (Ireland)	Patrick HUGHES, Tuam (IRL), 61
1972	Mazamet (France)	Pierre BORDES, Albi (F), 68
1986	Dromantine (Ireland)	Leo P McNEILL, Armagh (IRL), 68
1994	Dublin (Ireland)	+John REDDINGTON, Elphin (IRL), 84, Bishop of Jos Nigeria.
2010	Cadier en Keer (Netherlands)	Herman ENGBERINK, Utrecht (NL), 90
2015	Bangui (R. Centrafricaine)	Amos NGAÏZOURE, Bangui (RCA), 44
2023	Zinswald (France)	Arthur BECKER, Metz (F), 81

4

1990	Meerssen (Netherlands)	Jan HASSING, Groningen (NL), 85

5

1906	Cork (Ireland)	Auguste SIMON, Strasbourg (F), 37
1937	Jos (Nigeria)	Anthony O'DWYER, Clonfert (IRL), 27
1951	Saint-Pierre (France)	Albert ROESCH, Strasbourg (F), 42
2006	Dover (U.S.A.)	John J SHEEHAN, Hartford (USA), 90
2013	Haguenau (France)	Félix LUTZ, Strasbourg (F), 89
2018	St Jean le Vieux (France)	Bernard CURUTCHET, Bayonne (F), 88

6

1945	Colmar (France)	Joseph FAHRNER, Strasbourg (F), 47
1971	Ijebu-Ode (Nigeria)	William MURPHY, Cork (IRL), 62
1990	Assin Foso (Ghana)	Sef MOONEN, Roermond (NL), 63
2013	Tenaflay (USA)	Edward BIGGANE, Brooklyn (USA), 81
2014	Cork (Ireland)	Thomas FURLONG, Waterford & Lisimore (IRL), 90
2023	Montferrier (France)	Georges FONTENEAU, Luçon (F), 84

7

1960	La Croix-Valmer (France)	Ferdinand PRAUD, Luçon (F), 65
1961	Jacksonville (U.S.A.)	Daniel WATSON, Down & Connor (IRL), 50
1967	Helmond (Netherlands)	Mattheus van LIESHOUT, 's-Hertogenbosch (NL), 64, Brother Benedictus.
1973	Barclayville (Liberia)	Dominic DONOHUE, Kildare (IRL), 36
1992	Tralee (Ireland)	Thomas DEVANE, Kerry (IRL), 68
1996	Lutterbach (France)	Henri SCHNEIDER, Strasbourg (F), 85
2017	Cadier en Keer (Netherlands)	Gerard LUKASSEN, Groningen-Leeuwarden (NL), 88

8

1887	Lamage (France)	Eugène CHEVAL, Valence (F), 25, séminariste.
1966	La Croix-Valmer (France)	Barthélemy MONTEL, Clermont-Ferrand (F), 66, frère.
1974	Saint-Pierre (France)	Théodore FELLMANN, Strasbourg (F), 75
2003	Terwagne (Belgique)	Willy LEJEUNE, Malines Bruxelles (B), 81
2011	Cork (Ireland)	Hugh McKEOWN, Down & Connor (IRL), 86
2018	Cork (Ireland)	W Romuald BARRY, Cork & Ross (IRL), 73

9

1921	Mozac (France)	Prosper BACH, Strasbourg (F), 44
2004	Montpellier (France)	Pierre AUDOUIN, Laval (F), 58
2017	Schiltigheim (France)	André FUCHS, Strasbourg (F), 94
2023	Montferrier (France)	Raymond JOLY, Nantes (F), 87

10

1940	Sainte-Foy (France)	Émile Joseph SCHMITT, Strasbourg (F), 61
1980	Newry (Ireland)	+Francis CARROLL, Dromore (IRL), 68, Vicar Apostolic of Monrovia Liberia.
1990	Le Caire (Égypte)	Gabriel SCIAMMA, Héliopolis (ET), 77
1992	Yopougon (Côte d'Ivoire)	Jean MEYNIER, Saint-Claude (F), 61
1996	Cadier en Keer (Netherlands)	Hubert GIJSELAERS, Roermond (NL), 79
2014	Cork (Ireland)	Bridget Agatha FEELEY, Cork & Ross (IRL), 92, Honorary Member.

11

1941	Saint-Pierre (France)	Émile Nicolas SCHMITT, Strasbourg (F), 62
1954	Arnhem (Netherlands)	Martin KUIJPERS, 's-Hertogenbosch (NL), 50, brother.
1973	Asikuma (Ghana)	Cor van der PLAS, Haarlem (NL), 61

12

1948	Saint-Pierre (France)	+Ernest HAUGER, Strasbourg (F), 75, Vicaire Apostolique de la Côte-de-l'Or.
1978	Cork (Ireland)	Kevin O'SHEA, Cork (IRL), 70
2003	Clonmel (Ireland)	Owen F SWEENEY, Cork (IRL), 65
2006	Montferrier (France)	Pierre DIDELOT, Saint-Dié (F), 85
2017	Rustenburg (South Africa)	Pius AFIABOR O., Lagos (NGA), 45

13

1933	Gênes (Italie)	+Thomas BRODERICK, Kerry (IRL), 51, Vicar Apostolic of Western Nigeria.
1955	Salon-de-Provence (France)	Amédée CHIFFOLEAU, Nantes (F), 80
1973	Buitenkaag (Netherlands)	Kees BREUKEL, Rotterdam (NL), 70
1990	Montferrier (France)	Lucien NOURY, Nantes (F), 64
1995	Cadier en Keer (Netherlands)	Herman LUBBERS, Utrecht (NL), 77
2004	Ringwood (U.S.A.)	George LANDRY, Nicolet (CDN), 85
2008	Cork (Ireland)	James McCARTHY, Cork (IRL), 87

14

1871	Lagos (Nigeria)	Alexis VEYRET, Grenoble (F), 27
1940	Cotonou (Dahomey)	Michel BOURGET, Nantes (F), 55
1947	Abengourou (Côte d'Ivoire)	Léon KAPFER, Strasbourg (F), 35
1990	Breda (Netherlands)	Evert HEIJMANS, 's-Hertogenbosch (NL), 80
2008	Montpellier (France)	René MÉNARD, Poitiers (F), 84
2022	Abujia (Nigeria)	Matthew Shinkut BASSAH, Kaduna (NGA), 42

15

1872	Lagos (Nigeria)	Joseph BOURGUET, Nancy (F), 31
1912	Saint-Didier-sur-Doulon (France)	Jean BRESSOL, Le Puy (F), 24, séminariste.
1915	Sainte-Foy (France)	Henri LEGAL, Nantes (F), 33
1968	Dublin (Ireland)	Thomas CLONAN, Meath (IRL), 59
2007	Gênes (Italie)	Giacomo BARDELLI, Bergamo (I), 67

16

1892	Ronco-Scrivia (Italie)	Francesco BORGHERO, Gênes (I), 62
1940	Zifta (Égypte)	Joseph BORNE, Saint-Étienne (F), 35
1959	Bayonne (France)	Jean CURUTCHET, Bayonne (F), 49
1963	Soubré (Côte d'Ivoire)	Pierre BRUYAS, Lyon (F), 38, frère.
1980	Cork (Ireland)	Thomas DONOGHUE, Killaloe (IRL), 82
1997	Cork (Ireland)	Michael J COLLERAN, Tuam (IRL), 86
2014	Cork (Ireland)	Anthony J BUTLER, Dublin (IRL), 73

17

1880	Agoué (Dahomey)	Alphonse NOLAN, (IRL), brother.
1973	La Croix-Valmer (France)	Claude LAZINIER, Créteil (F), 66
1992	Leiden (Netherlands)	Gerard JOOSTEN, Utrecht (NL), 75
2015	Saint-Pierre (France)	Pierre JACQUOT, Besançon (F), 76
2016	Cadier en Keer (Netherlands)	Eduard HUBERT, Rotterdam (NL), 77
2020	Montferrier (France)	André PERRIN, Lyon (F), 75

18

1920	Grand-Bassam (Côte d'Ivoire)	Frédéric MARCHAIS, Nantes (F), 34
1921	Grand-Lahou (Côte d'Ivoire)	Pierre GARCIA, Bayonne (F), 38
1960	Carlow (Ireland)	Thomas F HUGHES, Tuam (IRL), 63
2016	Montferrier (France)	Maurice BIOTTEAU, Nantes (F), 84

19

1915	Niedercom (Luxembourg)	Aloyse NICOLAÏ, Luxembourg (LU), 29
1949	Kwa (Nigeria)	Francis SANDS, Dromore (IRL), 33
1980	Lyon (France)	Arthur CHAUVIN, Soissons (F), 67
1990	Strabane (Ireland)	Daniel J McCAULEY, Derry (IRL), 75
1999	Vero Beach, Florida (USA)	John F FLYNN, Ardagh (IRL), 70
2003	Amsterdam (Netherlands)	Wilhelmus HABITS, Haarlem (NL), 76
2006	Montferrier (France)	Pierre TRICHET, Auch (F), 82
2014	Cork (Ireland)	Daniel MURPHY, Cork & Ross (IRL), 82
2015	Montferrier (France)	Michel GIRARD, Paris (F), 91

20

1945	Ondo (Nigeria)	Patrick CLANCY, Limerick (IRL), 27
1948	Chamalières (France)	Marcel MÉTAYER, Rennes (F), 28
1958	Dabré (Côte d'Ivoire)	Pierre MÉRAUD, Limoges (F), 86
1960	Lauw (France)	Antoine WIEDER, Strasbourg (F), 55
1964	New York (U.S.A.)	Mgr William LITTLE, New York (USA), 78, Honorary Member.
1967	Allauch (France)	Denis CLOUET, Nantes (F), 67
1973	Cadier en Keer (Netherlands)	Kees BODEWES, Groningen (NL), 66
1982	Zinswald (France)	Hugues BRUN, Strasbourg (F), 71
1993	Cadier en Keer (Pays-Bas)	Andreas BRUINSMA, Groningen (NL), 75
1999	Cork (Ireland)	Hugh D CONLON, Cork (IRL), 78
2022	Colmar (France)	Georges SELZER, Strasbourg (F), 90

21

1891	Asaba (Nigeria)	Joseph PESSOZ, Tarentaise (F), 31
1900	Steinach (Suisse)	Jakob HOEGGER, Saint-Gall (CHE), 25
1907	Cape Coast (Ghana)	Auguste BANNWARTH, Strasbourg (F), 30
1916	Lyon (France)	Martin FRIEDRICH, Strasbourg (F), 44
1952	Zinswald (France)	Joseph STAUFFER, Strasbourg (F), 76
1972	Cork (Ireland)	Henry KENNY, Dublin (IRL), 80
1975	Oosterbeek (Netherlands)	Koos NADORP, Rotterdam (NL), 71, brother.
1981	Cork (Ireland)	Henry SHEPPARD, Cork (IRL), 73
1984	Lille (France)	Paul DEVIENNE, Lille (F), 73
2000	Maastricht (Netherlands)	Frits van VEIJFEIJKEN, 's-Hertogenbosch (NL), 73

22

1902	Grand-Bassam (Côte d'Ivoire)	Jean PERRAUD, Nantes (F), 24
1935	Mulhouse (France)	Bernard SCHMITT, Strasbourg (F), 60
1983	Montferrier (France)	Félix GOYHENETCHE, Bayonne (F), 68
1994	Cadier en Keer (Netherlands)	Coen EVERS, Rotterdam (NL), 88
2004	Cadier en Keer (Netherlands)	Leonardus van GASTEL, Breda (NL), 86

23

1942	Robbiano (Italie)	Berengario CERMENATI, Milano (I), 68
1951	Hohoe (Ghana)	Joseph COBBEN, Roermond (NL), 33
1969	Le Caire (Égypte)	Louis DEROCQ, Lille (F), 69, Frère Jean de Kenty.
1989	Montferrier (France)	Alphonse MARGUERIE, Coutances (F), 85

24

1900	Abeokuta (Nigeria)	Édouard LABORDE, Pamiers (F), 24
1916	Douaumont (France)	Louis LEROUX, Le Mans (F), 26, séminariste.
2008	Montferrier (France)	Bernard LAURENT, Laval (F), 89, frère.

25

1885	Lokoja (Nigeria)	Filippo FIORENTINI, Milano (I), 34
1961	Saint-Pierre (France)	Aimé SIMON, Strasbourg (F), 81
1976	Rome (Italie)	Ernst RIEDEL, Meissen (D), 77
2002	Cork (Ireland)	Martin HERAGHTY, Raphoe (IRL), 83
2015	Sarrebourg (France)	Ferdinand BLINDAUER, Metz (F), 83

26

1958	Pierre-Bénite (France)	Georges BLANDIN, Rennes (F), 38
1961	Hazebrouck (France)	Joseph WALLON, Lille (F), 62
1966	Tenafly (U.S.A.)	Joseph WERNERT, Strasbourg (F), 77
2015	Heerlen (PAYS-BAS)	Enricus (Harrie) HOEBEN, Roermond (NL), 81
2020	Montréal (Canada)	Thomas-Léon BOILY, Chicoutimi (CDN), 94

27

1918	Lagos (Nigeria)	Johann LANDOLT, Saint-Gall (CHE), 30
1954	Dublin (Ireland)	John DEANE, Kerry (IRL), 49
1965	Lagos (Nigeria)	+ Leo TAYLOR, Duluth (USA), 76, Archibishop of Lagos, Nigeria.
1988	Cadier en Keer (Netherlands)	Louis ZUIDWIJK, Haarlem (NL), 82
1995	Lille (France)	Étienne HUGOT, Arras (F), 86
2004	Montferrier (France)	Henri FRÉNEAU, Nantes (F), 67, frère.
2009	Asti (Italie)	Guido MONTANARO, Asti (I), 86, Membre Honoraire.

28

1927	Bufalo (U.S.A.)	Laurent BASTIAN, Strasbourg (F), 63
1938	Lagos (Nigeria)	+Francis O'ROURKE, Ardagh (IRL), 56, Vicair Apostolic of the Coast of Benin.
1940	Alexandria (Égypte)	Vincent MOORE, Dublin (IRL), 50
1962	Cork (Ireland)	Patrick Francis KELLY, Ossory (IRL), 50
1976	Corrundulla (Ireland)	Francis FALLON, Clonfert (IRL), 60
1976	Oosterbeek (Netherlands)	Jan ter LINDEN, 's-Hertogenbosch (NL), 69
1997	Saint-Pierre (France)	Camille STAUFF, Strasbourg (F), 78
2017	Sélestat (France)	Bernard VONDERSCHER, Saint-Dié (F), 87

29

1946	Akure (Nigeria)	Michael ROCHE, Tuam (IRL), 34
1952	La Croix-Valmer (France)	Jean VERT, Clermont-Ferrand (F), 69
1981	Sélestat (France)	Émile STADELWIESER, Strasbourg (F), 77
2013	Cork (Ireland)	William BURKE, Ossory (IRL), 87

30

| 1995 | Portlaoise (Ireland) | Matthew WALSH, Kildare & Leighlin (IRL), 85 |

31

1908	Axim (Ghana)	Arthur DUMOULIN, Roermond (NL), 29
1941	Bemelen (Netherlands)	Louis HELWEGEN, Roermond (NL), 32
2004	Cork (Ireland)	Robert HALES, Cork (IRL), 76

November/ Novembre

1

1980	Paris (France)	Jean THÉPAUT, Quimper (F), 73
1986	Nijmegen (Netherlands)	Leo OP't HOOG, 's-Hertogenbosch (NL), 59
2001	Hackensack (U.S.A.)	Michael J ROONEY, Tuam (IRL), 84

2

1962	Oosterbeek (Netherlands)	André HOMMA, Groningen (NL), 57, brother.
1962	Ibadan (Nigeria)	John Michael MONAHAN, Ferns (IRL), 28
1986	Heerlen (Netherlands)	Pierre KNOPS, Roermond (NL), 88
1999	Saint-Pierre (France)	Heinrich LATZ, Trèves (D), 74, frère.
2010	Ballygarriss (Ireland)	John FEENEY, Galway (IRL), 88

3

1978	Saint-Tropez (France)	Jean JESTIN, Quimper (F), 75
2000	Cork (Ireland)	Denis J O'DONOVAN, Cork (IRL), 86
2004	Montpellier (France)	Jean-Marie BAUDUCEL, Laval (F), 83

4

1955	Oosterbeek (Netherlands)	Piet COMINO, Utrecht (NL), 49, brother.
1962	Cork (Ireland)	Patrick Francis McKENNA, Kilmore (IRL), 73
1993	Montferrier (France)	Jean QUIGNON, Rennes (F), 76
1998	Montferrier (France)	Jean-Marie GAUTIER, Vannes (F), 79
2007	Montferrier (France)	Henri NEAU, Nantes (F), 68
2008	Amstelveen (Netherlands)	Johan VERSPEEK, Hertogenbosch (NL), 72

5

1934	Palimé (Togo)	Bernard van LEEUWEN, Haarlem (NL), 44
1935	New York (U.S.A.)	Michael O'DONOHUE, Kildare & Leighlin (IRL), 41
1960	Oosterbeek (Netherlands)	Louis van EERD, 's-Hertogenbosch (NL), 71
1963	Sunyani (Ghana)	Pierre LOOZEN, Roermond (NL), 40
1967	Zinswald (France)	Jérôme RIEMER, Strasbourg (F), 58
1973	Sainte-Foy (France)	Pascal COLICHET, Rennes (F), 73
1980	Montferrier (France)	Eugène Louis VENGEANT, Laval (F), 77, Frère Camille.
1986	Utrecht (Netherlands)	Wilhelmus de ROOY, Haarlem (NL), 75

6

1889	Nice (France)	Julien JAY, Tarentaise (F), 24
1936	Tilburg (Netherlands)	Harrie VUGTS, 's-Hertogenbosch (NL), 32
1966	Arnhem (Netherlands)	Laurent MEERTENS, Roermond (NL), 75, Frère Jean.
1985	Cork (Ireland)	Louis KINNANE, Down & Connor (IRL), 74
1994	Cork (Ireland)	Brendan HANNIFFY, Clonfert (IRL), 72
2016	Sotouboua (Togo)	Jean PERRIN, Strasbourg (F), 91
2019	Cotonou (Benin)	Albert TEVOEDJIRE, Porto-Novo (BEN), 90, Membre honoraire.

7

1883	Elmina (Ghana)	Pierre LEGEAY, Angers (F), 37
1907	Lyon (France)	Ferdinand TERRIEN, Nantes (F), 58
1935	Jos (Nigeria)	Florence O'DRISCOLL, Cork & Ross (IRL), 30
1962	La Croix-Valmer (France)	Joseph CORBEAU, Nantes (F), 80
1974	Saint-Colomban (France)	Théophile BOURSIN, Nantes (F), 77
1977	Haguenau (France)	Lucien KAPPS, Strasbourg (F), 68
1986	Soubré (Côte d'Ivoire)	Jean-Louis ROUMIER, Quimper (F), 63
1995	Saint-Pierre (France)	Joseph MEYER, Strasbourg (F), 81

8

1954	Le Caire (Égypte)	Michel GHALI, Héliopolis (ET), 79
1993	Guildford (Great Britain)	Richard D VEASEY, Clifton (GB), 45
1996	Cadier en Keer (Netherlands)	Wim RUIKES, Utrecht (NL), 80
2004	Saltpond (Ghana)	Jaap OBDAM, Haarlem (NL), 85
2010	Montferrier (France)	Joseph HÉRY, Nantes (F), 82
2022	Montferrier (France)	Pierre LEGENDRE, Nancy (F), 90

9

1912	Barcelona (Espagne)	Bartolomé SARRÁ, Barcelona (E), 71
1945	Bemelen (Pays Bas)	Charles LOUXEN, Luxembourg (LU), 81
1952	Los Vilos (Chile)	Nicolás BASTIDA, Burgos (E), 76
1989	Molenhoek (Netherlands)	André BODELIER, Roermond (NL), 55
1991	Oosterbeek (Netherlands)	Adrie A van BAAR, Haarlem (NL), 73
2018	Senlis (France)	Jean LEVEQUE, Nantes (F), 82
2020	Cork (Ireland)	James C FEGAN, Down & Connor (IRL), 72

10

| 1935 | Atlanta (U.S.A.) | Jérôme DOLLINGER, Strasbourg (F), 56 |

11

1907	Aboisso (Côte d'Ivoire)	Antoine CHALUS, Le Puy (F), 29
1926	Lyon (France)	François RÉNIER, Laval (F), 52
1942	Breda (Netherlands)	Henri ROTHOFF, 's-Hertogenbosch (NL), 39
1961	Arnhem (Netherlands)	Ate MONKEL, Utrecht (NL), 60
1975	Dublin (Ireland)	James HESSION, Tuam (IRL), 42
2014	Haguenau (France)	Jean-Paul GRASSER, Strasbourg (F), 77, Membre Honoraire.
2018	Montpellier (France)	Pierre BERGOT, Quimper (F), 89

12

1939	La Croix-Valmer (France)	Pierre MONNEY, Fribourg (CHE), 67, frère.
1949	Cotonou (Dahomey)	Eugène LIEUTAUD, Aix (F), 64
1967	Keta Ho (Ghana)	Jochem BOUMANS, Groningen (NL), 66
1975	near Ogbere (Nigeria)	Brendan DONOHUE, Kildare & Leighlin (IRL), 41
1991	Teaneck (U.S.A.)	Benedict BURKE, Cork (IRL), 69
2002	Castelbar (Ireland)	Henry J BELL, Tuam (IRL), 78
2008	Cork (Ireland)	John O'MAHONY, Dublin (IRL), 71

13

| 1911 | Ibadan (Nigeria) | Giuseppe FERRERIO, Milano (I), 29 |
| 2013 | Cadier en Keer (Netherlands) | Jacobus SMEELE, Rotterdam (NL), 67 |

14

| 1948 | Lyon (France) | René-François GUILCHER, Quimper (F), 67 |
| 1985 | Montferrier (France) | Benito IBARRETA, Vitoria (E), 75 |

15

1987	Montferrier (France)	René GUINOISEAU, Rennes (F), 87
1990	Cork (Ireland)	Michael A WALSH, Kilmore (IRL), 66, brother.
1994	Bangui (R Centrafrique)	Robert GUCWA, Tarnów (PL), 25, séminariste.
1994	Cork (Ireland)	+William MAHONY, Clonfert (IRL), 75, Bishop of Ilorin, Nigeria.
1996	Nantes (France)	Louis VIAUD, Nantes (F), 82
1998	Gênes (Italie)	Secondo CANTINO, Asti (I), 60
2010	Montferrier (France)	Pierre MESSNER, Nantes (F), 92

16

1931	Lyon (France)	+Jean OGÉ, Strasbourg (F), 63, Prefect Apostolic of Liberia.
1965	Grevenboïch (Germany)	Frits van DIJK, 's-Hertogenbosch (NL), 52
1979	Cork (Ireland)	Alphonsus O'SHEA, Armagh (IRL), 68
1990	Montferrier (France)	Jules BEDAULT, Rennes (F), 71
2017	Gênes (Italie)	Mario BOFFA, Alba (I), 85

17

1898	Porto-Novo (Dahomey)	Joseph PELLAT, Grenoble (F), 44
1943	Haguenau (France)	Clément BANNWARTH, Strasbourg (F), 66
1944	Saint-Pierre (France)	Victor BURG, Strasbourg (F), 66
2022	Lagos (Nigeria)	Mary Candy ONUSI, Kaduna (NGA), 68, Honorary Member.

18

| 1989 | Stadthagen (Germany) | Harrie SMITS, Utrecht (NL), 78 |
| 2005 | Maastricht (Netherlands) | Han van VELZEN, Rotterdam (NL), 83 |

19

1896	Hyères (France)	Henri PONCET, Lyon (F), 25
1911	Tanta (Égypte)	Isidore-Marie LOHIER, Rennes (F), 52, frère.
1959	Saint-Pierre (France)	Charles ONIMUS, Strasbourg (F), 73
1966	London (Great Britain)	Eugene McSWEENEY, Cloyne (IRL), 82
1980	Montferrier (France)	Joseph AUJOULAT, Mende (F), 78
1994	Tralee (Ireland)	Elisha O'SHEA, Kerry (IRL), 67
1997	Saint Beauzire (France)	Alfred ROPELEWSKI, Clermont-Ferrand (F), 71
2006	Dublin (Ireland)	John BURKE, Limerick (IRL), 64
2007	Abuja (Nigeria)	Cornelius GRIFFIN, Cork (IRL), 60
2013	Montferrier (France)	Nicolas MOUTERDE, Lyon (F), 85

20

1905	Zurich (Suisse)	+ Isidore KLAUSS, Saint-Gall (CHE), 41, Vicaire apostolique de la Côte de l'Or.
1910	Esure (Nigeria)	Joseph RIEFFEL, Strasbourg (F), 33
1960	Akure (Nigeria)	John MORTON, Down & Connor (IRL), 48
1997	Parakou (Bénin)	Michel AUFFRAY, Nantes (F), 67
1997	Cadier en Keer (Netherlands)	Ferdinand van LEEUWEN, Haarlem (NL), 77
2005	Cork (Ireland)	Cornelius O'DRISCOLL, Ross (IRL), 82
2017	Cadier en Keer (Nederlands)	Piet WENDERS, Roermond (NL), 81

21

1968	Arnhem (Netherlands)	Kees KOOLEN, 's-Hertogenbosch (NL), 66
1976	Eindhoven (Netherlands)	Leo BROUWER, Rotterdam (NL), 60
2003	Lomé (Togo)	Jeannine BROCHARD, Nantes (F),74, Soeur, Membre Honoraire.
2014	Nuth (Netherlands)	Lambert MEURDERS, Roermond (NL), 86
2016	Cork (Ireland)	Joseph MAGUIRE, Dublin (IRL), 94

22

1949	Hamilton (U.S.A.)	John AHERN, Cloyne (IRL), 58
1995	Montferrier (France)	Joseph GARNIER, Luçon (F), 83
2003	Newry (Ireland)	Thomas BLEE, Derry (IRL), 74
2016	Montferrier (France)	Dominique PEIRSEGAELE, Rouen (F), 82
2021	Ardee (Ireland)	Thomas KEARNEY, Armagh (IRL), 86

23

1926	Sekondi (Ghana)	Joseph HUBSTER, Strasbourg (F), 43
1972	Saint-Briac (France)	Adolphe SAUBAN, Quimper (F), 64
1988	Warri (Nigeria)	Jeremiah CADOGAN, Ross (IRL), 74
2016	Nantes (France)	Michel BERTONNEAU, Poitiers (F), 75

24

1966	Strasbourg (France)	Aloyse BLONDÉ, Strasbourg (F), 68
1989	Cork (Ireland)	Thomas MORAN, Tuam (IRL), 85
1996	Cadier en Keer (Netherlands)	Hubert JACOBI, Keulen (D), 85
2006	Lyon (France)	Xalbat MARCARIE, Bayonne (F), 69
2011	Sélestat (France)	Édouard DÉMÉRLÉ, Metz (F), 100

25

1902	Grand-Bassam (Côte d'Ivoire)	Théodore MESTER, Paderborn (D), 38, frère.
1962	Offiakaha (Côte d'Ivoire)	Robert PAULUS, Strasbourg (F), 48
1966	Le Caire (Égypte)	René MARZIN, Rennes (F), 58
2004	Gênes (Italie)	Gianfranco BRIGNONE, Mondovi (I), 59
2004	Matasia (Kenya)	John F HANNON, Killaloe (IRL), 65
2022	Gênes (Italie)	Eugenio BASSO, Mondovi (I), 78

26

1885	Porto-Novo (Dahomey)	Vicente BERENGUER, Valencia (E), 31
1959	Saint-Pierre (France)	Eugène SCHAEFFER, Strasbourg (F), 59
1960	Oosterbeek (Netherlands)	Gerardus van ROOIJ, 's-Hertogenbosch (NL), 68
2000	Cork (Ireland)	James HICKEY, Clonfert (IRL), 78
2003	Cork (Ireland)	Seán O'CONNELL, Cork (IRL), 77

27

1906	Mallow (Ireland)	Patrick SHEEHAN, Cloyne (IRL), 24, seminarian.
1937	Grenoble (France)	Jules NEU, Cambrai (F), 54
1965	Cadier en Keer (Netherlands)	Jan VERHAGEN, Rotterdam (NL), 68
1968	Lomé (Togo)	Aloyse RIEGERT, Strasbourg (F), 60
1974	Strasbourg (France)	Joseph MUCKENSTURM, Strasbourg (F), 74
2011	Montréal (Canada)	Charles-Henri BOUCHER, Québec (CDN), 81

28

1961	Cork (Ireland)	Alexander MATTHEWS, Down & Connor (IRL), 61
1968	Allerton Park (Ireland)	James TOBIN, Limerick (IRL), 49

29

1874	Bou-Thélis (Algérie)	Edouard DUBOSQ, Coutances (F), 31
1900	Athiémé (Dahomey)	Joseph SIMPLEX, Belley (F), 27
1942	La Croix-Valmer (France)	Francis VILLEVAUD, Tulle (F), 82
1976	Nijmegen (Netherlands)	Frans ROTHOFF, 's-Hertogenbosch (NL), 76
2009	Gostyn (Pologne)	Bernard MARIANSKI, Pelplin (PL), 95, Membre Honoraire.
2018	Cork (Ireland)	A Edward (Eamonn) KELLY, Elphin (IRL), 82

30

1863	Ouidah (Dahomey)	Francisco FERNANDEZ, Lugo (E), 38
1870	Mill Hill (Great Britain)	André PETIT, Clermont-Ferrand (F), 22, séminariste.
1909	Moossou (Côte d'Ivoire)	+Alexandre HAMARD, Angers (F), 55, Préfet apostolique de Côte d'Ivoire.
1913	Marseille (France)	Pierre BEISSON, Chambéry (F), 51
1935	Tenafly (U.S.A.)	Eugène PETER, Strasbourg (F), 63
1940	Sainte-Foy (France)	Germain GANDT de, Gand (B), 84
1970	La Croix-Valmer (France)	Edmond JAUFFRIT, Luçon (F), 59
1971	Castlebar (Ireland)	Patrick TOLAN, Achonry (IRL), 70, brother.
1977	Aix-en-Provence (France)	Roger DUQUESNE, Lille (F), 61
1983	Cadier en Keer (Netherlands)	Hubert van GASTEL, Roermond (NL), 77
1988	Lyon (France)	Jean-Baptiste AUDRAIN, Nantes (F), 79
1992	Glendalough (Australia)	Joseph MULLINS, Galway (IRL), 76
2009	Tarbes (France)	Eugène DUCASTAING, Bayonne (F), 72

December/ Décembre

1

1907	sur mer (naufragé)	Louis FAUVEL, Rennes (F), 39
1944	Monrovia (Liberia)	Martin LACEY, Tuam (IRL), 45
1962	West Palm Beach (U.S.A.)	Patrick LAVAN, Achonry (IRL), 56
1995	Cork (Ireland)	Peter J BENNETT, Tuam (IRL), 88
2002	Sélestat (France)	Marcel SINGER, Strasbourg (F), 75
2019	Besançon (France)	Gilbert PIRANDA, Besançon (F), 83

2

1933	London (Great Britain)	W. Gauthier BOUMANS, Utrecht (NL), 31
1946	Cork (Ireland)	James WARD, Down & Connor (IRL), 42
1956	Teaneck (U.S.A.)	Peter HARRINGTON, Ross (IRL), 67
1972	Bideford (Great Britain)	Francis CARDIFF, Dublin (IRL), 67
1988	Oosterbeek (Netherlands)	Jacobus VISSER, Haarlem (NL), 75
1996	Cadier en Keer (Netherlands)	Wim GRIFFIOEN, Haarlem (NL), 76
2008	Cork (Ireland)	John A CREAVEN, Tuam (IRL), 91

3

1927	Aledjo (Togo)	Luigi CAVAGNERA, Lodi (I), 47
1935	Dublin (Ireland)	John LAVELLE, Tuam (IRL), 37
1943	La Croix-Valmer (France)	Jean-Baptiste RAY, Clermont-Ferrand (F), 65
1962	en mer (Liberia)	Philip CARRIGAN, Boston (USA), 38
1973	Mahalla (Égypte)	Gabriel JOUANNE, Reims (F), 69
2006	Cork (Ireland)	Owen MAGINN, Down & Connor (IRL), 86
2021	Montferrier (France)	Albert ANDRE, Nantes (F), 95
2021	Borzecin Duzy (Pologne)	Józef OLCZAK, Warszawa (PL), 91, Honorary Member.

4

1937	Ibadan (Nigeria)	Edward MURPHY, Clogher (IRL), 27
1957	Fribourg (Suisse)	Jakob IMHOLZ, Saint-Gall (CHE), 80
2002	Cork (Ireland)	Edward J DONOVAN, Cork (IRL), 81
2005	Montferrier (France)	Théophile COGARD, Vannes (F), 85

5

1880	Lagos (Nigeria)	Jerome KILLEN, Westminster (GB), brother.
1929	Cadier en Keer (Netherlands)	Gaston DESRIBES, Tarbes (F), 81
1958	Oosterbeek (Pays-Bas)	Adrien SCHOONEN, Breda (NL), 61
1962	Cork (Ireland)	Martin FARRINGTON, Tuam (IRL), 63
1989	Englewood (U.S.A.)	Bartholomew KEOHANE, Cork (IRL), 85
2013	Cork (Ireland)	Thomas MULLAHY, Tuam (IRL), 79
2018	Maastricht (Netherlands)	Sr Mamerta DE LANGE, Rotterdam (NL), 92, Membre honoraire.
2022	Montferrier (France)	Jean CHARRIER, Nantes (F), 88

6

1900	Dabou (Côte d'Ivoire)	Charles BUMANN, Strasbourg (F), 23
1966	Nantes (France)	Augustin BARATHIEU, Mende (F), 84
1974	Cork (Ireland)	William BYRNE, Tuam (IRL), 64
1976	Saint-Pierre (France)	Eugène GASSER, Strasbourg (F), 90

7

1924	Abomey (Dahomey)	Joseph GIRERD, Lyon (F), 51
1934	Metz (France)	Georges VOGT, Strasbourg (F), 67
1976	Kerkrade (Netherlands)	Johannes BECKERS, Roermond (NL), 71

8

1953	Saint-Sulpice-des-Landes (France)	Jean-Marie RENOU, Nantes (F), 79
1976	Saint-Tropez (France)	Henri PICHON, Le Puy (F), 78
2002	Cork (Ireland)	Cornelius CLANCY, Cork (IRL), 88

9

1949	Ouidah (Dahomey)	Jacques IRIGOIN, Paris (F), 30, frère.
1976	Freemantle (Australia)	John GUILFOYLE, Ferns (IRL), 62
1985	Argentré-du-Plessis (France)	Arsène GANDON, Rennes (F), 87
1986	Montferrier (France)	Adolphe LEJEUNE, Namur (B), 65
1988	Montferrier (France)	Rogatien MARTINET, Nantes (F), 79
1999	Claremorris (Ireland)	Seán SWEENEY, Tuam (IRL), 90

10

1986	Arnhem (Netherlands)	Bernard EERDEN, Utrecht (NL), 80
1994	Cadier en Keer (Netherlands)	Petrus SANDERS, 's-Hertogenbosch (NL), 87
1999	Saint-Pierre (France)	Eugène BERNHART, Strasbourg (F), 78
2010	Colmar (France)	Albert WEBER, Strasbourg (F), 85, frère.

11

1967	Cork (Ireland)	Patrick CHRISTAL, Ardagh (IRL), 69
1969	Saint-Pierre (France)	Aloyse FRÉRING, Strasbourg (F), 65
2003	Hamilton (Canada)	Albert JAMES, Hamilton (CDN), 75
2004	Dromantine (Ireland)	Michael McGLINCHEY, Derry (IRL), 75
2017	Sélestat (France)	Jean KLEIN, Strasbourg (F), 79
2021	Cork (Ireland)	Thomas J TREACY, Tuam (IRL), 76

12

1903	Ouidah (Dahomey)	Jean MOUNIER, Le Puy (F), 27
1965	Lyon (France)	Alexandre LUSSON, Angers (F), 72
1984	Rezé (France)	Eugène LEAUTÉ, Nantes (F), 59, frère.
1987	Arnhen (Netherlands)	Johannes WATERREUS, Rotterdam (NL), 81
1997	Cadier en Keer (Netherlands)	Antoon van den DUNGEN, 's-Hertogenbosch (NL), 92, brother.
2007	Ingersheim (France)	Rolph ROTH, Strasbourg (F), 66
2009	Libramont (Belgique)	Jean EVRARD, Namur (B), 81
2012	Montpellier (France)	Alphonse ALLIRAND, Le Puy (F), 87

13

1941	Accra (Ghana)	Alfons TILLIE, Roermond (NL), 43
1958	Saint-Pierre (France)	Victor KERN, Strasbourg (F), 62
1964	La Croix-Valmer (France)	Charles ANÉZO, Nantes (F), 83
1985	Sittard (Netherlands)	Harrie NAUS, Roermond (NL), 73
1990	Montferrier (France)	Michel ROZE, Tours (F), 76

14

1943	Abidjan (Côte d'Ivoire)	Jean-Marie BEDEL, Saint-Brieuc (F), 72
1945	Paris (France)	Francis AUPIAIS, Nantes (F), 68
1986	Sarrebourg (France)	Victor WERLÉ, Strasbourg (F), 80
2006	Montferrier (France)	Jean LANDARRETCHE, Bayonne (F), 78
2016	Cadier en Keer (Pays Bas)	Harrie van HOOF, 's-Hertogenbosch (NL), 85
2016	Bayonne (France)	Jules LAHARGOU, Bayonne (F), 78

15

1903	Wurtzbourg (Germany)	+Maximilian ALBERT, Bamberg (D), 37, Vicaire Apostolique de la Côte de l'Or.
1963	Strasbourg (France)	Paul BUCHERT, Strasbourg (F), 67
1977	Cork (Ireland)	Richard TOBIN, Cork (IRL), 65
1995	Cadier en Keer (Netherlands)	Frans RAMAKERS, Roermond (NL), 85
2017	Gênes (Italie)	Andrea CABELLA, Gênes (I), 81, Membre honoraire.
2017	Gênes (Italie)	Zadio SENISE, Gênes (I), 96, Membre honoraire.

16

1969	Saint-Pierre (France)	Alphonse SCHAHL, Strasbourg (F), 85
1991	Arnhem (Pays-Bas)	Cornelius G HULSEN, 's-Hertogenbosch (NL), 78
1997	Cadier en Keer (Netherlands)	Martin KEINHORST, Haarlem (NL), 86
2000	Zinswald (France)	Michel CONVERS, Besançon (F), 81
2007	Montferrier (France)	Raymond DOMAS, Clermont-Ferrand (F), 82

17

1978	Marseille (France)	Joseph DELHOMMEL, Rennes (F), 93
1986	La Guerche (France)	Victor RUBLON, Rennes (F), 83
2006	Montferrier (France)	Antoine CAILHOUX, Clermont-Ferrand (F), 87
2013	Montpellier (France)	Albert BOGARD, Saint-Dié (F), 85

18

1955	Man (Côte d'Ivoire)	Jean MYARD, Autun (F), 37
1986	Nantes (France)	Jean ÉVAIN, Nantes (F), 62
1996	Cork (Ireland)	Laurence COLLINS, Cork (IRL), 66
1999	Embrun (France)	Mme Marie-Louise CHEVALIER, Gap (F), Membre Honoraire.
2007	Montpellier (France)	Jean GUITTENY, Nantes (F), 75

19

| 1982 | Sélestat (France) | Georges FIX, Strasbourg (F), 77 |
| 1996 | Teaneck (U.S.A.) | James O'SULLIVAN, Dublin (IRL), 67 |

20

1950	Dublin (Ireland)	John KENNEDY, Dublin (IRL), 48
1955	Nancy (France)	Claude MANSUY, Saint-Dié (F), 23, séminariste.
1961	Oosterbeek (Netherlands)	Johannes MAYS, Roermond (NL), 54
1962	Cork (Ireland)	Patrick McGIRR, Armagh (IRL), 69
1965	Saint-Pierre (France)	Jules HAENGGI, Strasbourg (F), 72
1966	Cork (Ireland)	Michael MAHONY, Clonfert (IRL), 66
2010	Cork (Ireland)	Anthony O'DONNELL, Raphoe (IRL), 84
2019	Tenafly (USA)	Daniel LYNCH, Bridgeport (USA), 71
2020	Saint-Pierre (France)	Paul SIMON, Strasbourg (F), 88

21

1953	La Croix-Valmer (France)	Auguste BRUHAT, Le Puy (F), 79, 6ème Supérieur Général.
1969	Lyon (France)	Albert HAAS, Strasbourg (F), 74
2006	Montferrier (France)	Raymond PEYLE, Lyon (F), 92

22

1894	Asaba (Nigeria)	Joseph VOLTZ, Strasbourg (F), 24
1983	Saint-Pierre (France)	Antoine ACKER, Strasbourg (F), 99
1999	Cadier en Keer (Netherlands)	Bernard WIEGGERS, Utrecht (NL), 82
2012	Maastricht (Netherlands)	Johannes FRANKENHUIJSEN, Utrecht (NL), 75
2016	Montferrier (France)	Félix RÉGNIER, Le Puy (F), 90

23

1894	Abeokuta (Nigeria)	Eugenio ARRIBAS, Burgos (E), 24
1979	Cadier en Keer (Netherlands)	Antoon BOUCHIER, Haarlem (NL), 67
2010	Dinan (France)	Yves LAGOUTTE, Saint-Brieuc (F), 90
2011	Cork (Ireland)	Sean MACCARTHY, Cork (IRL), 89

24

1902	Lagos (Nigeria)	Joseph HAMERS, Roermond (NL), 23
1914	La Boisselle (France)	Jean-Marie PAPIN, Nantes (F), 25
1944	Lyon (France)	Eugène MERLAUD, Luçon (F), 59
2012	Le Puy (France)	Paul VÉROT, Le Puy (F), 88
2021	Le Caire (Egypte)	Gennaro DI MARTINO, Alexandrie (ET), 85, Membre honoraire.

25

1880	Abeokuta (Nigeria)	François BOUÉ, Nantes (F), 31
1958	El-Milia (Algérie)	François SAPET, Viviers (F), 22, séminariste.
1964	Oosterbeek (Netherlands)	Harrie van de VEN, 's-Hertogenbosch (NL), 63
1984	Nantes (France)	Gabriel CHAUVET, Luçon (F), 81
1991	Bouzillé (France)	Marcel LEFORT, Angers (F), 88, frère.
1992	Tenafly (U.S.A.)	James GRIFFIN, Tuam (IRL), 93
2004	Cork (Ireland)	Thomas LINDON, Armagh (IRL), 71

26

1900	Moossou (Côte d'Ivoire)	Georges MEYER, Strasbourg (F), 23
1916	Cairo (Egitto)	François GUYOT, Lyon (F), 74
1930	Cork (Ireland)	Joseph BUTLER, Ossory (IRL), 51
1977	Cork (Ireland)	Daniel CORVIN, Down & Connor (IRL), 67
1985	Rome (Italie)	Henricus P MONDÉ, Rotterdam (NL), 76, 9ème Supérieur Général.
1993	Cork (Ireland)	John HACKETT, Ardagh & Clonmacnois (IRL), 69
1994	Hamilton (New Zealand)	Alexander LYNCH, Glasgow (GB), 56
1999	Saint Pierre (France)	Edouard VONWYL, Bale (CHE), 93

27

1889	Nice (France)	Ferdinando MERLINI, Milano (I), 35
1949	Saint-Tropez (France)	François COMTE, Mende (F), 71
1973	Saint-Pierre (France)	Ernest SAUER, Strasbourg (F), 79
1983	Cadier en Keer (Netherlands)	Henricus SANDERS, 's-Hertogenbosch (NL), 75, brother.
1991	Manchester (Great Britain)	Michael N GALLAGHER, Limerick (IRL), 72
1991	Medemblik (Netherlands)	Cornelius MANSHANDEN, Haarlem (NL), 72
2010	Cork (Ireland)	Gregory McGOVERN, Kilmore (IRL), 89
2020	Cadier en Keer (Netherlands)	Johan van BRAKEL, Utrecht (NL), 90

28

1864	Ouidah (Dahomey)	Jean-Baptiste BÉBIN, Reims (F), 34
1875	Saint-Maurice-sur-Loire (France)	Joseph THILLIER, Lyon (F), 39
1920	La Croix-Valmer (France)	Louis LANDAIS, Le Mans (F), 60
1921	Lokoja (Nigeria)	George LACEY, Tuam (IRL), 29
1939	Enugu (Nigeria)	Eugène STRUB, Strasbourg (F), 65
1943	Abidjan (Côte d'Ivoire)	Laurent JADÉ, Quimper (F), 34
1950	Bongouanou (Côte d'Ivoire)	Constant COUËDEL, Nantes (F), 26
1958	Metz (France)	Léon GRUNDLER, Strasbourg (F), 49
1958	Aalbeek (Netherlands)	Augustin BERRIÈRE, Roermond (NL), 68, brother.
1966	Porto-Novo (Benin)	Paul PERRIN, Strasbourg (F), 70
2016	Tenefly (Etats Unis)	Terence DOHERTY, Saint-Paul (USA), 81

29

1956	Nijmegen (Netherlands)	Antoon HARING, Rotterdam (NL), 57
1972	Maastricht (Netherlands)	Lambert ERKENS, Roermond (NL), 85
1985	Montferrier (France)	Roger BARTHÉLEMY, Nantes (F), 73
1997	Saint-Pierre (France)	Théodore FRITSCH, Strasbourg (F), 86
1998	Montferrier (France)	+André DUIRAT, Autun (F), 90, Évêque de Bouaké, Côte d'Ivoire.
2018	Montferrier (France)	Maurice PRAT, Viviers (F), 90

30

1926	La Croix-Valmer (France)	Hyacinthe BRICET, Rennes (F), 80, Préfet Apostolique du Dahomey.
1935	Dabou (Côte d'Ivoire)	Léon MOLY, Rodez (F), 60
1946	Le Rozay (France)	Jean-Louis CAËR, Quimper (F), 36
1967	Nantes (France)	Adrien MASSIOT, Rennes (F), 79
1969	Salon (France)	Jean-Marie TOURILLON, Nantes (F), 65
2003	Framingham (U.S.A.)	Francis GILLIS, Antigonish (CDN), 85

31

1875	Nantes (France)	Ernest JORET, Nantes (F), 27
1909	Le Mans (France)	Henri FOUQUET, Le Mans (F), 37
1916	Samos (Grèce)	Joachim FAVREAU, Nantes (F), 38
1942	Choubrah (Égypte)	François CAMILLERI, Héliopolis (ET), 67
1945	Savannah (U.S.A.)	John HAYES, Kerry (IRL), 44
1968	Tenefly (U.S.A.)	Martin BANE, Springfield (USA), 68
1981	Cadier en Keer (Netherlands)	Theodorus PRINCÉE, 's-Hertogenbosch (NL), 71
2012	Maastricht (Netherlands)	Joseph CRAMERS, Roermond (NL), 85

142

December/ Décembre

December/ Décembre

Chronological list

Liste chronologique

No	Date	Died in/Mort à	Name/Nom	Age
			1858	
1	03-Oct	France	Frère Pierre GUILLET	24
			1859	
2	02-Jun	Sierra Leone	Père Louis RIOCREUX	27
3	05-Jun	Sierra Leone	Père Jean-Baptiste BRESSON	47
4	13-Jun	Sierra Leone	Frère Gratien MONNOYEUR	29
5	25-Jun	Sierra Leone	Mgr Melchior Marie Joseph de MARION BRÉSILLAC	46
6	28-Jun	Sierra Leone	Père Louis REYMOND	36
			1861	
7	09-Apr	Sierra Leone	Père Louis EDDE	24
			1863	
8	20-Aug	France	Seminariste Laurent MATHON	29
9	30-Nov	Bénin	Père Francisco FERNANDEZ	38
			1864	
10	01-Jul	Bénin	Père Hector NOCHÉ	30
11	28-Dec	Bénin	Père Jean-Baptiste BÉBIN	34
			1866	
12	15-Feb	Bénin	Père Justin BURLATON	35
			1867	
13	28-Feb	Bénin	Père Alphée JOLANS	26
14	04-Mar	Naufragé	Père Joachim HALGAN	32
15	04-Mar	Naufragé	Père Barthélemy PUECH	57
			1869	
16	20-Apr	Nigeria	Père Claude VERMOREL	45
17	29-Apr	France	Père Jean VERDELET	32
			1870	
18	07-May	France	Frère Santiago BEAUVERT	39
19	06-Sep	France	Seminariste François LECAER	26
20	30-Nov	Great Britain	Seminariste André PETIT	22
			1871	
21	06-Mar	Nigeria	Père Gonzague THOLLON	32
22	01-Jul	Nigeria	Père Denis MEYRANX	26
23	14-Oct	Nigeria	Père Alexis VEYRET	27
			1872	

147

No	Date	Died in/Mort à	Name/Nom	Age
24	26-Apr	Nigeria	Père Giovanni Battista ARTERO	34
25	15-Oct	Nigeria	Père Joseph BOURGUET	31
		1873		
26	23-Apr	Bénin	Père Pierre VACHER	29
27	12-Jun	France	Père Etienne ARNAL	72
		1874		
28	07-Sep	France	Seminariste Léon LEBRUN	25
29	29-Nov	Algérie	Père Edouard DUBOSQ	31
		1875		
30	28-Dec	France	Père Joseph THILLIER	39
31	31-Dec	France	Père Ernest JORET	27
		1876		
32	02-Jun	Bénin	Père Édouard RUAULT	31
		1877		
33	06-May	France	Père Adolphe PAPETARD	69
		1878		
34	27-Mar	Égypte	Frère Auguste MANSOUR	
35	11-May	Nigeria	Père Alphonse POUSSIN	24
		1879		
36	22-Jan	France	Père François CLOUD	43
37	04-Jul	Bénin	Père Alphonse LEPOULTEL	26
38	30-Jul	Nigeria	Frère Jean PINEAU	
		1880		
39	07-Jul	Nigeria	Père Liguori PAGÉS	37
40	05-Aug	Ghana	Père Eugène MURAT	31
41	17-Oct	Bénin	Frère Alphonse NOLAN	
42	05-Dec	Nigeria	Frère Jerome KILLEN	
43	25-Dec	Nigeria	Père François BOUÉ	31
		1881		
44	22-Feb	Égypte	Père Michael O'CARROLL	29
45	23-May	Bénin	Père Auguste TULASNE	32
46	09-Sep	France	Seminariste Jean-Louis GUYOMAR	21
		1883		
47	20-Jan	Nigeria	Père Jean-Paul POURET	36
48	30-Apr	France	Père Arsène DARDENNE	30
49	10-Jun	Ghana	Père Peter MIESSEN	30
50	07-Nov	Ghana	Père Pierre LEGEAY	37
		1884		
51	10-Apr	France	Père Gustave BOUVET	26

No	Date	Died in/Mort à	Name/Nom	Age
52	17-May	Nigeria	Père Sébastien ANDRÉ	31
53	12-Aug	Nigeria	Père Antoine DURIEUX	35
54	30-Sep	Égypte	Frère Victor MANDONNET	24
		1885		
55	14-Jan	Égypte	Père Cyprien MALEN	38
56	11-Mar	Nigeria	Père Antonio TETTAMANTI	32
57	14-Apr	Nigeria	Père Théodore HOLLEY	33
58	16-Jul	Naufragé	Père James HENNEBERY	24
59	05-Sep	Nigeria	Père Louis BLANC	30
60	25-Oct	Nigeria	Père Filippo FIORENTINI	34
61	26-Nov	Bénin	Père Vicente BERENGUER	31
		1886		
62	10-Mar	Bénin	Père Hippolyte BOZON	28
63	21-Mar	Naufragé	Père Auguste MOREAU	39
64	22-May	Nigeria	Père Benoît VENESSY	26
65	27-May	Naufragé	Père Pierre PIOLAT	28
66	06-Aug	France	Père Louis POLYCARPE	21
67	17-Aug	Nigeria	Père Andrew DORNAN	30
68	29-Sep	France	Père Clément GUILLON	41
		1887		
69	13-Apr	Nigeria	Père William CONNAUGHTON	34
70	23-May	Ghana	Père Ange GAUDEUL	39
71	31-Jul	Égypte	Père Étienne CARAMBAUD	44
72	07-Aug	Togo	Père Jeremiah MORAN	28
73	07-Sep	Bénin	Père Pierre SADELER	28
74	29-Sep	France	Père Noël BAUDIN	43
75	08-Oct	France	Seminariste Eugène CHEVAL	25
		1888		
76	12-Mar	France	Seminariste Eugene COMBY	21
77	06-Apr	Bénin	Père Jean-Marie JACQUET	29
78	07-Apr	Ghana	Père Alexis FAGA	25
		1889		
79	26-Apr	France	Seminariste Pierre BLANCHON	23
80	30-Jun	Bénin	Père Jacques PASQUEREAU	42
81	16-Jul	Nigeria	Père Étienne COCHET	27
82	06-Nov	France	Père Julien JAY	24
83	27-Dec	France	Père Ferdinando MERLINI	35
		1891		
84	15-Jan	Ghana	Père Josef GROEBLI	26
85	17-Apr	Nigeria	Père Aimé BEAUQUIS	40
86	17-May	France	Père Vincenzo ROMEO	23
87	26-Jun	Ghana	Père Ernest GRANIER	32
88	18-Aug	France	Père Eugène ASTIER	28
89	20-Sep	Ghana	Père Cor van de PAVOORDT	30

No	Date	Died in/Mort à	Name/Nom	Age
90	21-Oct	Nigeria	Père Joseph PESSOZ	31

			1892	
91	20-Jan	France	Père Paul BREY	24
92	06-Feb	France	Père Georges ULRICH	28
93	08-Feb	Nigeria	Père Josué CRÉTAZ	34
94	24-Sep	France	Père Patrick DOWNEY	31
95	16-Oct	Italie	Père Francesco BORGHERO	62

			1893	
96	15-Mar	Ghana	Père Émile BURGEAT	25
97	28-Mar	Ghana	Père Philippe HEILIGENSTEIN	24
98	30-Mar	France	Seminariste Michael O'DONNELL	22
99	08-Apr	Nigeria	Père Pierre BALLAC	27
100	10-Jun	Ghana	Père Pierre DANIEL	27
101	05-Jul	Italie	Père Louis BOUTRY	43
102	07-Jul	France	Père Claude PAGNON	39
103	25-Sep	France	Seminariste Pierre KLAM	24

			1894	
104	17-Jan	France	Mgr Jean-Baptiste CHAUSSE	48
105	23-Jun	Égypte	Frère Louis DEVAUD	
106	22-Dec	Nigeria	Père Joseph VOLTZ	24
107	23-Dec	Nigeria	Père Eugenio ARRIBAS	24

			1895	
108	02-Feb	Nigeria	Père Pierre SÉDANT	35
109	03-Apr	Ghana	Père Emile MOSSER	25
110	03-Apr	Égypte	Frère Jean-Baptiste RIBAUD	61
111	09-Apr	Ghana	Père Joseph KAPFER	25
112	24-Apr	Ghana	Mgr Jean-Marie MICHON	43
113	30-Apr	Ghana	Père Alexandre RICHE	27
114	26-May	Great Britain	Seminariste Charles DRISCOLL	29
115	28-May	Nigeria	Père Justin FRANÇOIS	33
116	22-Jun	Bénin	Mgr Joseph LECRON	40
117	27-Sep	France	Seminariste Michel KIEFFER	20

			1896	
118	15-Feb	Nigeria	Père Jean-Marie CROHAS	30
119	10-Apr	Nigeria	Père Émile VERMOREL	31
120	18-Apr	Naufragé	Père John GARVEY	25
121	14-Aug	France	Père Joseph MORY	27
122	19-Nov	France	Père Henri PONCET	25

			1897	
123	24-May	France	Père Peter SCHENKEL	32

			1898	
124	21-Feb	Togo	Père Théodore VIALLE	32
125	15-Apr	Ghana	Père Michael WADE	36

150

No	Date	Died in/Mort à	Name/Nom	Age
126	27-Apr	France	Père Philibert COURDIOUX	60
127	05-May	Ghana	Père Joseph GUMY	26
128	07-May	Ghana	Père Ernest STEBER	25
129	24-Jul	Ghana	Père Othon HILBERER	34
130	02-Aug	Égypte	Père Charles KIEFFER	25
131	07-Aug	France	Père Pierre-Marie BARON	40
132	17-Nov	Bénin	Père Joseph PELLAT	44

			1899	
133	01-Mar	Ghana	Père Benjamin HAAS	25
134	29-Apr	Ghana	Père Jean LANG	26
135	13-May	Naufragé	Père Joseph PIED	51
136	13-May	Côte d'Ivoire	Mgr Matthieu RAY	51
137	17-May	Côte d'Ivoire	Père Albert VIGNA	26
138	18-May	Côte d'Ivoire	Père Louis TEYSSIER	33
139	22-May	Bénin	Père Louis MOLLIER	25
140	24-May	Côte d'Ivoire	Père Étienne PELLET	43
141	06-Jul	France	Père Antoine PROVENCHÈRE	41
142	22-Jul	Ghana	Père Michel DAHLENT	26

			1900	
143	23-Feb	France	Père Alexandre DORGÈRE	45
144	22-Mar	Ghana	Père Ernst SULTZBERGER	27
145	29-Mar	France	Père Joseph LATARD	29
146	12-Jun	Nigeria	Père Jacques WERLY	27
147	24-Sep	Nigeria	Père Alois SCHROD	25
148	21-Oct	Suisse	Père Jakob HOEGGER	25
149	24-Oct	Nigeria	Père Édouard LABORDE	24
150	29-Nov	Bénin	Père Joseph SIMPLEX	27
151	06-Dec	Côte d'Ivoire	Père Charles BUMANN	23
152	26-Dec	Côte d'Ivoire	Père Georges MEYER	23

			1901	
153	09-Apr	France	Père Irénée LAFITTE	64
154	30-Apr	Nigeria	Père Jean DEMERLÉ	32
155	30-May	Netherlands	Père Auguste VONVILLE	31
156	14-Jun	Nigeria	Père Alphonse VONAU	25
157	14-Aug	Nigeria	Père Jean-Baptiste VOIT	44

			1902	
158	09-Jan	Nigeria	Père Charles SPIESER	36
159	31-Jan	France	Frère Alexandre GAUZIC	38
160	14-Feb	Nigeria	Père Charles AUGIER	31
161	09-Mar	Bénin	Père Pierre PICHAUD	32
162	28-May	Côte d'Ivoire	Père Pierre MOLLIER	24
163	12-Aug	Côte d'Ivoire	Père Maurizio GROSJACQUES	34
164	22-Oct	Côte d'Ivoire	Père Jean PERRAUD	24
165	25-Nov	Côte d'Ivoire	Frère Théodore MESTER	38
166	24-Dec	Nigeria	Père Joseph HAMERS	23

No	Date	Died in/Mort à	Name/Nom	Age
			1903	
167	24-Mar	Côte d'Ivoire	Père Pierre RÉGUILLON	23
168	29-Mar	Côte d'Ivoire	Père Louis RAUSCHER	29
169	28-Apr	Ghana	Père Eugène-Bernard RAESS	34
170	15-Jul	Égypte	Seminariste Victor DROUAULT	20
171	10-Sep	France	Père Pierre-Bertrand BOUCHE	68
172	23-Sep	Nigeria	Père Victorin GALLAUD	49
173	12-Dec	Bénin	Père Jean MOUNIER	27
174	15-Dec	Germany	Mgr Maximilian ALBERT	37
			1904	
175	30-Jan	France	Frère Louis JAMET	26
176	05-Mar	Togo	Père Auguste CHOISNET	29
177	24-Mar	Nigeria	Père Joseph STUDER	28
178	30-Mar	Côte d'Ivoire	Père Joseph WOERTH	25
			1905	
179	03-Apr	Bénin	Mgr Louis DARTOIS	44
180	13-May	Égypte	Père Jean MÉNAGER	25
181	16-Jul	France	Père Paul GUINARD	28
182	21-Aug	Nigeria	Père Léon BRAUD	25
183	20-Nov	Suisse	Mgr Isidore KLAUSS	41
			1906	
184	07-Mar	Bénin	Père Clément LAUBIAC	25
185	14-Mar	Ghana	Père Nicolas SCHEIER	24
186	25-Jun	Bénin	Père Aristide MÉNAGER	24
187	24-Jul	France	Frère Auguste BRÉJÉ	27
188	24-Jul	France	Père Jean LICHTENAUER	37
189	05-Oct	Ireland	Père Auguste SIMON	37
190	27-Nov	Ireland	Seminariste Patrick SHEEHAN	24
			1907	
191	16-Jun	Nigeria	Père Paolo FERRERO	31
192	13-Aug	Nigeria	Père Ernest BELIN	26
193	21-Aug	France	Père Augustin PLANQUE	81
194	21-Oct	Ghana	Père Auguste BANNWARTH	30
195	07-Nov	France	Père Ferdinand TERRIEN	58
196	11-Nov	Côte d'Ivoire	Père Antoine CHALUS	29
197	01-Dec	naufragé	Père Louis FAUVEL	39
			1908	
198	07-Jan	Nigeria	Père Emile MUNCH	29
199	08-Apr	Bénin	Père Jules NOUVEL	44
200	16-May	Ghana	Père Kees MOLENAARS	30
201	31-Oct	Ghana	Père Arthur DUMOULIN	29
			1909	
202	15-Jan	Égypte	Père Claude CADOR	64
203	13-Mar	Nigeria	Père Pierre FOURAGE	33

152

No	Date	Died in/Mort à	Name/Nom	Age
204	24-Mar	Nigeria	Père Charles SCHUMACHER	25
205	10-Jun	Ghana	Père David FAESSLER	31
206	30-Nov	Côte d'Ivoire	Mgr Alexandre HAMARD	55
207	31-Dec	France	Père Henri FOUQUET	37
		1910		
208	27-Jun	Ireland	Père John Baptist BARRETT	66
209	02-Aug	France	Père Jérôme REINHARDT	36
210	28-Aug	Mexique	Père Eugène HATTEMER	31
211	20-Nov	Nigeria	Père Joseph RIEFFEL	33
		1911		
212	27-Apr	Nigeria	Père Joseph FERRIEUX	30
213	18-May	France	Père Georges KOCH	33
214	22-May	Bénin	Père Camille MALGOIRE	27
215	18-Aug	Côte d'Ivoire	Père Jean-Louis MÉHEUST	44
216	28-Aug	Suisse	Père Lucien BREITEL	59
217	13-Nov	Nigeria	Père Giuseppe FERRERIO	29
218	19-Nov	Égypte	Frère Isidore-Marie LOHIER	52
		1912		
219	02-Jan	France	Mgr Joseph LANG	43
220	09-Apr	Nigeria	Père Henri VANLEKE	35
221	27-Apr	Côte d'Ivoire	Père Casimir AMALRIC	26
222	14-Jun	France	Père Charles BONAPFEL	35
223	12-Jul	France	Père Auguste-Joseph MOREAU	39
224	15-Jul	Bénin	Père Jules GESLINIER	38
225	23-Aug	France	Père Paul FRÉRY	30
226	30-Sep	Belgique	Mgr Ernest-Marie MÉNAGER	64
227	15-Oct	France	Seminariste Jean BRESSOL	24
228	09-Nov	Espagne	Père Bartolomé SARRÁ	71
		1913		
229	24-May	Bénin	Père Jean-Marie GUÉGUEN	35
230	04-Aug	France	Père Léandre Le GALLEN	66
231	10-Sep	France	Père Charles BALTZ	36
232	21-Sep	Bénin	Père Jean-Marie PANNETIER	27
233	30-Nov	France	Père Pierre BEISSON	51
		1914		
234	11-Mar	France	Mgr Paul PELLET	54
235	09-May	Liberia	Père William SHINE	26
236	21-May	France	Seminariste Paul ROUFFIAC	26
237	29-Jul	France	Père Jean-Baptiste LIBS	40
238	27-Aug	France	Seminariste Joseph DESFONTAINES	26
239	06-Sep	France	Seminariste Ferdinand PIÉDALOS	22
240	10-Sep	Égypte	Père Albert LEGEARD	52
241	24-Dec	France	Père Jean-Marie PAPIN	25
		1915		

153

No	Date	Died in/Mort à	Name/Nom	Age
242	19-Feb	Netherlands	Frère Antoine VACHON	84
243	15-Mar	France	Père Alphonse GRASS	27
244	19-Apr	France	Père Eugène CHAUTARD	64
245	02-May	Turquie	Seminariste Marcel BUGNON	27
246	19-May	Mali	Père Louis TRANCHANT	27
247	13-Jul	Ghana	Père Valentin STOLZ	27
248	25-Sep	France	Frère Alexis SÉCHER	30
249	15-Oct	France	Père Henri LEGAL	33
250	19-Oct	Luxembourg	Père Aloyse NICOLAÏ	29
		1916		
251	06-Apr	France	Père François MOLLIER	34
252	26-Apr	France	Père Edouard RANCHIN	45
253	05-May	France	Père Ernest GUILLEMIN	28
254	24-May	France	Père Pierre BERTHELOT	38
255	07-Jul	Pologne	Frère Isidore CHRIST	38
256	08-Sep	Ireland	Père Count Llewellyn BLAKE	77
257	21-Oct	France	Père Martin FRIEDRICH	44
258	24-Oct	France	Seminariste Louis LEROUX	26
259	26-Dec	Égypte	Père François GUYOT	74
260	31-Dec	Grèce	Père Joachim FAVREAU	38
		1917		
261	30-Jan	Nigeria	Mgr Carlo ZAPPA	56
262	20-May	Suisse	Père Joseph BURGER	45
263	12-Aug	USA	Père Jean-Louis EHRET	36
		1918		
264	16-Feb	Bénin	Père Camille BEL	68
265	10-Jun	France	Père Émile GAUDEUL	30
266	20-Jul	France	Frère Henri GILOTEAU	33
267	27-Oct	Nigeria	Père Johann LANDOLT	30
		1919		
268	19-Sep	Nigeria	Père Donat SCHELCHER	31
		1920		
269	20-Jan	France	Père Casimir SCHIMPFF	82
270	10-May	USA	Père Joseph DAHLENT	44
271	10-Aug	France	Père Ignace MEDER	51
272	29-Aug	France	Mgr Auguste DURET	74
273	18-Oct	Côte d'Ivoire	Père Frédéric MARCHAIS	34
274	28-Dec	France	Père Louis LANDAIS	60
		1921		
275	12-Mar	France	Père Armand PERRAUD	36
276	17-Jul	France	Seminariste Henri CRESPEL	24
277	19-Jul	USA	Père Joseph ZIMMERMANN	72
278	01-Sep	Liberia	Père Denis O'HARA	29
279	09-Oct	France	Père Prosper BACH	44

No	Date	Died in/Mort à	Name/Nom	Age
280	18-Oct	Côte d'Ivoire	Père Pierre GARCIA	38
281	28-Dec	Nigeria	Père George LACEY	29
		1922		
282	07-Mar	France	Père Auguste LEBOUVIER	75
283	30-Mar	Liberia	Père Francis J McGOVERN	24
284	20-Jun	Togo	Père Alphonse LEDIS	33
285	10-Aug	Nigeria	Père Victor DELFOSSE	46
		1923		
286	10-Jan	France	Frère Georges OLLIER	72
287	30-Jan	Bénin	Père Charles VACHERET	58
288	15-Apr	France	Père André GEX	59
289	19-Jun	Ireland	Père Richard O'SULLIVAN	26
290	20-Jul	Espagne	Père Masimino GARCIA	51
291	17-Aug	France	Père Émile LEMAIRE	77
292	08-Sep	Nigeria	Père Victor WURTH	36
293	13-Sep	France	Seminariste Alexandre LECOMTE	31
		1924		
294	27-Feb	Côte d'Ivoire	Père Auguste GAULÉ	37
295	13-Mar	Ghana	Mgr Ignace HUMMEL	54
296	22-Mar	Nigeria	Père Pierre PIOTIN	57
297	28-Mar	Bénin	Frère Henri VERMULST	30
298	17-May	Bénin	Frère Emmanuel SERENNE	36
299	19-May	Côte d'Ivoire	Père Joseph GORJU	51
300	03-Jun	Togo	Père Charles HERVOUET	34
301	07-Dec	Bénin	Père Joseph GIRERD	51
		1925		
302	12-Jan	Liberia	Père John BARRY	24
303	04-Apr	Nigeria	Père Joseph GEELS	30
304	27-May	Naufragé	Père Xavier KUHN	36
305	14-Jun	Ghana	Père Henry de JONG	27
306	25-Sep	France	Père Jean PAY	48
		1926		
307	02-Feb	Ireland	Père Desmond RYAN	30
308	09-Apr	Côte d'Ivoire	Père Joseph REYMANN	54
309	28-May	Nigeria	Père Philip CASSIDY	38
310	28-May	Netherlands	Père Antoine BURG	53
311	12-Jul	France	Frère Jean-Baptiste ROUSSEAU	70
312	21-Jul	Nigeria	Père William BOND	30
313	11-Nov	France	Père François RÉNIER	52
314	23-Nov	Ghana	Père Joseph HUBSTER	43
315	30-Dec	France	Mgr Hyacinthe BRICET	80
		1927		
316	22-Apr	France	Père Louis FRIESS	50
317	22-Jun	France	Père Emile VALLÉE	26

No	Date	Died in/Mort à	Name/Nom	Age
318	31-Jul	Sénégal	Frère Matthieu BERRIÈRE	51
319	04-Aug	Belgique	Seminariste Xavier KELLER	20
320	08-Aug	Ghana	Père Philippe MUNTZINGER	39
321	28-Oct	USA	Père Laurent BASTIAN	63
322	03-Dec	Togo	Père Luigi CAVAGNERA	47
		1928		
323	17-Feb	Égypte	Père Alphonse BERLIOUX	45
324	07-Apr	Italie	Père Giovanni Battista FRIGERIO	59
325	17-May	France	Père Celso SIRONI	66
326	29-May	Italie	Père Natale RADAELLI	65
327	04-Jun	France	Frère Joseph HAUTBOIS	73
328	15-Jun	Bénin	Père Alexandre DURAFOUR	42
329	28-Aug	Côte d'Ivoire	Père Émile BONHOMME	75
		1929		
330	16-Jan	France	Frère Édouard ZIMMERMANN	66
331	02-Feb	France	Laïc Alfred-Marie-Alexandre DANJOU DE LA GARENNE	79
332	22-Feb	France	Mgr Pierre KERNIVINEN	53
333	26-Jul	France	Père Joseph PLANQUE	60
334	03-Aug	Naufragé	Mgr Ferdinand TERRIEN	52
335	05-Dec	Netherlands	Père Gaston DESRIBES	81
		1930		
336	17-Apr	France	Père François DEVOUCOUX	84
337	13-Jul	France	Père Daniel O'SULLIVAN	72
338	25-Jul	Côte d'Ivoire	Frère Ferdinand ALLAIN	43
339	25-Jul	Côte d'Ivoire	Père Louis SAECKINGER	37
340	28-Aug	Nigeria	Père Walter KEARY	29
341	16-Sep	France	Père Henri WELLINGER	83
342	22-Sep	France	Père Barthélemy SABOT	24
343	26-Dec	Ireland	Père Joseph BUTLER	51
		1931		
344	10-Jan	France	Frère Charles GOFFINET	60
345	20-Jun	Belgique	Père Yves L'ANTHOËN	64
346	18-Jul	France	Père Joseph MULLER	53
347	15-Sep	Niger	Père René GROSSEAU	30
348	24-Sep	Côte d'Ivoire	Père Alphonse LEBUS	33
349	16-Nov	France	Mgr Jean OGÉ	63
		1932		
350	17-Jan	Ireland	Père Francis YOUNG	36
351	04-Jun	France	Père Victor RAVOUX	61
352	09-Aug	Ireland	Frère Thomas KELLY	46
353	16-Sep	Nigeria	Père James McGETTIGAN	51
		1933		
354	08-Jan	France	Père Victor MOISON	80

No	Date	Died in/Mort à	Name/Nom	Age
355	10-Jan	France	Père Jules POIRIER	88
356	25-Mar	France	Père Jean-Marie CHABERT	59
357	27-Jun	Nigeria	Père Jean-Marie COQUARD	74
358	04-Jul	France	Père Stanislas DESRIBES	73
359	22-Aug	Ghana	Père Antoon SMETZERS	30
360	23-Aug	Égypte	Père Frédéric BRACHET	27
361	13-Oct	Italie	Mgr Thomas BRODERICK	51
362	02-Dec	Great Britain	Père W. Gauthier BOUMANS	31

1934

No	Date	Died in/Mort à	Name/Nom	Age
363	10-Jan	Belgique	Père Alphonse FURODET	67
364	04-Mar	France	Père Adrien BAUZIN	59
365	05-May	France	Père Alphonse MATHIVET	68
366	31-May	France	Frère Charles LISSNER	82
367	10-Jun	France	Père Eugène RICHARD	59
368	14-Jun	France	Père Jean-Baptiste DOURIS	64
369	14-Aug	USA	Père Eugène O'HEA	45
370	05-Nov	Togo	Père Bernard van LEEUWEN	44
371	07-Dec	France	Père Georges VOGT	67

1935

No	Date	Died in/Mort à	Name/Nom	Age
372	29-Mar	France	Mgr Jules MOURY	62
373	21-Jun	USA	Père Alphonse WOLFF	57
374	22-Oct	France	Père Bernard SCHMITT	60
375	05-Nov	USA	Père Michael O'DONOHUE	41
376	07-Nov	Nigeria	Père Florence O'DRISCOLL	30
377	10-Nov	USA	Père Jérôme DOLLINGER	56
378	30-Nov	USA	Père Eugène PETER	63
379	03-Dec	Ireland	Père John LAVELLE	37
380	30-Dec	Côte d'Ivoire	Père Léon MOLY	60

1936

No	Date	Died in/Mort à	Name/Nom	Age
381	20-Mar	USA	Père Joseph CRAWFORD	49
382	18-Apr	France	Père Eugène KELLER	54
383	30-Apr	Great Britain	Père Stephen WOODLEY	49
384	18-May	Tunisie	Père Adolphe ROUSSELET	68
385	20-May	France	Père Joseph DEFOIN	70
386	25-Jun	France	Père Jean-Baptiste THUET	76
387	07-Jul	Ghana	Père Kees FABRIE	29
388	06-Nov	Netherlands	Père Harrie VUGTS	32

1937

No	Date	Died in/Mort à	Name/Nom	Age
389	13-Feb	Ireland	Seminariste Eugene WYNNE	22
390	20-Mar	Bénin	Père Toussaint JOLIF	64
391	03-Jul	Pologne	Seminariste Aloyse KURACZ	22
392	21-Jul	France	Père André GRANGEON	57
393	12-Sep	Italie	Père Luigi TACCHINI	62
394	28-Sep	Nigeria	Père John MARREN	29
395	05-Oct	Nigeria	Père Anthony O'DWYER	27
396	27-Nov	France	Père Jules NEU	54

No	Date	Died in/Mort à	Name/Nom	Age
397	04-Dec	Nigeria	Père Edward MURPHY	27
			1938	
398	26-Mar	Nigeria	Père Thomas ROLT	26
399	28-Mar	France	Père Antonin BRESSOL	71
400	29-Jun	Côte d'Ivoire	Père Étienne VION	52
401	03-Jul	Liberia	Père Matthew McDONNELL	33
402	08-Jul	Bénin	Père Julien GUYOT	29
403	08-Jul	Côte d'Ivoire	Mgr François PERSON	48
404	04-Aug	Ireland	Père Patrick Joseph KELLY	42
405	29-Aug	Togo	Père Georges KRAUTH	52
406	29-Aug	Bénin	Père Emile GAUDIN	37
407	17-Sep	Netherlands	Frère Georges LANG	72
408	17-Sep	Great Britain	Seminariste Edward LEGGE	23
409	28-Oct	Nigeria	Mgr Francis O'ROURKE	56
			1939	
410	01-Jan	Ireland	Père James McNICHOLAS	44
411	02-Feb	France	Père Kilien ZERR	29
412	04-Feb	Égypte	Père Henri THIBAUD	53
413	08-Apr	Ireland	Père Michael ROWAN	62
414	21-Apr	Togo	Père Georges HARTMANN	29
415	27-May	Bénin	Père Jean-Baptiste TRUHAND	41
416	06-Jul	France	Mgr Oswald WALLER	73
417	15-Jul	Égypte	Père Jean FRANCIS	44
418	04-Aug	Côte d'Ivoire	Mgr Edmond WOLFF	40
419	19-Aug	Ghana	Père Leendert de KOK	31
420	04-Sep	Ghana	Père René van GOETHEM	31
421	13-Sep	France	Seminariste Jean GILORY	24
422	24-Sep	Ireland	Père Nicholas CLERY	54
423	12-Nov	France	Frère Pierre MONNEY	66
424	28-Dec	Nigeria	Père Eugène STRUB	65
			1940	
425	24-Jan	Netherlands	Seminariste Alfons HAKENS	25
426	06-Mar	Sénégal	Père Jean FUCHS	41
427	16-Apr	Nigeria	Père Andrew GERAGHTY	29
428	07-May	Côte d'Ivoire	Père Henri LACROIX	37
429	27-May	France	Père Michel SCHERRER	71
430	01-Jun	France	Père Maurice PARIS	27
431	14-Jun	France	Seminariste Henry PASQUERON de FOMMERVAULT	23
432	08-Jul	Ghana	Père Theo CUP	34
433	09-Jul	France	Seminariste Pierre DOUILLARD	21
434	18-Jul	Nigeria	Père Patrick BERMINGHAM	44
435	03-Aug	France	Seminariste Alphonse DRÉAN	23
436	03-Aug	Ireland	Père Michael McCAFFREY	64
437	30-Sep	Ireland	Père William BUTLER	59
438	10-Oct	France	Père Émile Joseph SCHMITT	61
439	14-Oct	Bénin	Père Michel BOURGET	55

No	Date	Died in/Mort à	Name/Nom	Age
440	16-Oct	Égypte	Père Joseph BORNE	35
441	28-Oct	Égypte	Père Vincent MOORE	50
442	30-Nov	France	Père Germain GANDT de	84
		1941		
443	16-Jan	USA	Père Célestin MONPOINT	57
444	24-Jan	France	Père Charles LAROCHE	81
445	19-Feb	France	Père Ernest ERHART	56
446	25-Feb	Côte d'Ivoire	Père Louis PARAGE	41
447	03-May	France	Père Robert FLESCH	51
448	29-May	France	Père Alphonse RIBER	65
449	16-Sep	France	Père Joseph QUICKERT	30
450	11-Oct	France	Père Émile Nicolas SCHMITT	62
451	31-Oct	Netherlands	Père Louis HELWEGEN	32
452	13-Dec	Ghana	Père Alfons TILLIE	43
		1942		
453	02-Jan	Ghana	Père Gerard REIMERT	38
454	07-Jan	France	Père Simeon ALBENIZ	67
455	16-Feb	Ireland	Frère Michael McKENNA	40
456	19-Feb	Ghana	Père Johan HEEMSKERK	28
457	05-Mar	France	Seminariste Michel BOILLON	23
458	02-Apr	USA	Père Denis O'SULLIVAN	65
459	20-Apr	Bénin	Père Firmin COLINEAUX	67
460	22-Apr	Ireland	Père Edward WARD	37
461	06-Jul	Ghana	Père Joseph VOGEL	58
462	15-Jul	France	Seminariste Joseph PHILIPPE	21
463	27-Jul	France	Père Joseph FUGIER	85
464	02-Aug	Bénin	Père Albert FECHTER	53
465	11-Aug	Togo	Père Hermann KEIMER	59
466	12-Aug	Côte d'Ivoire	Père Jean-Paul VOGEL	29
467	04-Sep	Nigeria	Père Thomas Sexton CAHILL	35
468	09-Sep	USA	Père Edmond SCHLECHT	49
469	25-Sep	France	Père Adolphe IMOBERDORF	71
470	23-Oct	Italie	Père Berengario CERMENATI	68
471	11-Nov	Netherlands	Père Henri ROTHOFF	39
472	29-Nov	France	Père Francis VILLEVAUD	82
473	31-Dec	Égypte	Père François CAMILLERI	67
		1943		
474	20-Jan	France	Père Edmond MUTSCHLER	65
475	26-Jan	Égypte	Père Ambroise LE CORRE	58
476	25-Feb	France	Père Albert PARTARRIEU	30
477	02-Mar	France	Père Henri HORN	68
478	15-Mar	France	Père Joseph GUÉNO	42
479	06-Apr	France	Frère Maurice FABLET	70
480	08-May	Bénin	Père Joseph PROU	33
481	16-Sep	France	Père Jean DUHAMEL	32
482	24-Sep	USA	Père Victor BAECHTEL	36
483	17-Nov	France	Père Clément BANNWARTH	66

No	Date	Died in/Mort à	Name/Nom	Age
484	03-Dec	France	Père Jean-Baptiste RAY	65
485	14-Dec	Côte d'Ivoire	Père Jean-Marie BEDEL	72
486	28-Dec	Côte d'Ivoire	Père Laurent JADÉ	34

1944

No	Date	Died in/Mort à	Name/Nom	Age
487	20-Jan	France	Père Joseph WERLÉ	61
488	28-Jan	France	Père Jean GRANDO	63
489	16-Mar	France	Père Ludan ANTZ	62
490	26-Mar	Netherlands	Père Rudolf HOEPPNER	59
491	04-Apr	France	Père Aristide BLAIN	72
492	22-Apr	Allemagne	Seminariste Maurice COUTIN	24
493	23-Apr	Égypte	Père Joseph DONAGHY	45
494	26-May	France	Père Justin STEINMETZ	38
495	02-Jun	France	Père Michel SCHUH	76
496	23-Jun	Nigeria	Père Patrick LEE	41
497	07-Aug	France	Père Victor HÉROLD	72
498	16-Aug	Algérie	Père Jean MICHAŁEK	32
499	23-Aug	Ireland	Père James McDONNELL	49
500	08-Sep	Italie	Seminariste Paul FLEITH	23
501	17-Nov	France	Père Victor BURG	66
502	01-Dec	Liberia	Père Martin LACEY	45
503	24-Dec	France	Père Eugène MERLAUD	59

1945

No	Date	Died in/Mort à	Name/Nom	Age
504	20-Jan	France	Laïc Mme Françoise Marguerite LAURENS	
505	25-Jan	Ireland	Père Patrick O'HERLIHY	53
506	31-Jan	France	Seminariste Michel HAY	28
507	07-Feb	France	Père Ambroise PRIOUL	53
508	02-Mar	USA	Père Joseph MARGREITHER	60
509	03-Mar	Togo	Mgr Jean-Marie CESSOU	61
510	01-Apr	Ireland	Père Martin LAVELLE	53
511	04-Apr	USA	Père John PRENDERGAST	67
512	08-Apr	Togo	Mgr Auguste HERMAN	65
513	09-Apr	Togo	Père Aloïse BALTZ	38
514	17-Apr	Allemagne	Père Joseph STAMM	63
515	18-May	USA	Père Patrick MOYLAN	56
516	08-Jun	Ghana	Père Willem HENDRIX	33
517	05-Jul	France	Père Jean-Marie HÉLIAS	38
518	12-Jul	Ireland	Père Patrick CAHILL	43
519	02-Sep	Ghana	Père Henri SCHOEN	64
520	06-Oct	France	Père Joseph FAHRNER	47
521	20-Oct	Nigeria	Père Patrick CLANCY	27
522	09-Nov	Netherlands	Père Charles LOUXEN	81
523	14-Dec	France	Père Francis AUPIAIS	68
524	31-Dec	USA	Père John HAYES	44

1946

No	Date	Died in/Mort à	Name/Nom	Age
525	01-Feb	USA	Père Francis WEISS	65
526	08-Feb	Égypte	Père Patrick LYNN	33
527	27-Mar	Allemagne	Seminariste Jean GOASDUFF	23

No	Date	Died in/Mort à	Name/Nom	Age
528	08-Apr	France	Père Ernest COMPAGNON	58
529	13-Apr	France	Père Eustache CHENU	81
530	20-May	Ghana	Père Servaas KERKHOFFS	35
531	24-May	Ireland	Père Martin John WALSH	42
532	09-Jun	France	Père Ferdinand FER	70
533	14-Sep	Great Britain	Père Jan HOUTMAN	79
534	29-Oct	Nigeria	Père Michael ROCHE	34
535	02-Dec	Ireland	Père James WARD	42
536	30-Dec	France	Père Jean-Louis CAËR	36
		1947		
537	21-Jan	France	Seminariste Firmin LOISEAU	23
538	30-Jan	Ireland	Mgr Stephen KYNE	75
539	05-Feb	France	Père Louis PIREYRE	68
540	20-Feb	France	Père Georges BRÉDIGER	71
541	22-Feb	France	Frère Jean-Baptiste BURGEL	62
542	27-Feb	France	Père Jules TIGEOT	78
543	01-Mar	Ireland	Père Peter ROGERS	38
544	03-May	France	Père Joseph GAGNAIRE	71
545	26-Sep	USA	Père Valentine BARNICLE	46
546	27-Sep	France	Père Joseph MONNEY	54
547	14-Oct	Côte d'Ivoire	Père Léon KAPFER	35
		1948		
548	12-Jan	France	Père Léon HÉRITEAU	29
549	21-Feb	France	Père Joseph HARTZ	63
550	01-Apr	France	Frère Aimé POUPLIN	68
551	15-Apr	France	Père Léon BURG	65
552	07-Aug	USA	Père Ignace LISSNER	81
553	13-Aug	France	Père Pierre BARON	67
554	12-Oct	France	Mgr Ernest HAUGER	75
555	20-Oct	France	Père Marcel MÉTAYER	28
556	14-Nov	France	Père René-François GUILCHER	67
		1949		
557	02-Jan	France	Père Alfred LAURENT	68
558	03-Jan	Nigeria	Père John HEALY	62
559	08-Feb	Ghana	Père Bertus BERNTS	46
560	12-Feb	France	Père Eugène NAEGEL	76
561	19-Apr	Togo	Père Louis FREYBURGER	74
562	19-Apr	France	Père Prosper CARTAL	69
563	11-Aug	Ireland	Père William COTTER	65
564	14-Sep	France	Frère Gustave BONNEFOY	74
565	27-Sep	USA	Père Alfred LAUBÉ	69
566	19-Oct	Nigeria	Père Francis SANDS	33
567	12-Nov	Bénin	Père Eugène LIEUTAUD	64
568	22-Nov	USA	Père John AHERN	58
569	09-Dec	Bénin	Frère Jacques IRIGOIN	30
570	27-Dec	France	Père François COMTE	71

No	Date	Died in/Mort à	Name/Nom	Age
			1950	
571	15-Jan	Suisse	Père Peter FUST	57
572	23-Feb	France	Père Joseph HAGENBACH	74
573	23-Mar	Égypte	Mgr Jules GIRARD	87
574	28-Mar	France	Frère Jean VINSONNEAU	79
575	16-Apr	Côte d'Ivoire	Père Henri BIGORGNE	31
576	15-May	France	Laïc Mlle Germaine GUTHMANN	
577	01-Jun	France	Père Séraphin MORON	72
578	23-Jul	France	Père Édouard LAQUEYRIE	72
579	06-Aug	France	Père Martin PFLEGER	78
580	07-Sep	Bénin	Père Joseph BARREAU	69
581	23-Sep	France	Père Louis COMBAT	44
582	20-Dec	Ireland	Père John KENNEDY	48
583	28-Dec	Côte d'Ivoire	Père Constant COUËDEL	26
			1951	
584	03-Feb	Côte d'Ivoire	Père Eugène THÈTE	30
585	08-Feb	France	Père Louis BRUGGER	61
586	08-Feb	Nigeria	Père Charles BURR	69
587	07-Apr	Netherlands	Père Harrie HOUSMANS	75
588	10-Aug	France	Père Joseph JOULORD	80
589	13-Aug	Égypte	Père Emile SCIAVI	70
590	18-Sep	Côte d'Ivoire	Père Laurens DANKERS	51
591	01-Oct	USA	Père Gustave OBRECHT	76
592	03-Oct	France	Père François-Xavier HIRSCH	60
593	05-Oct	France	Père Albert ROESCH	42
594	23-Oct	Ghana	Père Joseph COBBEN	33
			1952	
595	27-Jan	Ireland	Frère Patrick DEASY	67
596	30-Jan	Italie	Père Giovanni PIERGENTILI	70
597	03-Feb	France	Père Louis CAILLAUD	39
598	23-Mar	Bénin	Père Paul FERLANDIN	41
599	29-Mar	Bénin	Mgr François STEINMETZ	84
600	05-Apr	France	Père Lucien ARIAL	75
601	08-Apr	France	Père Joseph WINGERTSZAHN	71
602	18-Apr	France	Père Clovis OLIVE	76
603	26-Apr	Ireland	Père William HOLLAND	41
604	19-May	Belgique	Père François BACKER de	68
605	21-May	Côte d'Ivoire	Père Pierre PORTE	68
606	11-Jun	Ireland	Père Philip MAHON	45
607	21-Oct	France	Père Joseph STAUFFER	76
608	29-Oct	France	Père Jean VERT	69
609	09-Nov	Chile	Père Nicolás BASTIDA	76
			1953	
610	06-Jan	France	Père Joseph HÉGUY	47
611	31-Jan	Ireland	Père Michael O'FLYNN	56
612	06-Feb	Togo	Père Jacques HEGGER	34
613	19-Feb	Tunisie	Père Émile MALASSENET	55

No	Date	Died in/Mort à	Name/Nom	Age
614	22-Feb	France	Père Julien PRAUD	63
615	23-May	France	Père Joseph WOLFF	62
616	26-May	France	Père Pierre GOELLER	73
617	17-Jul	France	Père Jean GOUGEON	29
618	02-Aug	Bénin	Père Isidore PÉLOFY	79
619	15-Aug	Tunisie	Père Joseph SCHMIDT	76
620	09-Sep	Ireland	Père Edward BERMINGHAM	37
621	18-Sep	France	Père Simon FONTVIEILLE	72
622	08-Dec	France	Père Jean-Marie RENOU	79
623	21-Dec	France	Père Auguste BRUHAT	79
		1954		
624	01-Mar	Côte d'Ivoire	Père Jean-Baptiste VEST	64
625	10-Mar	France	Père Georges BADER	65
626	25-Apr	France	Père Joseph FREYBURGER	78
627	11-Aug	France	Père Jules LIEB	66
628	01-Oct	USA	Père Alphonse KOCH	54
629	11-Oct	Netherlands	Frère Martin KUIJPERS	50
630	27-Oct	Ireland	Père John DEANE	49
631	08-Nov	Égypte	Père Michel GHALI	79
		1955		
632	29-Jan	Italie	Père Louis GIRE	55
633	21-Mar	Ireland	Père Nicholas HEFFERNAN	79
634	25-Mar	Côte d'Ivoire	Mgr Alphonse KIRMANN	68
635	30-Mar	France	Père Auguste BONNET	71
636	19-Apr	France	Père Louis FUCHS	82
637	28-Apr	USA	Père James RAFFERTY	49
638	17-May	Togo	Père Georges FISCHER	70
639	12-Jul	Netherlands	Père Albert ROELOFS	52
640	25-Aug	Netherlands	Père Jan van den DONK	49
641	30-Aug	Côte d'Ivoire	Père Camille CHARRIER	34
642	13-Oct	France	Père Amédée CHIFFOLEAU	80
643	04-Nov	Netherlands	Frère Piet COMINO	49
644	18-Dec	Côte d'Ivoire	Père Jean MYARD	37
645	20-Dec	France	Seminariste Claude MANSUY	23
		1956		
646	23-Jan	Ireland	Père Thomas BARTLEY	58
647	04-Mar	France	Père François LEBERT	76
648	01-Apr	France	Père Théophile BOULANGER	72
649	05-Apr	Ireland	Père Patrick McHUGH	62
650	10-Apr	Ireland	Frère Joseph McCABE	78
651	16-Apr	Italie	Père Jacob MUYSER	60
652	02-Dec	USA	Père Peter HARRINGTON	67
653	29-Dec	Netherlands	Père Antoon HARING	57
		1957		
654	31-Mar	Côte d'Ivoire	Père André CARRÉ	32
655	02-Apr	Côte d'Ivoire	Père Gaston TEILLET	36

No	Date	Died in/Mort à	Name/Nom	Age
656	17-Apr	Ireland	Mgr Thomas P HUGHES	66
657	11-May	Ireland	Père Maurice SLATTERY	83
658	20-May	USA	Père Denis O'CONNOR	63
659	05-Aug	Ghana	Père Joseph-Benoît EVERS	47
660	19-Aug	Netherlands	Père Jan BEENKER	49
661	01-Oct	Côte d'Ivoire	Père Martin FÈVRE	45
662	04-Dec	Suisse	Père Jakob IMHOLZ	80

1958

No	Date	Died in/Mort à	Name/Nom	Age
663	06-Jan	Netherlands	Père Jacques van LEUVEN	69
664	19-Jan	Égypte	Père Alexandre PAGÉS	81
665	05-Feb	France	Père Célestin PAICHOUX	82
666	18-Mar	Égypte	Père Claude FAILLANT	85
667	08-Apr	USA	Père Claude TAYLOR	63
668	13-Apr	France	Père Louis RAST	64
669	14-Apr	France	Père Armand GUTKNECHT	64
670	16-Apr	France	Père Louis VOUILLON	85
671	12-Jun	France	Père Théodore TRANCHANT	72
672	27-Jul	Belgique	Père Sjeng LEMMENS	60
673	27-Aug	Netherlands	Père Piet MAURIKS	55
674	14-Sep	Bénin	Père Joseph DOUAUD	37
675	20-Oct	Côte d'Ivoire	Père Pierre MÉRAUD	86
676	26-Oct	France	Père Georges BLANDIN	38
677	05-Dec	Netherlands	Père Adrien SCHOONEN	61
678	13-Dec	France	Père Victor KERN	62
679	25-Dec	Algérie	Seminariste François SAPET	22
680	28-Dec	France	Père Léon GRUNDLER	49
681	28-Dec	Netherlands	Frère Augustin BERRIÈRE	68

1959

No	Date	Died in/Mort à	Name/Nom	Age
682	13-Jan	Netherlands	Père Gerard ELBERS	49
683	26-Jan	Ireland	Père Francis McNAMARA	65
684	02-Mar	USA	Père Charles CANAVAN	60
685	11-Mar	Naufragé	Père Philip CORISH	56
686	02-May	Naufragé	Père Justin ADRIAN	63
687	10-May	Côte d'Ivoire	Père Alphonse BERNUIZET	54
688	13-May	Ireland	Père Michael SCULLY	59
689	09-Jul	France	Père François-Xavier SITZMANN	80
690	12-Jul	Ireland	Père John O'FLAHERTY	58
691	16-Jul	Nigeria	Père William KEENAN	62
692	26-Jul	USA	Père William DUNNE	44
693	08-Aug	Nigeria	Père John P MOONEY	49
694	16-Oct	France	Père Jean CURUTCHET	49
695	19-Nov	France	Père Charles ONIMUS	73
696	26-Nov	France	Père Eugène SCHAEFFER	59

1960

No	Date	Died in/Mort à	Name/Nom	Age
697	13-Jan	USA	Père Robert STITT	62
698	17-Feb	France	Père Jean-André COLOMBET	58
699	05-Mar	Ireland	Père Henry BAKER	70

No	Date	Died in/Mort à	Name/Nom	Age
700	21-Apr	Bénin	Mgr Louis PARISOT	75
701	13-Jun	Ireland	Frère Gerald COLLINS	58
702	29-Jul	France	Père Louis-Pierre MALLET	79
703	10-Aug	France	Père André PÉRÉS	74
704	27-Aug	Netherlands	Père Willem MEELBERG	65
705	20-Sep	Ireland	Père Thomas DEELEY	57
706	07-Oct	France	Père Ferdinand PRAUD	65
707	18-Oct	Ireland	Père Thomas F HUGHES	63
708	20-Oct	France	Père Antoine WIEDER	55
709	05-Nov	Netherlands	Père Louis van EERD	71
710	20-Nov	Nigeria	Père John MORTON	48
711	26-Nov	Netherlands	Père Gerardus van ROOIJ	68

		1961		
712	07-Jan	France	Père Auguste BAUMANN	71
713	13-Jan	France	Père Antoine BRUNGARD	64
714	27-Jan	Netherlands	Frère Julien TILLEMAN	72
715	06-Feb	France	Père Émile BARRIL	87
716	20-Feb	France	Père Antoine CLEYET-MAREL	57
717	03-Mar	Liberia	Mgr John M COLLINS	72
718	20-May	Ghana	Père Patrick O'LEARY	38
719	02-Jun	Netherlands	Père Piet MAASSEN	59
720	08-Jun	France	Père Xavier RASSER	71
721	07-Jul	Ireland	Père Alfred GLYNN	50
722	12-Jul	Great Britain	Père Michael McENIRY	65
723	07-Oct	USA	Père Daniel WATSON	50
724	25-Oct	France	Père Aimé SIMON	81
725	26-Oct	France	Père Joseph WALLON	62
726	11-Nov	Netherlands	Père Ate MONKEL	60
727	28-Nov	Ireland	Père Alexander MATTHEWS	61
728	20-Dec	Netherlands	Père Johannes MAYS	54

		1962		
729	14-Feb	Belgique	Père Julien LE GLOAHEC	88
730	22-Feb		Seminariste Gérard CHAUVINEAU	23
731	13-Mar	Netherlands	Père Mathieu WOUTERS	79
732	17-Mar	Netherlands	Père Antoon MEEUWSEN	68
733	26-Apr	Netherlands	Père Joseph MULDERS	55
734	07-May	France	Frère Nicolas MULLER	71
735	21-May	Great Britain	Père James B McCARTHY	59
736	08-Jul	Togo	Père Johann Baptist RIMLÉ	76
737	15-Jul	Ireland	Père Patrick O'HARA	51
738	19-Aug	France	Père Albert GAYMARD	72
739	22-Aug	Ireland	Père Vincent FINNEGAN	48
740	22-Sep	Great Britain	Mgr William LUMLEY	64
741	28-Oct	Ireland	Père Patrick Francis KELLY	50
742	02-Nov	Netherlands	Frère André HOMMA	57
743	02-Nov	Nigeria	Père John Michael MONAHAN	28
744	04-Nov	Ireland	Père Patrick Francis McKENNA	73
745	07-Nov	France	Père Joseph CORBEAU	80

165

No	Date	Died in/Mort à	Name/Nom	Age
746	25-Nov	Côte d'Ivoire	Père Robert PAULUS	48
747	01-Dec	USA	Père Patrick LAVAN	56
748	03-Dec	Liberia	Père Philip CARRIGAN	38
749	05-Dec	Ireland	Père Martin FARRINGTON	63
750	20-Dec	Ireland	Père Patrick McGIRR	69

1963

No	Date	Died in/Mort à	Name/Nom	Age
751	12-Feb	Côte d'Ivoire	Père Jean-Claude DENNIEL	36
752	26-Feb	Netherlands	Père Wim van HOUT	49
753	02-Mar	France	Père Joseph VALLÉE	88
754	03-Mar	France	Père Henri MOUËZY	64
755	06-Mar	France	Père Camille RIEDLIN	57
756	10-Mar	France	Frère Jean LECORNO	69
757	21-Mar	Netherlands	Père Anno REEKERS	64
758	20-Jun	France	Père Bernard GUILLIEN	39
759	24-Jun	Ireland	Père Patrick Joseph DUFFY	54
760	18-Jul	Bénin	Père Jean-Marie FAVIER	37
761	07-Aug	Ghana	Père Denis FLORACK	47
762	09-Aug	France	Père Auguste GASSER	53
763	22-Aug	Netherlands	Père Jo BEUMERS	46
764	24-Aug	Ireland	Père John Patrick GRANT	49
765	05-Sep	France	Mgr François FAROUD	78
766	12-Sep	France	Père Georges OLLIER	80
767	15-Sep	France	Mgr Joseph DISS	85
768	16-Sep	France	Père Darius DUHILL	72
769	29-Sep	Ireland	Père John O'NEILL	53
770	16-Oct	Côte d'Ivoire	Frère Pierre BRUYAS	38
771	05-Nov	Ghana	Père Pierre LOOZEN	40
772	15-Dec	France	Père Paul BUCHERT	67

1964

No	Date	Died in/Mort à	Name/Nom	Age
773	09-Jan	Ireland	Père Thomas HURST	86
774	16-Jan	Ireland	Père James HOLLAND	47
775	17-Mar	Great Britain	Père John WOOD	61
776	28-Mar	Côte d'Ivoire	Père Alfred LEICHTNAM	46
777	01-Apr	France	Père Guy RABILLAT	43
778	28-Apr	Nigeria	Père John LYONS	52
779	19-Jun	Great Britain	Père Patrick O'CONNELL	71
780	22-Jun	France	Père Michel COUSTEIX	70
781	02-Jul	Ireland	Frère Thomas W HUGHES	72
782	16-Aug	France	Père Gabriel CLAMENS	57
783	20-Aug	Great Britain	Père John P MURPHY	60
784	24-Aug	Netherlands	Père Jan SEVRIENS	68
785	25-Aug	France	Père Eugène MASSON	64
786	03-Oct	Ireland	Père Patrick HUGHES	61
787	20-Oct	USA	Père Mgr William LITTLE	78
788	13-Dec	France	Père Charles ANÉZO	83
789	25-Dec	Netherlands	Père Harrie van de VEN	63

1965

166

No	Date	Died in/Mort à	Name/Nom	Age
790	07-Jan	France	Père Claudius ROUSSEL	57
791	12-Mar	France	Père Armand BOURASSEAU	71
792	16-Mar	Côte d'Ivoire	Père Paul LARVOR	47
793	27-Apr	France	Père Joseph FURST	54
794	14-May	Ghana	Père Gerrit van der LEEUW	62
795	19-Jun	USA	Père George McCORMACK	64
796	24-Jun	France	Père Joseph FISCHER	66
797	26-Jun	France	Père Joseph HERVOUET	86
798	06-Jul	Ireland	Père John SHEEHAN	58
799	27-Oct	Nigeria	Mgr Leo TAYLOR	76
800	16-Nov	Germany	Père Frits van DIJK	52
801	27-Nov	Netherlands	Père Jan VERHAGEN	68
802	12-Dec	France	Frère Alexandre LUSSON	72
803	20-Dec	France	Père Jules HAENGGI	72

		1966		
804	26-Jan	Côte d'Ivoire	Père Clément AUDRAIN	58
805	26-Jan	Bénin	Frère Jean-Marie BAUDU	71
806	31-Jan	Netherlands	Père Cornelius de ROY	60
807	15-Feb	Ireland	Père James McGUIRK	77
808	18-Feb	France	Père Frédéric KURZ	63
809	01-Mar	Côte d'Ivoire	Père Georges MINKER	38
810	02-Mar	USA	Père Patrick FITZSIMONS	57
811	24-Mar	Ireland	Père Thomas J HUGHES	67
812	26-Apr	Belgique	Père Bernard van den BERG	57
813	07-Jun	Netherlands	Père Joseph COUENBERG	64
814	16-Jun	Great Britain	Mgr William PORTER	79
815	04-Jul	Togo	Père Paul WELSCH	51
816	22-Jul	France	Père René BOTHUA	60
817	22-Jul	Ireland	Père John McELGUNN	45
818	12-Aug	Netherlands	Mgr HUBERT PAULISSEN	85
819	15-Aug	France	Père Georges KNAEBEL	50
820	25-Aug	Bénin	Père Antonin GAUTIER	82
821	13-Sep	France	Père Émile HEBTING	78
822	22-Sep	USA	Père John SHEEHY	66
823	08-Oct	France	Frère Barthélemy MONTEL	66
824	26-Oct	USA	Père Joseph WERNERT	77
825	06-Nov	Netherlands	Frère Laurent MEERTENS	75
826	19-Nov	Great Britain	Père Eugene McSWEENEY	82
827	24-Nov	France	Père Aloyse BLONDÉ	68
828	25-Nov	Égypte	Père René MARZIN	58
829	06-Dec	France	Père Augustin BARATHIEU	84
830	20-Dec	Ireland	Père Michael MAHONY	66
831	27-Dec	Bénin	Père Paul PERRIN	70

		1967		
832	08-Jan	Ireland	Père Andrew O'ROURKE	54
833	11-Jan	Ghana	Père Piet van STRIEN	45
834	01-Apr	USA	Père Pierre HESS	95
835	14-Apr	France	Père Raymond ESCHENBRENNER	44

No	Date	Died in/Mort à	Name/Nom	Age
836	31-May	Ireland	Père Michael FOLEY	54
837	16-Jun	France	Père Marius MICOUD	75
838	24-Jun	USA	Père John CORCORAN	85
839	21-Jul	France	Père Arthur HECK	80
840	07-Oct	Netherlands	Frère Mattheus van LIESHOUT	64
841	20-Oct	France	Père Denis CLOUET	67
842	05-Nov	France	Père Jérôme RIEMER	58
843	12-Nov	Ghana	Père Jochem BOUMANS	66
844	11-Dec	Ireland	Père Patrick CHRISTAL	69
845	30-Dec	France	Père Adrien MASSIOT	79

		1968		
846	15-Feb	Netherlands	Père Hubert JANSSEN	67
847	20-Apr	France	Père Louis JOLIF	86
848	26-Apr	France	Père Louis ROMAGON	82
849	30-Apr	Netherlands	Père Harrie SEVRIENS	62
850	02-May	Côte d'Ivoire	Père Charles VANDAELE	42
851	03-May	Israël	Père Robert SIMON	59
852	13-May	France	Père Alfred LEGRAND	73
853	25-Jun	Togo	Père Edmond GASSER	54
854	01-Jul	France	Frère Désiré LIENHARDT	79
855	02-Jul	France	Père Pierre ZERRINGER	61
856	06-Jul	France	Père François PEYVEL	61
857	25-Jul	Ireland	Père John O'HARA	55
858	16-Sep	Côte d'Ivoire	Père Raymond ÉVAIN	44
859	23-Sep	France	Père Joseph LEGRAND	84
860	26-Sep	France	Père Gabriel LELIÈVRE	87
861	15-Oct	Ireland	Père Thomas CLONAN	59
862	21-Nov	Netherlands	Père Kees KOOLEN	66
863	27-Nov	Togo	Père Aloyse RIEGERT	60
864	28-Nov	Great Britain	Père James TOBIN	49
865	31-Dec	USA	Père Martin BANE	68

		1969		
866	02-Feb	Ireland	Père John LEVINS	78
867	06-Feb	Ireland	Père Patrick KILLEEN	46
868	08-Feb	France	Frère Pierre BRÉTÉCHÉ	82
869	25-Feb	France	Père Henri BARTHÉLEMY	55
870	03-Mar	Ireland	Père John CONNOLLY	58
871	08-Mar	Netherlands	Père Johannes ROTHOFF	72
872	13-Mar	France	Père Henri GIRARD	80
873	25-Mar	France	Père Mélaine ROUGER	69
874	08-Apr	Ireland	Père Michael CUMMINS	71
875	22-Apr	France	Père Alexandre DESBOIS	74
876	23-Apr	Ireland	Père John LUPTON	81
877	25-Apr	Netherlands	Père Rudolf ZIJLSTRA	74
878	21-May	Great Britain	Père Maurice WALSH	60
879	15-Jun	Côte d'Ivoire	Père Bernard REVEL	39
880	16-Jun	France	Père Joseph LEIBENGUTH	60
881	21-Jun	France	Père Jean-Pierre SPRUNCK	50

No	Date	Died in/Mort à	Name/Nom	Age
882	04-Jul	Allemagne	Père Michael CONVEY	54
883	25-Jul	Netherlands	Père Gerrit van DIJK	72
884	03-Aug	France	Père Aloïse BLANCK	64
885	30-Aug	Ireland	Frère Charles WEST	71
886	08-Sep	Ireland	Frère Paul HURST	75
887	23-Oct	Égypte	Frère Louis DEROCQ	69
888	11-Dec	France	Père Aloyse FRÉRING	65
889	16-Dec	France	Père Alphonse SCHAHL	85
890	21-Dec	France	Père Albert HAAS	74
891	30-Dec	France	Père Jean-Marie TOURILLON	65
		1970		
892	02-Jan	France	Père François LE PORT	80
893	07-Jan	France	Père André HUCHET	46
894	08-Jan	France	Père Benoît DESSARCE	68
895	27-Jan	Netherlands	Père Laurens VERMULST	65
896	29-Jan	Ireland	Père Stephen HARRINGTON	70
897	08-Feb	Bénin	Père Maxime CHAZAL	73
898	11-Mar	Ireland	Père Francis O'SHEA	60
899	22-Mar	Ireland	Père John O'DOHERTY	70
900	17-Apr	Great Britain	Père Martin NADORP	64
901	24-Apr	France	Mgr Jean-Baptiste BOIVIN	72
902	27-May	USA	Père James STANLEY	80
903	27-May	France	Père Jean-Baptiste CASTANCHOA	60
904	01-Jul	France	Frère Pierre GAUTRAIS	71
905	21-Jul	France	Père Ignace GOYHENETCHE	59
906	26-Jul	Netherlands	Père Antoon PEETERS	60
907	12-Aug	USA	Père Georges LAUGEL	83
908	02-Sep	Ireland	Père Michael WALKER	29
909	25-Sep	France	Père Bernard SOULÉ	40
910	30-Nov	France	Père Edmond JAUFFRIT	59
		1971		
911	07-Jan	France	Frère Claude BALLIGAND	70
912	16-Feb	Ghana	Père Kees KLAVER	57
913	22-Feb	Nigeria	Père Thomas MURRAY	65
914	17-Apr	France	Père Jean ALLEZARD	78
915	19-Apr	Belgique	Père Albert FRANÇOIS	67
916	27-Apr	France	Père André GUILLO	53
917	04-May	France	Père Alfred COLIN	72
918	11-May	Ireland	Père John O'SHEA	69
919	17-May	Ireland	Père Bernard CUNNINGHAM	54
920	24-May	France	Père Joseph FRANCK	58
921	26-May	Nigeria	Père Patrick CULLIGAN	64
922	24-Jun	Ireland	Père Joseph HILLIARD	57
923	24-Jun	France	Frère Joseph BONNANT	66
924	19-Aug	Ireland	Père Patrick DORR	64
925	12-Sep	Ireland	Père John LYNOTT	72
926	13-Sep	France	Père Paul EZANNO	83
927	06-Oct	Nigeria	Père William MURPHY	62

No	Date	Died in/Mort à	Name/Nom	Age
928	30-Nov	Ireland	Frère Patrick TOLAN	70

1972

No	Date	Died in/Mort à	Name/Nom	Age
929	04-Jan	France	Père Alphonse STECK	79
930	04-Feb	Nigeria	Père Thomas HASSETT	35
931	05-Feb	France	Père Pierre BERNARD	70
932	07-Feb	France	Père Joseph MIET	71
933	08-Feb	France	Frère Jean POTIRON	37
934	12-Mar	Ireland	Père Robert O'LEARY	72
935	18-Mar	Ireland	Père Peter GILROY	62
936	27-Mar	Ireland	Père William FEGAN	75
937	30-Mar	Égypte	Père Alexandre GAIGNOUX	70
938	03-Apr	Great Britain	Père Patrick McKAY	61
939	14-Apr	Great Britain	Mgr Joseph Gerald HOLLAND	67
940	28-May	Ireland	Père Patrick McKENNA	79
941	01-Jul	Netherlands	Père Wim van LIESHOUT	76
942	05-Jul	France	Père André CHASSAIGNON	71
943	19-Jul	Great Britain	Père James McEVOY	63
944	05-Aug	France	Père Jean DAUPHIN	65
945	05-Aug	Ireland	Père Edward RICE	61
946	19-Aug	France	Père Joseph ANGIBAUD	75
947	21-Aug	Italie	Père Giuseppe MONTICONE	86
948	03-Oct	France	Père Pierre BORDES	68
949	21-Oct	Ireland	Père Henry KENNY	80
950	23-Nov	France	Père Adolphe SAUBAN	64
951	02-Dec	Great Britain	Père Francis CARDIFF	67
952	29-Dec	Netherlands	Père Lambert ERKENS	85

1973

No	Date	Died in/Mort à	Name/Nom	Age
953	04-Jan	Côte d'Ivoire	Père André LOMBARDET	54
954	08-Jan	Netherlands	Père Kees TUKKER	59
955	20-Jan	USA	Père Anthony McANDREW	73
956	17-Feb	USA	Père Alphonse SITTLER	79
957	18-Feb	Bénin	Père Jean CLOUET	41
958	20-Mar	France	Frère Jean-Marie COSSET	83
959	26-Mar	Netherlands	Père Jan van den BROEK	64
960	13-Apr	France	Père Ernest DESSEILLE	53
961	25-May	Nigeria	Père Joseph CAREW	60
962	02-Jun	Great Britain	Père John DUFFY	67
963	06-Jun	France	Père Henri POIDEVINEAU	69
964	15-Jun	Italie	Père Michael DREW	52
965	21-Jun	Netherlands	Père Jacques ten HAVE	78
966	28-Jun	France	Père Jean-Pierre BITTMANN	37
967	14-Jul	France	Frère Louis ROUÉ	61
968	21-Jul	France	Mgr Robert CHOPARD-LALLIER	52
969	23-Jul	Ireland	Père Michael COLLINS	90
970	14-Aug	Nigeria	Père Eric WHITE	54
971	16-Aug	France	Père Joseph BARDOL	73
972	16-Aug	France	Père Marcel CALMET	50
973	20-Aug	Ireland	Père Patrick HARMON	87

No	Date	Died in/Mort à	Name/Nom	Age
974	24-Aug	Italie	Mgr Pietro ZUCCARINO	75
975	28-Aug	France	Père Jules MEYER	63
976	19-Sep	Great Britain	Père Michael HOLTON	58
977	07-Oct	Liberia	Père Dominic DONOHUE	36
978	11-Oct	Ghana	Père Cor van der PLAS	61
979	13-Oct	Netherlands	Père Kees BREUKEL	70
980	17-Oct	France	Père Claude LAZINIER	66
981	20-Oct	Netherlands	Père Kees BODEWES	66
982	05-Nov	France	Père Pascal COLICHET	73
983	03-Dec	Égypte	Père Gabriel JOUANNE	69
984	27-Dec	France	Père Ernest SAUER	79
		1974		
985	01-Jan	Ireland	Père Michael CAVANAGH	55
986	05-Jan	France	Père Roger COLLIN	56
987	25-Jan	Bénin	Père Raymond MALO	69
988	28-Feb	France	Père Emile RIEBSTEIN	83
989	11-Apr	Ireland	Père Malachy MORRIS	66
990	21-Apr	USA	Père Thomas LARKIN	57
991	22-Apr	Netherlands	Père Jan VAES	70
992	02-Jun	Ireland	Père William DEELEY	67
993	26-Jun	France	Père Théophile BLIN	76
994	28-Jun	Nigeria	Père Michael HARRISON	70
995	15-Jul	Netherlands	Frère Franciscus VERHAGEN	72
996	01-Aug	France	Père Bruno HAUSHERR	62
997	08-Aug	France	Père Joseph PORCHEROT	77
998	22-Aug	France	Père Joseph ÉVAIN	50
999	27-Sep	Ghana	Père Jan BACKES	54
1000	27-Sep	Germany	Père Adrie SUIJKERBUIJK	62
1001	29-Sep	Ireland	Père John MORAN	68
1002	08-Oct	France	Père Théodore FELLMANN	75
1003	07-Nov	France	Père Théophile BOURSIN	77
1004	27-Nov	France	Père Joseph MUCKENSTURM	74
1005	06-Dec	Ireland	Père William BYRNE	64
		1975		
1006	17-Jan	France	Père Joseph BOULAIRE	51
1007	29-Jan	Netherlands	Père Joseph MOUREN	93
1008	24-Feb	Liberia	Père Alfred LOVE	63
1009	26-Feb	Ireland	Père John G O'NEILL	67
1010	16-Mar	Bénin	Père Jean PRIGENT	50
1011	18-Mar	Ireland	Père Denis MAGUIRE	55
1012	19-Mar	Ireland	Père Maurice B KELLY	70
1013	26-Apr	Ireland	Père Michael DRUMMOND	70
1014	28-Apr	Netherlands	Père Rudolf van OOIJEN	83
1015	09-Jun	France	Père Claude MORISSEAU	75
1016	11-Jun	Ireland	Mgr John McCARTHY	73
1017	27-Jun	Netherlands	Frère Theo HOLLANDER	61
1018	22-Jul	Ireland	Père Patrick McCARTHY	78
1019	05-Aug	Netherlands	Père Wim BOND	74

171

No	Date	Died in/Mort à	Name/Nom	Age
1020	07-Aug		Père Piet FISCHER	71
1021	11-Aug	France	Père Pierre HÉNAFF	73
1022	11-Aug	Netherlands	Père Frans PAS	61
1023	22-Aug	Ireland	Père Patrick SHINE	75
1024	21-Oct	Netherlands	Frère Koos NADORP	71
1025	11-Nov	Ireland	Père James HESSION	42
1026	12-Nov	Nigeria	Père Brendan DONOHUE	41
			1976	
1027	03-Feb	Côte d'Ivoire	Père Jean ALLOATTI	48
1028	13-Feb	Netherlands	Père Gerard HOMBERGEN	64
1029	24-Feb	France	Frère Théodore KALBERMATTEN	84
1030	12-Mar	Ireland	Père Florence O'RIORDAN	56
1031	07-Apr	France	Frère Xavier WELTERLIN	86
1032	15-Apr	Nigeria	Père Richard FITZGERALD	69
1033	22-Apr	Espagne	Père Zacharias REMIRO	63
1034	13-May	France	Père Jean LE GOFF	69
1035	16-May	France	Mgr Jean-Marie ÉTRILLARD	76
1036	17-May	USA	Père Alphonse BARTHLEN	95
1037	03-Jun	Ireland	Père Ambrose O'HAIRE	76
1038	08-Jun	France	Père Pierre CHIPOT	55
1039	23-Jun	Ireland	Père Peter MOORE	65
1040	26-Jun	Great Britain	Père John COLEMAN	80
1041	26-Jul	France	Père Louis BOUVIER	76
1042	29-Jul	Ireland	Père Justin McCARTHY	61
1043	30-Jul	Ireland	Frère Jeremiah RING	53
1044	11-Aug	Nigeria	Père Michael BRENNAN	26
1045	12-Sep	USA	Père Laurence CARR	56
1046	25-Oct	Italie	Frère Ernst RIEDEL	77
1047	28-Oct	Ireland	Père Francis FALLON	60
1048	28-Oct	Netherlands	Père Jan ter LINDEN	69
1049	21-Nov	Netherlands	Père Leo BROUWER	60
1050	29-Nov	Netherlands	Père Frans ROTHOFF	76
1051	06-Dec	France	Père Eugène GASSER	90
1052	07-Dec	Netherlands	Père Johannes BECKERS	71
1053	08-Dec	France	Père Henri PICHON	78
1054	09-Dec	Australia	Père John GUILFOYLE	62
			1977	
1055	24-Jan	France	Père Victor CHOIMET	91
1056	31-Jan	Ireland	Père John HEANEY	80
1057	31-Jan	France	Père Aloyse KOELTZ	70
1058	11-Mar	USA	Père Louis IMBACH	85
1059	23-Mar	France	Frère Charles WOISSELIN	74
1060	06-Apr	Ireland	Père Patrick KERR	65
1061	12-Apr	France	Père Désiré CUQ	63
1062	24-Apr	Nigeria	Père John M MURPHY	47
1063	09-May	France	Père Jacques MONTAGUT	54
1064	28-May	France	Père François PELTIER	69
1065	02-Jul	France	Père Jean-Baptiste BRUYAS	66

No	Date	Died in/Mort à	Name/Nom	Age
1066	11-Jul	France	Père Simon-Pierre COSSÉ	79
1067	27-Jul	France	Père Élie COUSSEAU	63
1068	17-Aug	France	Père François BRÉGAINT	60
1069	20-Aug	France	Père Henri BAROTTIN	73
1070	23-Aug	France	Père Prosper MALO	69
1071	22-Sep	Nigeria	Père John KILBEY	85
1072	07-Nov	France	Père Lucien KAPPS	68
1073	30-Nov	France	Père Roger DUQUESNE	61
1074	15-Dec	Ireland	Père Richard TOBIN	65
1075	26-Dec	Ireland	Père Daniel CORVIN	67
			1978	
1076	04-Jan	Ireland	Père Daniel O'CONNELL	82
1077	21-Jan	Netherlands	Père Arie de KOK DE	70
1078	07-Mar	Ireland	Père James SAUL	80
1079	12-Mar	Belgique	Père Jean BRUGGEMANS	82
1080	14-Mar	Belgique	Père Joseph AALBERS	78
1081	19-Mar	France	Père Louis NOËL	65
1082	10-Apr	France	Père Eugène SIRLINGER	91
1083	11-Apr	Netherlands	Père Jan OOSTENBACH	58
1084	03-May	Great Britain	Père William BRESLIN	54
1085	03-May	Netherlands	Père Frits van TRIGT	68
1086	26-May	Ireland	Père Jeremiah HIGGINS	70
1087	31-May	Liberia	Père Edward McCROREY	31
1088	02-Jun	France	Père Joseph DASTILLUNG	58
1089	23-Jun	France	Père Eugène WICKY	82
1090	30-Aug	France	Père Jules SAVÉAN	68
1091	12-Oct	Ireland	Père Kevin O'SHEA	70
1092	03-Nov	France	Père Jean JESTIN	75
1093	17-Dec	France	Père Joseph DELHOMMEL	93
			1979	
1094	18-Jan	Égypte	Père Jean-Paul NÉDÉLEC	57
1095	25-Jan	Netherlands	Frère Franz GEIER	82
1096	04-Feb	France	Frère Gabriel VAUTHIER	75
1097	08-Feb	France	Frère Jean-Marie MAISONNEUVE	88
1098	09-Feb	Ireland	Père Martin KENNY	71
1099	24-Feb	Ireland	Père Thomas DUFFY	81
1100	26-Feb	Netherlands	Père Jacques VERHEUGD	79
1101	16-Mar	France	Frère Raymond GAVILLET	74
1102	18-Mar	Scotland	Père Denis HORGAN	83
1103	29-Mar	Ghana	Père Thijs WESTENBROEK	59
1104	21-Apr	Great Britain	Père Patrick GUINAN	62
1105	14-May	Netherlands	Père Joseph BASTIAENS	74
1106	16-May	France	Père Joseph DUBOIS	78
1107	04-Jun	Ireland	Père John J COLLINS	71
1108	05-Aug	France	Père Gervais KÉROUANTON	72
1109	08-Sep	Ireland	Père Malachy GATELY	73
1110	20-Sep	France	Père Francis VERGER	56
1111	02-Oct	France	Père Eugene CHRIST	67

173

No	Date	Died in/Mort à	Name/Nom	Age
1112	16-Nov	Ireland	Père Alphonsus O'SHEA	68
1113	23-Dec	Netherlands	Père Antoon BOUCHIER	67

1980

No	Date	Died in/Mort à	Name/Nom	Age
1114	16-Jan	USA	Père Thomas O'DONNELL	47
1115	03-Feb	Netherlands	Père Antoon BERGERS	81
1116	09-Feb	France	Père Joseph RAINGEARD	77
1117	10-Feb	Netherlands	Père Adriaan KEIJSERS	75
1118	14-Feb	France	Frère Jean-Marie SALAÜN	76
1119	24-Feb	France	Frère Antoine RICHARD	80
1120	28-Mar	Netherlands	Frère Joannes BRANTJES	84
1121	15-Apr	Netherlands	Frère Gerard van de PASCH	60
1122	23-Apr	Netherlands	Père Jan van der KOOY	73
1123	12-May	France	Père Claude DAUVERGNE	70
1124	15-May	France	Père Paul BRUNET	64
1125	17-May	France	Père Joseph SPAMPINATI	71
1126	24-May	Ireland	Père Daniel CANNON	64
1127	02-Jun	Ireland	Père John MURTAGH	67
1128	04-Jul	USA	Père John GALVIN	75
1129	08-Jul	Netherlands	Père Jan van den HOUT	83
1130	12-Jul	Ireland	Père John MAHON	77
1131	17-Jul	France	Père René JUNGMANN	45
1132	21-Jul	France	Père Amand HUBERT	80
1133	07-Aug	France	Père Paul FALCON	63
1134	28-Aug	Netherlands	Père Frans HERTSIG	79
1135	30-Aug	Netherlands	Père Johannes de ROOY	74
1136	11-Sep	Scotland	Père Gerard PHILLIPS	73
1137	02-Oct	France	Père Ignace DELANNOY	54
1138	10-Oct	Ireland	Mgr Francis CARROLL	68
1139	16-Oct	Ireland	Père Thomas DONOGHUE	82
1140	19-Oct	France	Père Arthur CHAUVIN	67
1141	01-Nov	France	Père Jean THÉPAUT	73
1142	05-Nov	France	Frère Eugène Louis VENGEANT	77
1143	19-Nov	France	Père Joseph AUJOULAT	78

1981

No	Date	Died in/Mort à	Name/Nom	Age
1144	27-Jan	Netherlands	Père Piet DERICKX	75
1145	30-Jan	France	Père Édouard BEILLEVAIRE	80
1146	05-Feb	Great Britain	Père James O'REILLY	39
1147	10-Feb	Ireland	Père Kevin McKEOWN	73
1148	11-Feb	Ghana	Père Nico STEEMERS	55
1149	02-Mar	France	Père Jean ANGST	68
1150	05-Mar	France	Père Joseph HUCHET	80
1151	08-Mar	Great Britain	Père John DESMOND	72
1152	17-Apr	Ireland	Père James MURPHY	62
1153	23-Apr	Netherlands	Père Frits KOOLEN	92
1154	30-Apr	France	Père Germain BOUCHEIX	70
1155	06-May	Ireland	Père John McGUINNESS	53
1156	26-May	France	Père Albert MEY	80
1157	20-Jun	France	Père Jean-Marie FAVIER	75

174

No	Date	Died in/Mort à	Name/Nom	Age
1158	24-Jun	Nigeria	Père Michael Anthony GLYNN	66
1159	27-Jun	Allemagne	Père Jan ENGELEN	65
1160	02-Jul	France	Père Paul REY	79
1161	03-Jul	Ireland	Père Jerome SHEEHAN	87
1162	18-Jul	France	Père Séraphin VINET	69
1163	21-Jul	Ireland	Père William McAULEY	71
1164	29-Jul	France	Père Joseph GUÉRIN	80
1165	02-Aug	Netherlands	Père Bernard GOOTZEN	72
1166	03-Aug	France	Père Joseph VOGEL	92
1167	11-Aug	Ireland	Père Francis DOYLE	65
1168	12-Aug	Ireland	Père Patrick HURST	78
1169	20-Sep	Ireland	Père John O'MALLEY	63
1170	21-Oct	Ireland	Père Henry SHEPPARD	73
1171	29-Oct	France	Père Émile STADELWIESER	77
1172	31-Dec	Netherlands	Père Theodorus PRINCÉE	71
			1982	
1173	10-Jan	USA	Père Albert TURCOTTE	62
1174	11-Jan	Netherlands	Père Gerard POT	82
1175	13-Jan	Côte d'Ivoire	Père Angelo BIANCO	38
1176	13-Jan	France	Frère Robert KREMSER	75
1177	23-Jan	Bénin	Père Mgr Moïse DURAND	86
1178	01-Feb	Netherlands	Père Emmanuel KENNIS	87
1179	02-Mar	Great Britain	Père Cornelius D MURPHY	60
1180	02-Mar	Belgique	Père Jean TOUSSAINT	60
1181	18-Mar	Netherlands	Frère Hendrik RUBIE	88
1182	26-Mar	Netherlands	Frère Cornelius COMMANDEUR	98
1183	26-Apr	Netherlands	Frère Kees van GENNIP	76
1184	19-Jun	Canada	Père Gabriel HADDAD	59
1185	23-Jun	Netherlands	Père Theo SLOOTS	84
1186	30-Jun	France	Père Aloyse BISCHOFBERGER	85
1187	07-Jul	France	Père François GALLIOU	76
1188	18-Jul	France	Père Henri PERNOT	78
1189	05-Aug	France	Père Kees LIGTVOET	67
1190	11-Aug	France	Père Paul LOMELET	67
1191	21-Aug	Netherlands	Père John van HEESEWIJK	85
1192	21-Aug	Netherlands	Père Piet WOUTERS	80
1193	01-Sep	Ireland	Frère James AHERN	69
1194	20-Oct	France	Père Hugues BRUN	71
1195	19-Dec	France	Père Georges FIX	77
			1983	
1196	16-Jan	France	Père Henri THOMAS	59
1197	23-Jan	France	Père Jean JACOBY	73
1198	28-Jan	USA	Père Maurice McCARTHY	63
1199	17-Mar	Germany	Père Theo VENHOVENS	73
1200	27-Mar	France	Père Jacques MARSTEAU	59
1201	04-Apr	Ireland	Père Michael CAROLAN	70
1202	09-Apr	France	Mgr Louis WACH	75
1203	01-May	France	Père Joseph Le ROCH	54

175

No	Date	Died in/Mort à	Name/Nom	Age
1204	03-May	Bénin	Père Daniel VERHILLE	57
1205	18-May	France	Père Eugène GESTER	73
1206	18-Jun	France	Père Paul BAUDU	68
1207	24-Jun	France	Père Raymond COTTEZ	83
1208	24-Jun	France	Père René MOCKERS	73
1209	11-Jul	France	Père Alphonse GUÉRIN	78
1210	13-Jul	USA	Père John HARRINGTON	65
1211	15-Jul	Ireland	Père Timothy O'DRISCOLL	76
1212	23-Jul	France	Père Joseph-Arthur ESCHLIMANN	76
1213	28-Jul	Nigeria	Père Michael McLOUGHLIN	78
1214	12-Aug	France	Père Louis GOMMEAUX	70
1215	17-Aug	France	Père Émile ALLAINMAT	75
1216	03-Sep	France	Père Eugène OLIVAIN	85
1217	02-Oct	Ireland	Père Richard BEAUSANG	61
1218	22-Oct	France	Père Félix GOYHENETCHE	68
1219	30-Nov	Netherlands	Père Hubert van GASTEL	77
1220	22-Dec	France	Père Antoine ACKER	99
1221	27-Dec	Netherlands	Frère Henricus SANDERS	75
		1984		
1222	17-Jan	USA	Père Peter J O'CONNELL	48
1223	17-Jan	Ireland	Père Philip O'SHEA	72
1224	29-Jan	Ireland	Père Michael J O'SHEA	63
1225	05-Feb	Ireland	Père Timothy CADOGAN	87
1226	13-Feb	Ireland	Frère James GARRETT	71
1227	12-Mar	France	Mgr Joseph STREBLER	91
1228	12-Mar	France	Père Rémi BRUNGARD	95
1229	15-Mar	France	Père Charles HAEFFNER	76
1230	27-Mar	Ireland	Père James V YOUNG	80
1231	23-Apr	Pologne	Père Bolesław SZMANIA	76
1232	31-May	USA	Père Patrick FLEMING	80
1233	01-Jun	France	Père Louis AGUILHON	64
1234	10-Jun	Nigeria	Père John Henry JONES	61
1235	13-Jun	Ireland	Père Gerard Q McGAHAN	61
1236	14-Jun	France	Père Paul FRÉRING	68
1237	20-Jun	Netherlands	Père Henk SMETS	81
1238	25-Jun	Togo	Père Ernest KRAUTH	63
1239	13-Aug	France	Père René ROBERT	83
1240	23-Aug	France	Père Louis DELBAERE	87
1241	21-Oct	France	Père Paul DEVIENNE	73
1242	12-Dec	France	Frère Eugène LEAUTÉ	59
1243	25-Dec	France	Père Gabriel CHAUVET	81
		1985		
1244	03-Jan	France	Frère Joseph ZIELIŃSKI	79
1245	07-Jan	Ireland	Père James A McAFEE	75
1246	13-Jan	Netherlands	Père Wout SAMUELS	77
1247	01-Feb	Ireland	Père Florence McCARTHY	77
1248	06-Mar	Ghana	Père Hans van de VEN	37
1249	16-Mar	Côte d'Ivoire	Père Jean GRETER	47

No	Date	Died in/Mort à	Name/Nom	Age
1250	29-Mar	Ireland	Père Stephen MURPHY	73
1251	03-May	France	Mgr Jérôme LINGENHEIM	78
1252	07-May	France	Mgr Noël BOUCHEIX	84
1253	13-Jul	France	Père Joseph PETER	65
1254	18-Jul	France	Frère Jean-Marie ROCHERY	79
1255	20-Jul	France	Père Alfred DUFOUR	65
1256	20-Jul	Belgique	Père Jean LEJEUNE	61
1257	07-Aug	Ireland	Père Thomas J GALVIN	83
1258	17-Aug	France	Père Yves DUVAL	63
1259	21-Aug	France	Père Joseph ROTH	68
1260	06-Nov	Ireland	Père Louis KINNANE	74
1261	14-Nov	France	Père Benito IBARRETA	75
1262	09-Dec	France	Père Arsène GANDON	87
1263	13-Dec	Netherlands	Père Harrie NAUS	73
1264	26-Dec	Italie	Père Henricus P MONDÉ	76
1265	29-Dec	France	Père Roger BARTHÉLEMY	73

			1986	
1266	03-Jan	France	Frère Louis MARCHANT	75
1267	21-Jan	Netherlands	Père Henk SOUTBERG	74
1268	26-Jan	France	Père Henri BOUIX	79
1269	01-Feb	France	Père Wendelin HEINRICH	75
1270	13-Feb	France	Père Albert DIEBOLD	75
1271	17-Feb	France	Père Victor HOLLENDER	78
1272	28-Feb	Ireland	Père Thomas M GREENE	83
1273	03-Mar	Ireland	Père Thomas O'CONNOR	62
1274	03-Apr	USA	Père Philip C BAGNASCO	59
1275	08-Apr	Netherlands	Père Henk SMEELE	76
1276	26-Apr	Espagne	Père Candido TROCONIZ	76
1277	03-May	France	Frère Joseph FEDERSPIEL	89
1278	28-May	France	Père Jean-Baptiste BAUWENS	63
1279	06-Jun	Ireland	Père John J KEAVENEY	74
1280	07-Jul	Espagne	Père Juan Maria CÁMARA	63
1281	14-Aug	France	Père Jacques KNAEBEL	77
1282	03-Oct	Ireland	Père Leo P McNEILL	68
1283	01-Nov	Netherlands	Père Leo OP't HOOG	59
1284	02-Nov	Netherlands	Père Pierre KNOPS	88
1285	05-Nov	Netherlands	Père Wilhelmus de ROOY	75
1286	07-Nov	Côte d'Ivoire	Père Jean-Louis ROUMIER	63
1287	09-Dec	France	Père Adolphe LEJEUNE	65
1288	10-Dec	Netherlands	Père Bernard EERDEN	80
1289	14-Dec	France	Père Victor WERLÉ	80
1290	17-Dec	France	Père Victor RUBLON	83
1291	18-Dec	France	Père Jean ÉVAIN	62

			1987	
1292	05-Jan	Netherlands	Père Adriaan JUYN	74
1293	10-Jan	France	Père Léon TAVERNIER	76
1294	12-Feb	Suisse	Père Jacques FISCHER	117
1295	14-Feb	Netherlands	Frère Chris FILIPPINI	81

177

No	Date	Died in/Mort à	Name/Nom	Age
1296	25-Feb	France	Père Roger JOYEAU	72
1297	05-Apr	Ireland	Père Patrick Joseph KETT	79
1298	09-Apr	USA	Père Patrick O'DONOGHUE	78
1299	29-Apr	Togo	Père André WIDLOECHER	67
1300	11-May	Ghana	Père Leo BEKEMA	69
1301	30-May	Netherlands	Père Jacques GEURTS	90
1302	06-Jun	France	Père Jean PALLARÈS	59
1303	15-Jun	France	Père Louis GESTER	78
1304	24-Jul	France	Père Ange BOULO	72
1305	06-Aug	Ireland	Père John McANDREW	71
1306	15-Aug	France	Père Pierre GUÉGADEN	79
1307	01-Sep	Ireland	Père Thomas O'ROURKE-HUGHES	82
1308	15-Nov	France	Père René GUINOISEAU	87
1309	12-Dec	Netherlands	Père Johannes WATERREUS	81
		1988		
1310	21-Jan	France	Père Pierre PETITJEAN	76
1311	03-Feb	Ireland	Mgr William R FIELD	80
1312	10-Feb	Great Britain	Père Patrick M KELLY	83
1313	13-Mar	Ireland	Père John MOORHEAD	69
1314	21-May	France	Père Lucien REIBEL	79
1315	28-Jun	Netherlands	Père Theo BLOM	67
1316	29-Jun	France	Père Yves PIRIOU	80
1317	10-Jul	Côte d'Ivoire	Frère Octave HOUTMANN	85
1318	23-Aug	Netherlands	Père Sjef GIESEN	78
1319	24-Sep	France	Père Frédéric MÉNARD	71
1320	27-Oct	Netherlands	Père Louis ZUIDWIJK	82
1321	23-Nov	Nigeria	Père Jeremiah CADOGAN	74
1322	30-Nov	France	Père Jean-Baptiste AUDRAIN	79
1323	02-Dec	Netherlands	Père Jacobus VISSER	75
1324	09-Dec	France	Père Rogatien MARTINET	79
		1989		
1325	04-Jan	Ireland	Père Richard FINN	76
1326	07-Jan	Nigeria	Père Michael GRACE	70
1327	13-Jan	Ireland	Père John HORAN	67
1328	20-Jan	Netherlands	Père Louis MOONEN	83
1329	05-Feb	Nigeria	Père Joseph STEPHENS	73
1330	17-Mar	France	Père Czesław SWIERKOWSKI	71
1331	26-Mar	Netherlands	Père Piet MEEUWENOORD	81
1332	06-Apr	USA	Père Daniel LOONEY	58
1333	11-Apr	France	Père Antoine HICKENBICK	90
1334	17-Apr	France	Père Jean DRIOT	60
1335	27-Apr	France	Père Jean-Paul SCHUR	53
1336	28-Apr	USA	Père Eugène GEISSER	84
1337	10-May	France	Père Basilio SEGUROLA	77
1338	20-May	Netherlands	Père Jan DOESWIJK	85
1339	30-May	Australia	Père Donal CONNOLLY	48
1340	21-Jun	Ireland	Père Martin WHYTE	70
1341	24-Jun	France	Père Jean-François MARTEL	76

No	Date	Died in/Mort à	Name/Nom	Age
1342	12-Jul	France	Frère Jacques RICARD	94
1343	18-Jul	Ireland	Père James BYRNE	73
1344	03-Aug	Ireland	Père Michael O'KEEFFE	66
1345	21-Aug	France	Frère Jean MAURER	80
1346	10-Sep	France	Frère Edouard BLARER	90
1347	23-Oct	France	Père Alphonse MARGUERIE	85
1348	09-Nov	Netherlands	Père André BODELIER	55
1349	18-Nov	Germany	Père Harrie SMITS	78
1350	24-Nov	Ireland	Père Thomas MORAN	85
1351	05-Dec	USA	Père Bartholomew KEOHANE	85

1990

No	Date	Died in/Mort à	Name/Nom	Age
1352	02-Jan	Ireland	Père Francis CONVEY	77
1353	05-Jan	Ireland	Père Luke CARNEY	74
1354	12-Feb	Ireland	Père Denis MINIHANE	84
1355	02-Mar	France	Père Jacques BERTHO	87
1356	29-Mar	France	Père Pierre LE GUEN	82
1357	20-Apr	Nigeria	Père Martin McDONNELL	80
1358	30-Apr	Great Britain	Père Joseph G CONBOY	75
1359	08-May	France	Laïc Mme Georgette LEFEUVRE	0
1360	11-May	Ireland	Père William SHEEHAN	62
1361	26-May	Netherlands	Frère James TRIEPELS	98
1362	03-Jun	USA	Père Owen O'SULLIVAN	60
1363	04-Jul	France	Père Joseph AYOUL	78
1364	04-Aug	France	Père François KAPUŠCIK	72
1365	10-Aug	Netherlands	Père Jo LEFERINK	73
1366	02-Sep	Ireland	Père James CARROLL	80
1367	16-Sep	Netherlands	Père Wim van de LAAR	72
1368	22-Sep	Netherlands	Père Hubert LEHAEN	85
1369	23-Sep	France	Père Nicolas WEBER	79
1370	24-Sep	France	Frère François NOËL	79
1371	04-Oct	Netherlands	Père Jan HASSING	85
1372	06-Oct	Ghana	Père Sef MOONEN	63
1373	10-Oct	Égypte	Père Gabriel SCIAMMA	77
1374	13-Oct	France	Père Lucien NOURY	64
1375	14-Oct	Netherlands	Père Evert HEIJMANS	80
1376	19-Oct	Ireland	Père Daniel J McCAULEY	75
1377	15-Nov	Ireland	Frère Michael A WALSH	66
1378	16-Nov	France	Père Jules BEDAULT	71
1379	13-Dec	France	Père Michel ROZE	76

1991

No	Date	Died in/Mort à	Name/Nom	Age
1380	15-Jan	Ireland	Père Patrick J MURPHY	78
1381	24-Jan	USA	Père Adolph GALL	93
1382	28-Jan	Belgique	Père Hubert WIJNANS	82
1383	26-Feb	France	Père Jean-Louis BRÉHIER	88
1384	04-Mar	France	Père Jean-Marie FÉRA	59
1385	08-Mar	France	Frère Martin BATO	79
1386	12-Mar	France	Père Camille CHIROL	85
1387	19-Apr	Côte d'Ivoire	Père Richard BROWN	45

179

No	Date	Died in/Mort à	Name/Nom	Age
1388	03-May	France	Père François-Xavier RASSER	55
1389	06-May	USA	Père Aloysius RAMSTEIN	90
1390	11-May	Netherlands	Mgr Antoon KONINGS	81
1391	24-Jul	Netherlands	Père Theodorus de ROOY	76
1392	31-Jul	France	Frère Johannes Mattheus GEUSKENS	53
1393	08-Aug	Ireland	Père John James BRESLIN	75
1394	17-Aug	France	Père Jacques CLARISSE	73
1395	18-Aug	Ireland	Mgr Patrick J KELLY	96
1396	05-Sep	USA	Père Laurier W HAINES	56
1397	13-Sep	Ireland	Père David MULCAHY	84
1398	09-Nov	Netherlands	Père Adrie A van BAAR	73
1399	12-Nov	USA	Père Benedict BURKE	69
1400	16-Dec	Netherlands	Père Cornelius G HULSEN	78
1401	25-Dec	France	Frère Marcel LEFORT	88
1402	27-Dec	Great Britain	Père Michael N GALLAGHER	72
1403	27-Dec	Netherlands	Père Cornelius MANSHANDEN	72
		1992		
1404	12-Jan	Ireland	Père John G LEE	86
1405	08-Feb	Togo	Père Albert REIFF	72
1406	03-Mar	Netherlands	Père Harrie PORTIER	76
1407	12-Mar	Togo	Père Guy KRAEMER	58
1408	14-Mar	Côte d'Ivoire	Père Joseph PFISTER	81
1409	23-Mar	Netherlands	Père Piet FEIJEN	57
1410	30-Mar	USA	Père Henry P J RUSSELL	79
1411	04-Apr	France	Père Pie SEILER	73
1412	07-Apr	France	Père Joseph LABROSSE	84
1413	27-Apr	Great Britain	Père Martin O'MEARA	80
1414	03-May	France	Père Joseph FUCHS	59
1415	19-May	Netherlands	Père Johan MENSINK	66
1416	11-Jun	Ireland	Père Joseph DONNELLY	75
1417	17-Jun	Ireland	Père Richard O KELLEHER	43
1418	19-Jun	Ireland	Père Thomas O'SHAUGHNESSY	81
1419	23-Jun	France	Père Bernard FORTIN	71
1420	27-Jun	Ireland	Père John POWER	64
1421	30-Jun	France	Père Joseph ROUX	71
1422	06-Jul	Ireland	Père Denis MANNING	92
1423	10-Jul	France	Père Philippe NUSS	74
1424	22-Jul	Ireland	Père S Joseph STYLES	78
1425	13-Aug	Ireland	Père Michael MOORHEAD	80
1426	26-Aug	Netherlands	Père Jan van DEUN	71
1427	07-Sep	Ghana	Père Piet NEEFJES	58
1428	12-Sep	France	Père Eugène WOELFFEL	82
1429	14-Sep	USA	Père Hugh A McLAUGHLIN	88
1430	20-Sep	Netherlands	Père Jan GOOREN	74
1431	01-Oct	France	Père Jean-Dominique CHATTOT	49
1432	07-Oct	Ireland	Père Thomas DEVANE	68
1433	10-Oct	Côte d'Ivoire	Père Jean MEYNIER	61
1434	17-Oct	Netherlands	Père Gerard JOOSTEN	75
1435	30-Nov	Australia	Père Joseph MULLINS	76

180

No	Date	Died in/Mort à	Name/Nom	Age
1436	25-Dec	USA	Père James GRIFFIN	93

			1993	
1437	12-Jan	Nigeria	Père Kevin CARROLL	72
1438	13-Jan	France	Père Joseph NONNENMACHER	85
1439	15-Jan	Ireland	Père Bernard DERVIN	76
1440	15-Feb	France	Père Jules KRAUSS	85
1441	02-Mar	Nigeria	Père Maurice MAGUIRE	75
1442	02-Mar	Netherlands	Père Cor van OERS	79
1443	06-Mar	Netherlands	Frère Jan BOVENMARS	75
1444	15-Mar	Côte d'Ivoire	Père Adrien JEANNE	55
1445	17-Mar	France	Père Antoine JUNG	75
1446	07-Apr	Ireland	Père Jeremiah COAKLEY	80
1447	10-Apr	Ireland	Père Thomas KENNEDY	65
1448	25-Apr	Ireland	Père Martin CONBOY	72
1449	28-Apr	France	Père Henri GRUNENWALD	69
1450	06-May	USA	Père John Vincent MULVEY	94
1451	11-May	France	Père Frédéric STEINER	81
1452	07-Jun	France	Mgr Patient REDOIS	68
1453	06-Aug	Ireland	Père Bernard DOLAN	72
1454	19-Aug	Netherlands	Père Wim RECKMANN	79
1455	30-Aug	USA	Laïc Freda M WALTER	82
1456	24-Sep	Ireland	Père Edward F COLEMAN	78
1457	20-Oct	Netherlands	Père Andreas BRUINSMA	75
1458	04-Nov	France	Père Jean QUIGNON	76
1459	08-Nov	Great Britain	Père Richard D VEASEY	45
1460	26-Dec	Ireland	Père John HACKETT	69

			1994	
1461	08-Jan	USA	Père Cyril J DONNELLY	83
1462	23-Jan	Ireland	Père Anthony McDONAGH	76
1463	24-Jan	France	Père Gustave KLERLEIN	76
1464	02-Mar	France	Père Joseph LEMARIÉ	89
1465	12-Mar	France	Mgr Émile DURRHEIMER	84
1466	14-Mar	Ireland	Père Gerard FERGUS	70
1467	09-Apr	Netherlands	Père Harry van NULAND	88
1468	19-Apr	Germany	Père Theo MAESSEN	75
1469	28-May	USA	Père William J ELLIOTT	67
1470	02-Jun	Ireland	Père Michael TONER	74
1471	01-Jul	France	Père Maurice GRENOT	78
1472	19-Jul	France	Frère Dominique MAUGARD	49
1473	18-Aug	France	Père Jacques DUJARDIN	68
1474	23-Aug	France	Père Claude SCHNEIDER	63
1475	30-Aug	USA	Père James MORRISON	71
1476	03-Sep	Ireland	Père Patrick BRANIFF	89
1477	03-Oct	Ireland	Mgr John REDDINGTON	84
1478	22-Oct	Netherlands	Père Coen EVERS	88
1479	06-Nov	Ireland	Père Brendan HANNIFFY	72
1480	15-Nov	RCA	Seminariste Robert GUCWA	25
1481	15-Nov	Ireland	Mgr William MAHONY	75

181

No	Date	Died in/Mort à	Name/Nom	Age
1482	19-Nov	Ireland	Père Elisha O'SHEA	67
1483	10-Dec	Netherlands	Père Petrus SANDERS	87
1484	26-Dec	New Zealand	Père Alexander LYNCH	56

		1995		
1485	19-Jan	R D Congo	Père Edouard GRAAS	65
1486	23-Jan	France	Père Marcel LICKEL	76
1487	04-Feb	Ireland	Père James WHITTAKER	80
1488	14-Mar	France	Père Albert CHAIZE	82
1489	14-Apr	Netherlands	Père Toon DOMENSINO	98
1490	04-May	Ireland	Père Francis O'MAHONY	78
1491	12-May	Nigeria	Père John GUBBINS	63
1492	18-May	France	Père Germain FLOURET	62
1493	19-May	R D Congo	Père Faustin MANZANZA	40
1494	09-Jun	Ireland	Mgr Nicholas GRIMLEY	77
1495	13-Jun	France	Père Paul RIVAL	67
1496	21-Jun	Netherlands	Père Antoon van HOUT	83
1497	29-Jun	Netherlands	Père Sjeng JACOBS	73
1498	27-Aug	France	Frère René WACHT	61
1499	20-Sep	France	Père Jean BRIENS	86
1500	28-Sep	France	Père Maxime GAUME	84
1501	13-Oct	Netherlands	Père Herman LUBBERS	77
1502	27-Oct	France	Père Étienne HUGOT	86
1503	30-Oct	Ireland	Père Matthew WALSH	85
1504	07-Nov	France	Père Joseph MEYER	81
1505	22-Nov	France	Père Joseph GARNIER	83
1506	01-Dec	Ireland	Père Peter J BENNETT	88
1507	15-Dec	Netherlands	Père Frans RAMAKERS	85

		1996		
1508	01-Jan	Netherlands	Père Pierre CRUTS	83
1509	26-Jan	France	Père Pierre ROMANIAK	78
1510	27-Jan	Netherlands	Père Piet GIEBELS	81
1511	17-Feb	Ireland	Père John J MACKLE	80
1512	29 Feb	France	Père Jean HER	68
1513	07-Mar	Zambia	Frère Brendan MURRAY	58
1514	30-Mar	France	Père Bernard CHAPEAU	68
1515	17-May	USA	Père Sylvester John MURRAY	67
1516	28-May	France	Père Alphonse HAEUSSLER	89
1517	01-Jun	Ireland	Père Francis HUGHES	82
1518	06-Jun	Ireland	Père Vincent O'NEILL	52
1519	10-Jun	Netherlands	Père Jan BERGERVOET	86
1520	02-Jul	France	Père Clovis NIEL	71
1521	02-Jul	France	Père Joël ROY	69
1522	22-Jul	France	Père Antonin BRUYAS	88
1523	15-Aug	Ireland	Père Benno WOLFF	71
1524	30-Aug	France	Père Robert THIBAUD	61
1525	12-Sep	France	Père Bertrand HELLEUX	69
1526	13-Sep	Ireland	Père Michael McCOY	74
1527	13-Sep	Netherlands	Père Hein VERSPEEK	69

No	Date	Died in/Mort à	Name/Nom	Age
1528	07-Oct	France	Père Henri SCHNEIDER	85
1529	10-Oct	Netherlands	Père Hubert GIJSELAERS	79
1530	08-Nov	Netherlands	Père Wim RUIKES	80
1531	15-Nov	France	Père Louis VIAUD	82
1532	24-Nov	Netherlands	Père Hubert JACOBI	85
1533	02-Dec	Netherlands	Père Wim GRIFFIOEN	76
1534	18-Dec	Ireland	Père Laurence COLLINS	66
1535	19-Dec	USA	Père James O'SULLIVAN	67

1997

No	Date	Died in/Mort à	Name/Nom	Age
1536	23-Jan	France	Père Georges CADEL	85
1537	31-Jan	USA	Père Louis NASSER	71
1538	17-Feb	France	Père Louis ALLIBE	69
1539	23-Feb	Ireland	Père Michael CONWAY	79
1540	19-Mar	Ireland	Père James HEALY	83
1541	02-Apr	Netherlands	Père Jan MEULEPAS	78
1542	07-Apr	Ireland	Père Anthony J FOLEY	80
1543	08-Apr	France	Père Pierre BONY	66
1544	15-Apr	France	Père Konrad WALKOWIAK	79
1545	20-Apr	Égypte	Seminariste René SAGNI	31
1546	05-May	France	Frère Joseph BOHN	86
1547	08-May	France	Père François PRUAL	82
1548	13-May	Netherlands	Mgr André van de BRONK	89
1549	17-May	Scotland	Père Thomas Anthony DUKE	68
1550	01-Jun	Ireland	Père John CANTILLON	75
1551	02-Jun	France	Laïc Pierre LÉVÈQUE	73
1552	04-Jun	Ireland	Père John B DONNELLY	82
1553	09-Jun	France	Père André ROUX	69
1554	15-Jun	Ireland	Père Laurence DOLAN	89
1555	15-Jun	France	Père Joseph PUAUT	71
1556	20-Jun	Ireland	Père Benedict NOLAN	82
1557	01-Jul	USA	Père Ernest MAGEE	74
1558	08-Jul	Ireland	Père Patrick J MURPHY	67
1559	22-Jul	Germany	Père Joseph LOCHTMAN	80
1560	28-Aug	Ireland	Père Michael McFADDEN	81
1561	29-Aug	Netherlands	Père Jeu FLORACK	78
1562	16-Sep	Ireland	Père Thomas DRUMMOND	75
1563	29-Sep	France	Père Louis PANIS	79
1564	16-Oct	Ireland	Père Michael J COLLERAN	86
1565	28-Oct	France	Père Camille STAUFF	78
1566	19-Nov	France	Père Alfred ROPELEWSKI	71
1567	20-Nov	Bénin	Père Michel AUFFRAY	67
1568	20-Nov	Netherlands	Père Ferdinand van LEEUWEN	77
1569	12-Dec	Netherlands	Frère Antoon van den DUNGEN	92
1570	16-Dec	Netherlands	Père Martin KEINHORST	86
1571	29-Dec	France	Père Théodore FRITSCH	86

1998

No	Date	Died in/Mort à	Name/Nom	Age
1572	14-Jan	Netherlands	Père Gerard van de WEIJDEN	87
1573	26-Jan	France	Père Jean Baptiste URVOY	89

183

No	Date	Died in/Mort à	Name/Nom	Age
1574	15-Feb	France	Père Jean Marie HUET	83
1575	09-Mar	Ireland	Père Terence BERMINGHAM	65
1576	11-Mar	France	Père Gilbert BREM	66
1577	11-Mar	France	Père Paul GACHET	93
1578	24-Mar	France	Père Jacques DALBIN	84
1579	10-Apr	Bénin	Père Joseph NEYME	64
1580	15-Apr	Ireland	Père Maurice BURKE	70
1581	16-Apr	Bénin	Père Gabriel HOUÉZÉ	105
1582	22-Apr	France	Père Gabriel EUVRARD	63
1583	02-May	Ireland	Père Anthony JENNINGS	75
1584	25-Jun	Ireland	Père John V O'BRIEN	78
1585	25-Jun	Netherlands	Frère Wim van LEEUWEN	90
1586	20-Jul	Ireland	Père Joseph D BARRETT	87
1587	08-Aug	France	Père Noël DOUAU	75
1588	21-Aug	Ireland	Père John J DUNNE	72
1589	04-Nov	France	Père Jean-Marie GAUTIER	79
1590	15-Nov	Italie	Père Secondo CANTINO	60
1591	29-Dec	France	Mgr André DUIRAT	90
			1999	
1592	09-Jan	France	Père Michel KERDERRIEN	66
1593	19-Jan	Netherlands	Père Huub LEMMERLING	83
1594	19-Jan	Ireland	Père Fintan P NELLY	79
1595	29-Jan	Ireland	Père Vincent E BOYLE	78
1596	01-Feb	Great Britain	Père Alfred BICKERTON	85
1597	05-Feb	France	Père Georges KERLÉVÉO	86
1598	14-Feb	Netherlands	Père Gerard van HOUT	80
1599	26-Feb	Ireland	Père Francis P McGOVERN	78
1600	22-Mar	France	Père Henri KUENEMANN	74
1601	02-Apr	Ireland	Père Anthony L MURPHY	84
1602	04-Apr	India	Seminariste SAHAYARAJ	25
1603	05-Apr	Côte d'Ivoire	Père François HUMBERT	64
1604	12-Apr	Côte d'Ivoire	Père Léopold LACROIX	53
1605	26-Apr	France	Père Victor LERDOU	85
1606	01-May	Netherlands	Père Cor BEURSKENS	74
1607	11-Jul	Netherlands	Père Martin GEELEN	73
1608	28-Jul	Ireland	Père James HAYES	70
1609	03-Aug	France	Père Modeste BILLOTTE	65
1610	10-Aug	Liberia	Laïc Paul DICKRELL	37
1611	19-Oct	USA	Père John F FLYNN	70
1612	20-Oct	Ireland	Père Hugh D CONLON	78
1613	02-Nov	France	Frère Heinrich LATZ	74
1614	09-Dec	Ireland	Père Seán SWEENEY	90
1615	10-Dec	France	Père Eugène BERNHART	78
1616	18-Dec	France	Laïc Mme Marie-Louise CHEVALIER	
1617	22-Dec	Netherlands	Père Bernard WIEGGERS	82
1618	26-Dec	France	Père Edouard VONWYL	93
			2000	
1619	20-Jan	Netherlands	Père Nico PRONK	79

184

No	Date	Died in/Mort à	Name/Nom	Age
1620	31-Jan	Ireland	Père Patrick O'NEILL	87
1621	10-Mar	USA	Père Francis HYNES	81
1622	20-Mar	France	Père Georges GROS	86
1623	30-Apr	Scotland	Père Michael J WALSH	85
1624	07-Jun	France	Frère Paul CORBINEAU	70
1625	10-Jun	France	Père Joseph PARRIAUX	75
1626	17-Jun	Ireland	Père Bartholomew McCARTHY	76
1627	18-Jun	Ireland	Père Thomas LENNON	79
1628	20-Jun	France	Père Joseph MALVAL	84
1629	02-Jul	Suisse	Frère Marcel ROULIN	89
1630	31-Jul	Netherlands	Père Jacques van VEEN	74
1631	01-Aug	Belgique	Père Jacques TOUSSAINT	73
1632	25-Aug	France	Père Lucien REYSER	91
1633	12-Sep	France	Père Jean DURIF	78
1634	21-Oct	Netherlands	Père Frits van VEIJFEIJKEN	73
1635	03-Nov	Ireland	Père Denis J O'DONOVAN	86
1636	26-Nov	Ireland	Père James HICKEY	78
1637	16-Dec	France	Père Michel CONVERS	81

No	Date	Died in/Mort à	Name/Nom	Age
			2001	
1638	25-Jan	Scotland	Laïc Mlle Margaret ASPINALL	
1639	05-Feb	Germany	Père Cornelius POTTERS	90
1640	07-Feb	France	Laïc Joseph MICHAUD	77
1641	17-Feb	Ireland	Père Edward HARRINGTON	85
1642	26-Feb	Great Britain	Laïc Leonard WALKER	90
1643	11-Mar	France	Père André CASSARD	88
1644	14-Apr	USA	Père Kevin SCANLAN	70
1645	04-Jun	Ireland	Frère Peter HOULIHAN	86
1646	28-Jun	Great Britain	Laïc Mlle Anne TIMOTHY	0
1647	29-Jun	Great Britain	Père Patrick McANALLY	92
1648	29-Jun	France	Père Jean-Luc GUILBAUD	62
1649	30-Jun	Netherlands	Père Kees KONIJN	77
1650	02-Jul	USA	Père Michael MAUGHAN	83
1651	11-Jul	Ireland	Père Michael J FEELEY	83
1652	24-Jul	Belgique	Père Albert Georges LEROY	75
1653	06-Aug	Netherlands	Père Jan COOLEN	87
1654	07-Aug	Ireland	Père Seán O'MAHONY	81
1655	08-Aug	Ireland	Père John RODGERS	76
1656	09-Aug	France	Mgr Noël TEKRY KOKORA	79
1657	16-Aug	France	Père Michel ROBERT	87
1658	22-Sep	Netherlands	Père Wynand RUYLING	74
1659	23-Sep	Netherlands	Père Sjef LENNERTZ	84
1660	01-Nov	USA	Père Michael J ROONEY	84

No	Date	Died in/Mort à	Name/Nom	Age
			2002	
1661	06-Jan	Ireland	Père Patrick GANTLY	82
1662	08-Jan	France	Père Henri BANNWARTH	82
1663	25-Jan	France	Père Gérard ALTHUSER	69
1664	29-Jan	Togo	Père André BOUHELIER	60
1665	07-Feb	Netherlands	Père Frits BOLLEN	94

185

No	Date	Died in/Mort à	Name/Nom	Age
1666	27-Feb	France	Laïc John A FEELEY	82
1667	02-Mar	Bénin	Père René FAURITE	61
1668	14-Mar	Ireland	Père John J BROWNE	86
1669	15-Mar	Ghana	Père Frits HEBBEN	69
1670	10-Jun	France	Père Hubert GRIENEISEN	91
1671	11-Jun	France	Père Joseph DANIEL	96
1672	09-Jul	Ireland	Père Francis McARDLE	89
1673	29-Jul	Ireland	Père Patrick J GLYNN	82
1674	19-Aug	Ireland	Frère Francis MURPHY	86
1675	28-Aug	Ireland	Père Daniel J O'CONNOR	72
1676	04-Sep	Belgique	Père Bernard DODENBIER	98
1677	05-Sep	Wales	Père P Gerard SCANLAN	82
1678	25-Oct	Ireland	Père Martin HERAGHTY	83
1679	12-Nov	Ireland	Père Henry J BELL	78
1680	01-Dec	France	Père Marcel SINGER	75
1681	04-Dec	Ireland	Père Edward J DONOVAN	81
1682	08-Dec	Ireland	Père Cornelius CLANCY	88

			2003	
1683	02-Jan	Ireland	Père Michael A HIGGINS	72
1684	21-Jan	France	Père Yves CALVEZ	79
1685	29-Jan	Ireland	Père Robert V WISEMAN	73
1686	02-Feb	Netherlands	Père Theo GÖRTZ	89
1687	10-Feb	France	Père Ambroise VEILLARD	84
1688	17-Feb	Ghana	Père Antonius MANSHANDEN	69
1689	24-Feb	Netherlands	Père Stef KERSTEN	82
1690	25-Feb	France	Frère Pascal MARIN	66
1691	01-Mar	Canada	Père Fernand ALAIN	66
1692	13-Mar	Ireland	Père William POWER	79
1693	23-Mar	France	Père Joseph MITTAINE	78
1694	18-Apr	France	Père Pierre SCHMITT	88
1695	19-Apr	France	Père Joseph GASS	90
1696	01-May	France	Père Bernard KLAMBER	77
1697	01-May	France	Père Joseph SPEITEL	82
1698	09-May	France	Père Roger STÉPHAN	77
1699	11-May	France	Père Pierre LAMANDÉ	81
1700	21-May	Netherlands	Père Theodorus VELDBOER	95
1701	27-May	Netherlands	Père Cornelius SCHELTINGA	89
1702	09-Jun	Great Britain	Père Jeremiah CROWE	76
1703	11-Jun	France	Père Charles LOTZ	74
1704	22-Jun	France	Père Yves ROCHER	85
1705	26-Jun	France	Père Raymond BINOCHE	79
1706	07-Jul	Ireland	Père James B HILL	86
1707	07-Jul	Ireland	Père Denis SLATTERY	87
1708	08-Jul	France	Père René GAUTHIER	73
1709	08-Oct	Belgique	Père Willy LEJEUNE	81
1710	12-Oct	Ireland	Père Owen F SWEENEY	65
1711	19-Oct	Netherlands	Père Wilhelmus HABITS	76
1712	21-Nov	Togo	Sr Jeannine BROCHARD	
1713	22-Nov	Ireland	Père Thomas BLEE	74

No	Date	Died in/Mort à	Name/Nom	Age
1714	26-Nov	Ireland	Père Seán O'CONNELL	77
1715	11-Dec	Canada	Père Albert JAMES	75
1716	30-Dec	USA	Père Francis GILLIS	85

			2004	
1717	10-Jan	Ireland	Père Matthew GILMORE	88
1718	11-Jan	France	Père Gabriel CHOTARD	80
1719	04-Feb	Ireland	Père James FLANAGAN	84
1720	07-Feb	France	Père Casimir BADOC	86
1721	11-Feb	France	Père Victor MERCIER	90
1722	19-Feb	France	Père Maurice DUQUESNE	82
1723	04-Mar	France	Père André DEUTSCH	70
1724	10-Mar	France	Père Jean-Paul GUILLARD	66
1725	19-Mar	Netherlands	Père Tamis WEVER	67
1726	05-Apr	Netherlands	Père André STOFFELS	93
1727	28-Apr	Ireland	Père Eugene CASEY	75
1728	30-Jun	France	Père Jean-Baptiste ROSIER	82
1729	14-Jul	France	Père Joseph DEMEYÈRE	100
1730	22-Jul	Australia	Père Petrus de VRIES	89
1731	18-Sep	France	Père Jean-Louis GUÉNOLÉ	86
1732	09-Oct	France	Père Pierre AUDOUIN	58
1733	13-Oct	USA	Père George LANDRY	85
1734	22-Oct	Netherlands	Père Leonardus van GASTEL	86
1735	27-Oct	France	Frère Henri FRÉNEAU	67
1736	31-Oct	Ireland	Père Robert HALES	76
1737	03-Nov	France	Père Jean-Marie BAUDUCEL	83
1738	08-Nov	Ghana	Père Jaap OBDAM	85
1739	25-Nov	Italie	Père Gianfranco BRIGNONE	59
1740	25-Nov	Kenya	Père John F HANNON	65
1741	11-Dec	Ireland	Père Michael McGLINCHEY	75
1742	25-Dec	Ireland	Père Thomas LINDON	71

			2005	
1743	20-Jan	Ireland	Père Laurence SKELLY	78
1744	20-Jan	France	Père Michel DURAND	85
1745	01-Feb	Ireland	Père Thomas HIGGINS	86
1746	23-Feb	Netherlands	Père Jan TILLIE	79
1747	17-Mar	France	Frère François Marie ABGUILLERM	97
1748	06-Apr	Ireland	Père Oliver SMITH	84
1749	08-Apr	Ireland	Père Robert J MOLLOY	92
1750	08-Apr	France	Père Julien GAILLARD	90
1751	24-Apr	Ireland	Père John J (Sean) KELLY	70
1752	02-May	France	Père Albert HAAS	71
1753	19-May	France	Père Robert LANOË	80
1754	22-May	France	Père Maurice PAVAGEAU	82
1755	11-Jun	Ireland	Père Richard DEVINE	73
1756	27-Jun	France	Père André NETH	89
1757	12-Jul	Ireland	Père Daniel DALY	95
1758	18-Nov	Netherlands	Père Han van VELZEN	83
1759	20-Nov	Ireland	Père Cornelius O'DRISCOLL	82

No	Date	Died in/Mort à	Name/Nom	Age
1760	04-Dec	France	Père Théophile COGARD	85

			2006	
1761	04-Jan	France	Frère Pierre FRITSCH	84
1762	17-Jan	Zambia	Père Fergus CONLAN	66
1763	18-Jan	France	Père Joseph CHOPARD	83
1764	16-Feb	France	Frère François-Marie FLOCH	91
1765	18-Feb	France	Père Joseph COLSON	85
1766	20-Feb	Ireland	Père James G LEE	81
1767	01-Mar	Ireland	Père Joseph BRENNAN	80
1768	22-Apr	Ireland	Père John BREHENY	74
1769	03-May	Ireland	Père Thomas EGAN	80
1770	04-May	France	Père Yves GUILLOU	83
1771	24-May	France	Père Antoine BRUNNER	71
1772	05-Jun	USA	Père Francis Thomas GILFETHER	82
1773	14-Jun	Netherlands	Père Frans SPRONCK	84
1774	14-Jun	France	Père Albert MATHIEU	91
1775	01-Jul	France	Père Jean-Baptiste CORBINEAU	70
1776	27-Jul	India	Père Joseph RAMESH	33
1777	08-Aug	Italie	Père Luigi FINOTTI	73
1778	08-Aug	France	Père Antoine VALÉRO	80
1779	14-Aug	France	Sr Marie-Marthe PORTIER	82
1780	05-Oct	USA	Père John J SHEEHAN	90
1781	12-Oct	France	Père Pierre DIDELOT	85
1782	19-Oct	France	Père Pierre TRICHET	82
1783	19-Nov	Ireland	Père John BURKE	64
1784	24-Nov	France	Père Xalbat MARCARIE	69
1785	03-Dec	Ireland	Père Owen MAGINN	86
1786	14-Dec	France	Père Jean LANDARRETCHE	78
1787	17-Dec	France	Père Antoine CAILHOUX	87
1788	21-Dec	France	Père Raymond PEYLE	92

			2007	
1789	06-Jan	France	Père Georges ERHARD	91
1790	13-Jan	Ireland	Père David HUGHES	89
1791	28-Jan	Netherlands	Père Wim JANSMAN	77
1792	30-Jan	Ireland	Père Christopher MURPHY	88
1793	31-Jan	Great Britain	Père Joseph McANDREW	79
1794	02-Feb	France	Père Francis PLUMELET	90
1795	23-Feb	France	Père Paul AILLERIE	75
1796	27-Feb	Ireland	Père John McCREANOR	87
1797	19-Mar	Côte d'Ivoire	Père René HOC	67
1798	23-Mar	Ireland	Père Peter DEVINE	73
1799	26-Mar	Ireland	Père Michael KENNEDY	80
1800	02-Apr	Netherlands	Père Jacques van den BRONK	88
1801	03-Apr	Netherlands	Père Herman van de LAAR	88
1802	12-Apr	Ireland	Père Bernard HORAN	71
1803	01-Jun	France	Père Gilbert WILHELM	73
1804	17-Jul	France	Père Georges YÈCHE	91
1805	25-Jul	France	Père René LEMASSON	83

No	Date	Died in/Mort à	Name/Nom	Age
1806	07-Aug	RCA	Frère Paul FLAGEUL	62
1807	04-Sep	Ireland	Père Francis McCABE	89
1808	21-Sep	Netherlands	Père James van OUDHEUSDEN	92
1809	15-Oct	Italie	Père Giacomo BARDELLI	67
1810	04-Nov	France	Père Henri NEAU	68
1811	19-Nov	Nigeria	Père Cornelius GRIFFIN	60
1812	12-Dec	France	Père Rolph ROTH	66
1813	16-Dec	France	Père Raymond DOMAS	82
1814	18-Dec	France	Père Jean GUITTENY	75
			2008	
1815	11-Jan	France	Père Roger ERHEL	87
1816	12-Jan	Italie	Père Mme Tina STEFANACHI	
1817	17-Feb	Belgique	Père Henri THEIZEN	72
1818	08-Mar	Netherlands	Père Chris DOUMA	83
1819	02-Apr	Italie	Père Giacomo UBBIALI	74
1820	07-Apr	Ireland	Père Dominic KEARNS	83
1821	26-Apr	USA	Père Edward RICHARDSON	89
1822	13-May	France	Mgr Bernardin GANTIN	86
1823	14-May	France	Père Charles CUENIN	73
1824	19-May	France	Père Ugo BOSETTI	93
1825	03-Jun	France	Père Maurice ACHARD	84
1826	27-Jun	Netherlands	Père Jaap BAKKER	86
1827	06-Jul	France	Père Michel WACK	95
1828	24-Jul	France	Père Gérard VIAUD	77
1829	05-Aug	Ireland	Père Jeremiah DWYER	84
1830	15-Sep	USA	Père James Harold SULLIVAN	74
1831	27-Sep	France	Père Michel DENIAUD	73
1832	13-Oct	Ireland	Père James McCARTHY	87
1833	14-Oct	France	Père René MÉNARD	84
1834	24-Oct	France	Frère Bernard LAURENT	89
1835	04-Nov	Netherlands	Père Johan VERSPEEK	72
1836	12-Nov	Ireland	Père John O'MAHONY	71
1837	02-Dec	Ireland	Père John A CREAVEN	91
			2009	
1838	09-Jan	Canada	Laïc Mme Anne-Marie LOUBIER	30
1839	17-Jan	France	Père Alexandre COLSON	84
1840	28-Jan	Ireland	Père Patrick CARROLL	84
1841	06-Feb	Ireland	Père Henry CASEY	67
1842	13-Feb	France	Laïc Gilbert JUNG	63
1843	20-Feb	France	Père Yves LE MIGNON	85
1844	22-Mar	Netherlands	Père Dionysius van de LAAK	72
1845	22-Mar	France	Père Louis GONON	78
1846	18-Apr	India	Père Anthony RAJAREEGAM	73
1847	20-Jun	USA	Sr Sr Claire TYNAN	78
1848	16-Jul	Ireland	Père Seaghan RAFFERTY	85
1849	02-Aug	France	Père Georges LEGRAND	89
1850	04-Aug	Ireland	Père James O'CONNELL	72
1851	12-Aug	Netherlands	Père Jan KOENDERS	92

No	Date	Died in/Mort à	Name/Nom	Age
1852	20-Aug	France	Père Paul-Henri DUPUIS	83
1853	30-Aug	France	Père Antoine GOETZ	87
1854	30-Aug	Ireland	Père James HARROLD	91
1855	27-Oct	Italie	Laïc Mgr Guido MONTANARO	86
1856	29-Nov	Pologne	Père Bernard MARIANSKI	95
1857	30-Nov	France	Père Eugène DUCASTAING	72
1858	12-Dec	Belgique	Père Jean EVRARD	81

		2010		
1859	18-Jan	France	Frère Joseph LASKA	94
1860	20-Jan	Ireland	Mgr John MOORE	68
1861	20-Jan	Belgique	Père Georges LEJEUNE	87
1862	01-Feb	Ireland	Laïc Christopher (Christy) O'SULLIVAN	90
1863	17-Feb	Ghana	Père Robertus CLOBUS	72
1864	06-Mar	France	Père Ange MABON	86
1865	27-Mar	Great Britain	Père Richard Douglas BLUETT	75
1866	26-Apr	Suisse	Père Pierre Canisius ZOSSO	97
1867	27-Apr	Ireland	Père Paul D'ARCY	65
1868	27-Jun	Netherlands	Père Theodorus BROCKHOFF	94
1869	29-Jun	France	Père Gérard VOLARD	75
1870	15-Jul	USA	Père James PERRONE	82
1871	16-Jul	France	Père Marius KRUTT	75
1872	22-Sep	Ireland	Père Martin McNEELY	77
1873	02-Oct	Belgique	Père Jean-Marie LAMOTTE	78
1874	03-Oct	Netherlands	Père Herman ENGBERINK	90
1875	02-Nov	Ireland	Père John FEENEY	88
1876	08-Nov	France	Père Joseph HÉRY	82
1877	15-Nov	France	Père Pierre MESSNER	92
1878	10-Dec	France	Frère Albert WEBER	85
1879	20 Dec	Ireland	Père Anthony O'DONNELL	84
1880	23-Dec	France	Père Yves LAGOUTTE	90
1881	27-Dec	Ireland	Père Gregory McGOVERN	89

		2011		
1882	22-Jan	France	Père Gilbert ANTHONY	78
1883	05-Feb	Netherlands	Père Maarten WESSELING	73
1884	02-Mar	France	Laïc Jean BIAU	95
1885	31-Mar	Ireland	Père Gerard HACKETT	80
1886	03-Apr	Ireland	Père James CONLON	83
1887	11-Apr	France	Père Marcel MAHY	85
1888	28-Apr	Ireland	Père Eugene CONNOLLY	87
1889	08-May	Netherlands	Père Johannes SMITS	76
1890	18-May	France	Père Marcel HUNTZINGER	89
1891	02-Jun	Ireland	Père Christopher McKEOGH	76
1892	07-Jul	Philippines	Père Bembolio de los SANTOS	37
1893	07-Jul	Belgique	Père Louis MAHY	89
1894	22-Jul	Netherlands	Père Henricus KONING	72
1895	07-Aug	France	Père Paul ROSTOUCHER	82
1896	22-Aug	Belgique	Père Paulus van WINDEN	44
1897	19-Sep	Ireland	Père Bernard RAYMOND	79

No	Date	Died in/Mort à	Name/Nom	Age
1898	08-Oct	Ireland	Père Hugh McKEOWN	86
1899	24-Nov	France	Père Édouard DÉMÉRLÉ	100
1900	27-Nov	Canada	Père Charles-Henri BOUCHER	81
1901	23-Dec	Ireland	Père Sean MacCARTHY	89
		2012		
1902	02-Jan	France	Père Denys BELLUT	86
1903	04-Jan	France	Père Pierre BONNET	91
1904	05-Jan	France	Père Francis HÉRY	87
1905	23-Jan	Niger	Père Yves PELLETIER	62
1906	30-Jan	Ireland	Père Mary (Sadie) McDONAGH	87
1907	04-Feb	France	Mgr Pierre ROUANET	94
1908	10-Feb	Ireland	Père Patrick WHELAN	79
1909	15-Feb	Ireland	Père Michael CAHILL	75
1910	17-Feb	France	Père Raymond PASCAL	97
1911	22-Feb	France	Père Henri CHALOPIN	91
1912	25-Feb	Ireland	Frère James REDMOND	80
1913	10-Mar	Côte d'Ivoire	Père Gérard BARBIER	73
1914	22-Mar	Canada	Père Jean-Paul PARISEAU	80
1915	30-Mar	Ireland	Père Dermot HEALY	86
1916	04-Apr	France	Père André GUILLARD	84
1917	27-Apr	France	Père Aloyse RAUNER	94
1918	20-May	France	Père André MARTIN	89
1919	29-May	France	Père Paul GAUTRET	86
1920	25-Jul	France	Père Fernand BIORET	88
1921	26-Jul	Ireland	Laïc Mrs Ellen GALVIN	87
1922	21-Aug	Ireland	Père Robert O'REGAN	97
1923	02-Sep	France	Père Jean-Baptiste DUFFÈS	88
1924	06-Sep	France	Père Paul AUBRY	79
1925	19-Sep	Netherlands	Père Johannes Maria KOEK	67
1926	20-Sep	India	Père Aarokiasamy GNANAPRAGASAM	84
1927	23-Sep	France	Père Petrus REYNARD	83
1928	12-Dec	France	Père Alphonse ALLIRAND	87
1929	22-Dec	Netherlands	Père Johannes FRANKENHUIJSEN	75
1930	24-Dec	France	Père Paul VÉROT	88
1931	31-Dec	Netherlands	Père Joseph CRAMERS	85
		2013		
1932	03-Jan	USA	Père Clark YATES	87
1933	18-Jan	France	Père Guy OLLIVAUD	74
1934	19-Jan	Netherlands	Père Cornelis Z PRIEMS	92
1935	29-Jan	Ireland	Père Martin NOLAN	78
1936	01-Feb	France	Père Michel DURIF	88
1937	05-Feb	France	Père Joseph ARSAC	81
1938	18-Feb	France	Père Jacques VAROQUI	64
1939	20-Feb	Netherlands	Père Antonius J HULSHOF	86
1940	25-Mar	Ireland	Père Billy O'SULLIVAN	79
1941	30-Mar	France	Père Clément CADIEU	98
1942	31-Mar	France	Père Jaël Joseph ISOLÉRI	84
1943	17-Apr	France	Père Louis BOIRON	86

No	Date	Died in/Mort à	Name/Nom	Age
1944	10-May	Ireland	Père Michael DARCY	78
1945	13-May	Ireland	Père Hugh McLAUGHLIN	82
1946	13-May	France	Père Jean-Marie SÉBILO	88
1947	31-May	Ireland	Père Donal Michael O'CONNOR	80
1948	01-Jun	Canada	Père Benoît BOUCHARD	83
1949	19-Jun	France	Père Jean-Baptiste LEBRUN	83
1950	01-Jul	France	Père Jean-Paul FELDER	79
1951	24-Aug	France	Laïc Mlle Philomène CROS	100
1952	24-Sep	Netherlands	Père Willebrordus HUISMAN	92
1953	05-Oct	France	Père Félix LUTZ	89
1954	06-Oct	USA	Père Edward BIGGANE	81
1955	29-Oct	Ireland	Père William BURKE	87
1956	13-Nov	Netherlands	Père Jacobus SMEELE	67
1957	19-Nov	France	Père Nicolas MOUTERDE	85
1958	05-Dec	Ireland	Père Thomas MULLAHY	79
1959	17-Dec	France	Père Albert BOGARD	85

2014

No	Date	Died in/Mort à	Name/Nom	Age
1960	02-Jan	Netherlands	Père Wilhelmus van FRANKENHUIJSEN	84
1961	24-Jan	France	Père Paul GOTTE	87
1962	27-Jan	Bénin	Laïc Théophile VILLAÇA	84
1963	22-Feb	Ireland	Père Sean RYAN	80
1964	05-Apr	Ireland	Père Liam O'CALLAGHAN	95
1965	09-May	USA	Père John GUINEY	82
1966	19-May	Canada	Père Raymond LORTIE	89
1967	16-Jun	France	Père Marcel RANCHIN	88
1968	18-Jun	Ireland	Père Michael McEGAN	80
1969	24-Jun	France	Père Louis ROLLAND	88
1970	06-Jul	France	Père Claude MASSON	81
1971	15-Jul	Ireland	Père Sean HAYES	78
1972	25-Jul	France	Père Pierre MORILLON	75
1973	29-Jul	Ireland	Père Martin J WALSH	86
1974	30-Jul	Ireland	Père William FOLEY	78
1975	30-Jul	France	Père Claude TEMPLE	71
1976	02-Aug	France	Laïc Mme Colette GRIVEL	83
1977	16-Aug	Togo	Père Gérard BRETILLOT	76
1978	19-Aug	Netherlands	Père Josephus Petrus VALENTIN	74
1979	31-Aug	USA	Père Thomas E HAYDEN	82
1980	09-Sep	Ireland	Père Thomas S DORAN	81
1981	16-Sep	RCA	Père Barthélémy NAMDEGANAMNA	49
1982	23-Sep	France	Père Elie COCHO	82
1983	26-Sep	France	Père Michel LOIRET	77
1984	06-Oct	Ireland	Père Thomas FURLONG	90
1985	10-Oct	Ireland	Laïc Bridget Agatha FEELEY	92
1986	16-Oct	Ireland	Père Anthony J BUTLER	73
1987	19-Oct	Ireland	Père Daniel MURPHY	82
1988	11-Nov	France	Laïc Jean-Paul GRASSER	77
1989	21-Nov	Netherlands	Père Lambert MEURDERS	86

2015

192

No	Date	Died in/Mort à	Name/Nom	Age
1990	02-Mar	Ireland	Père John CASEY	84
1991	06-Mar	Côte d'Ivoire	Père Francesco ARNOLFO	69
1992	16-Mar	Netherlands	Père Johannes Th WAGEMAKERS	98
1993	03-May	Netherlands	Frère Hubertus VERREUSSEL	93
1994	18-May	Ireland	Père William KENNEDY	88
1995	04-Jun	Ireland	Père Patrick McGOVERN	85
1996	03-Jul	France	Laïc Mlle Elise GILROY	106
1997	09-Jul	USA	Père John F MURRAY	92
1998	13-Jul	Canada	Père Jean-Guy MARTEL	74
1999	26-Jul	Ireland	Père T Vincent LAWLESS	84
2000	31-Jul	Bénin	Père Chabi Emile BIAOU	35
2001	05-Sep	Denmark	Père Theodorus L BAKKER	83
2002	06-Sep	France	Père Jacques LALANDE	88
2003	10-Sep	France	Père Jean-Charles RAMIN	91
2004	17-Sep	Netherlands	Père Petrus G KESSELS	88
2005	03-Oct	RCA	Père Amos NGAÏZOURE	44
2006	17-Oct	France	Père Pierre JACQUOT	76
2007	19-Oct	France	Père Michel GIRARD	91
2008	25-Oct	France	Père Ferdinand BLINDAUER	83
2009	26-Oct	Netherlands	Père Henricus C HOEBEN	80
			2016	
2010	21-Jan	France	Laïc M. Antoine THOMAS	91
2011	29-Jan	Liberia	Laïc Beth OTTING	52
2012	04-Feb	Ireland	Père Thomas GORMAN	93
2013	26-Feb	Italie	Père Giuseppe, Don CAVALLI	86
2014	30-Mar	France	Laïc Mme Dominique PILLARD	64
2015	03-Apr	Ireland	Père James J HIGGINS	92
2016	05-Apr	USA	Père Daniel CULLEN	95
2017	05-Apr	France	Père Michel IRIQUIN	66
2018	05-Apr	France	Père Joseph FOLMER	90
2019	19-Apr	France	Laïc Jean BOUHELIER	79
2020	08-Jul	France	Laïc Josée POLOCE	91
2021	09-Jul	France	Frère Jean-Paul BAUMANN	76
2022	17-Jul	Ireland	Père Eugene RIORDAN	93
2023	02-Aug	France	Père Yves BLOT	82
2024	17-Aug	Ireland	Père Jeremiah P O'CONNELL	84
2025	27-Aug	Ireland	Père Daniel J O'NEILL	78
2026	05-Sep	Ireland	Père Vincent LAWLESS	84
2027	13-Sep	France	Père Pierre TRICHET	82
2028	30-Sep	France	Père Louis-Marie MOREAU	85
2029	17-Oct	Netherlands	Père Eduard HUBERT	77
2030	18-Oct	France	Père Maurice BIOTTEAU	84
2031	06-Nov	Togo	Père Jean PERRIN	91
2032	21-Nov	Ireland	Père Joseph MAGUIRE	94
2033	22-Nov	France	Père Dominique PEIRSEGAELE	82
2034	23-Nov	France	Père Michel BERTONNEAU	75
2035	14-Dec	Netherlands	Père Harrie van HOOF	85
2036	14-Dec	France	Père Jules LAHARGOU	78
2037	22-Dec	France	Père Félix RÉGNIER	90

No	Date	Died in/Mort à	Name/Nom	Age
2038	28-Dec	USA	Père Terence DOHERTY	81
			2017	
2039	08-Jan	France	Père Jean-Paul GOURNAY	73
2040	14-Jan	Netherlands	Père Joseph van UUM	87
2041	22-Jan	France	Père Rene GROSSEAU	84
2042	23-Jan	India	Père Peter Pandi NAYAGAM	51
2043	23-Jan	Ireland	Père James F KIRSTEIN	81
2044	06-Feb	France	Père Louis PERROCHAUD	93
2045	15-Feb	Ireland	Père Edward CASEY	89
2046	23-Feb	France	Père Albert LIROT	79
2047	18-Mar	France	Père Hubert DAUDE	82
2048	06-Apr	Great Britain	Michael McPARTLAND	77
2049	06-Apr	Espagne	Laïc José PÉREZ GÓMEZ	73
2050	23-Apr	France	Père Yves BERGERON	75
2051	25-Apr	Italie	Père Carmine CARMINATI	86
2052	25-Jun	Ireland	Père Vincent GLENNON	70
2053	30-Jun	France	Père Paul LE GOFF	90
2054	25-Jul	France	Père Camille ALLAIN	80
2055	30-Jul	France	Laïc Marie Reine SCHNEIDER	72
2056	18-Aug	Ireland	Père Francis MEEHAN	88
2057	25-Aug	Netherlands	Père Arjen RIJPKEMA	90
2058	06-Sep	Togo	Père Andre CHAUVIN	84
2059	30-Sep	France	Père Francis KUNTZ	86
2060	01-Oct	France	Père Charles SANDERS	87
2061	02-Oct	Ireland	Père John A TRAVERS	91
2062	07-Oct	Netherlands	Père Gerard LUKASSEN	88
2063	09-Oct	France	Père André FUCHS	94
2064	12-Oct	South Africa	Père Pius AFIABOR O.	45
2065	28-Oct	France	Père Bernard VONDERSCHER	87
2066	16-Nov	Italie	Père Mario BOFFA	85
2067	20-Nov	Netherlands	Père Piet WENDERS	81
2068	11-Dec	France	Père Jean KLEIN	79
2069	15-Dec	Italie	Laïc Andrea CABELLA	81
2070	15-Dec	Italie	Laïc Zadio SENISE	96
			2018	
2071	02-Jan	Netherlands	Père Jan DEKKER	93
2072	11-Jan	France	Père Marcel DUSSUD	82
2073	23-Jan	France	Père Louis JACQUOT	105
2074	01-Feb	Ireland	Frère Thomas (Bro) FITZGERALD	99
2075	20-Mar	Tanzania	Père Adam BARTKOWICZ	34
2076	28-Mar	France	Père Paul BRION	85
2077	28-Mar	Nigeria	Père Sylvester OGBOGU	45
2078	29-Apr	France	Frère Andre ANDRE	88
2079	10-Jun	Canada	Père Léo LATENDRESSE	85
2080	07-Jul	USA	Père Donatien DJOHOSSOU	54
2081	26-Aug	Ireland	Père Cornelius O'LEARY	88
2082	05-Oct	France	Père Bernard CURUTCHET	88
2083	08-Oct	Ireland	Père W Romuald BARRY	73

No	Date	Died in/Mort à	Name/Nom	Age
2084	09-Nov	France	Père Jean LEVEQUE	82
2085	11-Nov	France	Père Pierre BERGOT	89
2086	29-Nov	Ireland	Père A Edward (Eamonn) KELLY	82
2087	05-Dec	Netherlands	Soeur Mamerta DE LANGE	92
2088	29-Dec	France	Père Maurice PRAT	90
			2019	
2089	05-Feb	France	Père François MARGERIT	90
2090	17-Feb	Ireland	Père Michael BRADY	77
2091	13-Apr	France	Père Antoine BRUNGARD	79
2092	17-Apr	Ireland	Père Alberto OLIVONI	82
2093	21-Apr	Great Britain	Père Peter B HERSEY	77
2094	23-Apr	Ireland	Laïc Margaret McMAHON	92
2095	30-Apr	France	Père Joseph MOULIAN	70
2096	04-May	Ireland	Père William CUSACK	78
2097	08-Jun	France	Père Ernest MOULIN	77
2098	13-Jun	Ireland	Père T Patrick MACKLE	94
2099	29-Jun	France	Père Roger MORITZ	87
2100	08-Jul	Ireland	Père Johnie HAVERTY	83
2101	10-Aug	France	Père Andre DESBOIS	92
2102	06-Nov	Bénin	Laïc Albert TEVOEDJIRE	90
2103	01-Dec	France	Père Gilbert PIRANDA	83
2104	20-Dec	USA	Père Daniel LYNCH	71
			2020	
2105	01-Jan	France	Père Bernard GUILLARD	80
2106	14-Jan	Ireland	Père Patrick J. M. KELLY	65
2107	17-Jan	France	Père Max VIVIER	77
2108	30-Jan	Ireland	Père Francis E FUREY	77
2109	08-Feb	Bénin	Père Jesús FERNANDEZ DE TROCONIZ	76
2110	10-Feb	Ireland	Père Terence GUNN	84
2111	22-Feb	Ireland	Père Michael M EVANS	88
2112	06-Mar	France	Laïc Jean-Baptiste ZANCHI	82
2113	11-Mar	Espagne	Laïc María Auxiliadora FERNÁNDEZ GARCÍA	65
2114	17-Mar	Ireland	Père James O'HEA	92
2115	20-Mar	Italie	Père Dario FALCONE	81
2116	24-Mar	Ireland	Père John Mc CORMACK	75
2117	02-Apr	France	Père Roger LE ROCH	92
2118	05-Apr	Ireland	Père Patrick JENNINGS	95
2119	07-Apr	Ireland	Père Daniel J O'BRIEN	74
2120	13-Apr	Ireland	Père Brendan DUNNING	76
2121	18-Apr	Ireland	Père John CLANCY	89
2122	23-Apr	Nigeria	Père Robert OBRO	57
2123	26-Apr	Zambia	Père Brian KATUNANSA	43
2124	03-May	Ireland	Père John (Seán) KILBANE	88
2125	06-May	France	Père Jean CHENEVIER	97
2126	21-May	France	Père Jean COMBY	89
2127	28-May	France	Père Gabriel MOUESCA	91
2128	04-Jun	France	Père Louis KUNTZ	89

No	Date	Died in/Mort à	Name/Nom	Age
2129	05-Jun	Togo	Père Bernard BARDOUILLET	83
2130	09-Jul	France	Père Edmond COLSON	93
2131	16-Jul	Ireland	Père John QUINLAN	84
2132	10-Aug	France	Père Roger VÉRICEL	86
2133	18-Aug	France	Père Jean Baptiste FOLMER	100
2134	25-Aug	France	Laïc Jean PICHAT	77
2135	26-Aug	France	Père Claude GAVARD	73
2136	07-Sep	Ireland	Père James HICKEY	96
2137	10-Sep	France	Père Bernard FAVIER	86
2138	17-Oct	France	Père André PERRIN	75
2139	26-Oct	Canada	Père Thomas-Léon BOILY	93
2140	09-Nov	Ireland	Père James C FEGAN	72
2141	20-Dec	France	Père Paul SIMON	88
2142	27-Dec	Netherlands	Père Johan van BRAKEL	90

			2021	
2143	27-Jan	France	Père Athanase LE BERRE	85
2144	17-Feb	Ireland	Père Michael BOYLE	96
2145	31-Mar	Ireland	Père Daniel BURKE	88
2146	15-Apr	Netherlands	Père Herman BOMMER	84
2147	16-Apr	Ireland	Père Leo E SILKE	93
2148	02-May	Italie	Père Gerardo BOTTARLINI	86
2149	20-May	France	Père Pierre BROSSAUD	94
2150	09-Jun	United Kingdom	Père Darryl Peter BURROWS	81
2151	12-Jun	France	Père Alphonse RAPION	85
2152	25-Jun	France	Père Bernard RAYMOND	87
2153	28-Jun	France	Père Bernard GUICHARD	95
2154	12-Jul	France	Père Materne HUSSHERR	88
2155	27-Jul	Netherlands	Père Rinke de VREEZE	98
2156	14-Aug	France	Père Jean DHUMEAU	95
2157	22-Nov	Ireland	Père Thomas KEARNEY	86
2158	03-Dec	France	Père Albert ANDRE	95
2159	03-Dec	Pologne	Père Józef OLCZAK	91
2160	11-Dec	Ireland	Père Thomas J TREACY	76
2161	24-Dec	Égypte	Père Gennaro DI MARTINO	85

			2022	
2162	06-Jan	Netherlands	Père Koos JANSSEN	84
2163	14-Jan	France	Père Jean THÉBAULT	89
2164	10-Apr	France	Père Andre GUERET	90
2165	21-Apr	Great Britain	Père Gerald A J TONER	78
2166	02-May	Ireland	Père Owen MCKENNA	86
2167	15-May	France	Père Marcel SCHNEIDER	79
2168	03-Jun	France	Père Jean PAUGAM	97
2169	05-Jun	Italie	Père Giovanni AIMETTA	84
2170	17-Jun	France	Père Paul CHATAIGNE	81
2171	22-Jun	Ireland	Père John FLYNN	91
2172	04-Jul	France	Père Louis GENEVAUX	77
2173	15-Jul	France	Père Emile POTTIER	93
2174	29-Jul	France	Père Charles CHEVALIER	82

No	Date	Died in/Mort à	Name/Nom	Age
2175	30-Jul	France	Père Michel CARTERON	85
2176	02-Aug	Netherlands	Père Wiel van EIJK	92
2177	10-Aug	Ireland	Père Maurice KELLEHER	84
2178	16-Aug	Netherlands	Père Arjen van BALEN	98
2179	31-Aug	Kenya	Père Lawrence N. ONGOMA	41
2180	26-Sep	France	Père Jacques SICARD	86
2181	27-Sep	Ireland	Père Michael NOHILLY	76
2182	14-Oct	Nigeria	Père Matthew Shinkut BASSAH	42
2183	20-Oct	France	Père Georges SELZER	90
2184	08-Nov	France	Père Pierre LEGENDRE	90
2185	17-Nov	Nigeria	Laïc Mary Candy ONUSI	68
2186	25-Nov	Italie	Père Eugenio BASSO	78
2187	05-Dec	France	Père Jean CHARRIER	88
		2023		
2188	21-Jan	France	Père Michel DUJARIER	91
2189	28-Jan	Netherlands	Père Willy ZIJLSTRA	91
2190	22-Feb	Ireland	Père Fintan D DALY	85
2191	10-Mar	Netherlands	Père Gé BUURMAN	84
2192	28-Mar	France	Père Jean-Pierre MICHAUD	91
2193	14-Apr	Ireland	Père John DUNLEAVY	86
2194	01-May	Pologne	Père Władysław PENKALA	75
2195	05-Jun	Italie	Père Marco PRADA	64
2196	21-Jun	France	Père Georges LABORDE-BARBANEGRE	90
2197	21-Aug	France	Père Jean RASSINOUX	90
2198	03-Oct	France	Père Arthur BECKER	81
2199	06-Oct	France	Père Georges FONTENEAU	84
2200	09-Oct	France	Père Raymond JOLY	87

Alphabetical list

Liste alphabétique

Alphabetical list / Liste alphabétique

Alphabetical list / Liste alphabétique

A

AALBERS Joseph	14-Mar-1978
ABGUILLERM François Marie	17-Mar-2005
ACHARD Maurice	03-Jun-2008
ACKER Antoine	22-Dec-1983
ADRIAN Justin	02-May-1959
AFIABOR O. Pius	12-Oct-2017
AGUILHON Louis	01-Jun-1984
AHERN James	01-Sep-1982
AHERN John	22-Nov-1949
AILLERIE Paul	23-Feb-2007
AIMETTA Giovanni	05-Jun-2022
ALAIN Fernand	01-Mar-2003
ALBENIZ Simeon	07-Jan-1942
ALBERT +Maximilian	15-Dec-1903
ALLAIN Camille	25-Jul-2017
ALLAIN Ferdinand	25-Jul-1930
ALLAINMAT Émile	17-Aug-1983
ALLEZARD Jean	17-Apr-1971
ALLIBE Louis	17-Feb-1997
ALLIRAND Alphonse	12-Dec-2012
ALLOATTI Jean	03-Feb-1976
ALTHUSER Gérard	25-Jan-2002
AMALRIC Casimir	27-Apr-1912
ANDRE Albert	03-Dec-2021
ANDRE Andre	29-Apr-2018
ANDRÉ Sébastien	17-May-1884
ANÉZO Charles	13-Dec-1964
ANGIBAUD Joseph	19-Aug-1972
ANGST Jean	02-Mar-1981
ANTHONY Gilbert	22-Jan-2011
ANTZ Ludan	16-Mar-1944
ARIAL Lucien	05-Apr-1952
ARNAL Etienne	12-Jun-1873
ARNOLFO Francesco	06-Mar-2015
ARRIBAS Eugenio	23-Dec-1894
ARSAC Joseph	05-Feb-2013
ARTERO Giovanni Battista	26-Apr-1872
ASPINALL Mlle Margaret	25-Jan-2001
ASTIER Eugène	18-Aug-1891
AUBRY Paul	06-Sep-2012
AUDOUIN Pierre	09-Oct-2004
AUDRAIN Clément	26-Jan-1966
AUDRAIN Jean-Baptiste	30-Nov-1988
AUFFRAY Michel	20-Nov-1997
AUGIER Charles	14-Feb-1902
AUJOULAT Joseph	19-Nov-1980
AUPIAIS Francis	14-Dec-1945
AYOUL Joseph	04-Jul-1990

B

BAAR Adrie A van	09-Nov-1991
BACH Prosper	09-Oct-1921
BACKER de François	19-May-1952
BACKES Jan	27-Sep-1974
BADER Georges	10-Mar-1954
BADOC Casimir	07-Feb-2004
BAECHTEL Victor	24-Sep-1943
BAGNASCO Philip C	03-Apr-1986
BAKER Henry	05-Mar-1960
BAKKER Jaap	27-Jun-2008
BAKKER Theodorus L (Dick)	05-Sep-2015
BALEN Arjen van	16-Aug-2022
BALLAC Pierre	08-Apr-1893
BALLIGAND Claude	07-Jan-1971
BALTZ Aloïse	09-Apr-1945
BALTZ Charles	10-Sep-1913
BANE Martin	31-Dec-1968
BANNWARTH Auguste	21-Oct-1907
BANNWARTH Clément	17-Nov-1943
BANNWARTH Henri	08-Jan-2002
BARATHIEU Augustin	06-Dec-1966
BARBIER Gérard	10-Mar-2012
BARDELLI Giacomo	15-Oct-2007
BARDOL Joseph	16-Aug-1973
BARDOUILLET Bernard	05-Jun-2020
BARNICLE Valentine	26-Sep-1947
BARON Pierre	13-Aug-1948
BARON Pierre-Marie	07-Aug-1898
BAROTTIN Henri	20-Aug-1977
BARREAU Joseph	07-Sep-1950
BARRETT John Baptist	27-Jun-1910
BARRETT Joseph D	20-Jul-1998
BARRIL Émile	06-Feb-1961
BARRY John	12-Jan-1925
BARRY W Romuald	08-Oct-2018
BARTHÉLEMY Henri	25-Feb-1969
BARTHÉLEMY Roger	29-Dec-1985
BARTHLEN Alphonse	17-May-1976

BARTKOWICZ Adam	20-Mar-2018
BARTLEY Thomas	23-Jan-1956
BASSAH Matthew Shinkut	14-Oct-2022
BASSO Eugenio	25-Nov-2022
BASTIAENS Joseph	14-May-1979
BASTIAN Laurent	28-Oct-1927
BASTIDA Nicolás	09-Nov-1952
BATO Martin	08-Mar-1991
BAUDIN Noël	29-Sep-1887
BAUDU Jean-Marie	26-Jan-1966
BAUDU Paul	18-Jun-1983
BAUDUCEL Jean-Marie	03-Nov-2004
BAUMANN Auguste	07-Jan-1961
BAUMANN Jean-Paul	09-Jul-2016
BAUWENS Jean-Baptiste	28-May-1986
BAUZIN Adrien	04-Mar-1934
BEAUQUIS Aimé	17-Apr-1891
BEAUSANG Richard	02-Oct-1983
BEAUVERT Santiago	07-May-1870
BÉBIN Jean-Baptiste	28-Dec-1864
BECKER Arthur	03-Oct-2023
BECKERS Johannes	07-Dec-1976
BEDAULT Jules	16-Nov-1990
BEDEL Jean-Marie	14-Dec-1943
BEENKER Jan	19-Aug-1957
BEILLEVAIRE Édouard	30-Jan-1981
BEISSON Pierre	30-Nov-1913
BEKEMA Leo	11-May-1987
BEL Camille	16-Feb-1918
BELIN Ernest	13-Aug-1907
BELL Henry J	12-Nov-2002
BELLUT Denys	02-Jan-2012
BENNETT Peter J	01-Dec-1995
BERENGUER Vicente	26-Nov-1885
BERG Bernard van den	26-Apr-1966
BERGERON Yves	23-Apr-2017
BERGERS Antoon	03-Feb-1980
BERGERVOET Jan	10-Jun-1996
BERGOT Pierre	11-Nov-2018
BERLIOUX Alphonse	17-Feb-1928
BERMINGHAM Edward	09-Sep-1953
BERMINGHAM Patrick	18-Jul-1940
BERMINGHAM Terence	09-Mar-1998
BERNARD Pierre	05-Feb-1972
BERNHART Eugène	10-Dec-1999
BERNTS Bertus	08-Feb-1949
BERNUIZET Alphonse	10-May-1959
BERRIÈRE Augustin	28-Dec-1958
BERRIÈRE Matthieu	31-Jul-1927
BERTHELOT Pierre	24-May-1916
BERTHO Jacques	02-Mar-1990
BERTONNEAU Michel	23-Nov-2016
BEUMERS Jo	22-Aug-1963
BEURSKENS Cor	01-May-1999
BIANCO Angelo	13-Jan-1982
BIAOU Chabi Emile	31-Jul-2015
BIAU Jean	02-Mar-2011
BICKERTON Alfred	01-Feb-1999
BIGGANE Edward	06-Oct-2013
BIGORGNE Henri	16-Apr-1950
BILLOTTE Modeste	03-Aug-1999
BINOCHE Raymond	26-Jun-2003
BIORET Fernand	25-Jul-2012
BIOTTEAU Maurice	18-Oct-2016
BISCHOFBERGER Aloyse	30-Jun-1982
BITTMANN Jean-Pierre	28-Jun-1973
BLAIN Aristide	04-Apr-1944
BLAKE Count Llewellyn	08-Sep-1916
BLANC Louis	05-Sep-1885
BLANCHON Pierre	26-Apr-1889
BLANCK Aloïse	03-Aug-1969
BLANDIN Georges	26-Oct-1958
BLARER Edouard	10-Sep-1989
BLEE Thomas	22-Nov-2003
BLIN Théophile	26-Jun-1974
BLINDAUER Ferdinand	25-Oct-2015
BLOM Theo	28-Jun-1988
BLONDÉ Aloyse	24-Nov-1966
BLOT Yves	02-Aug-2016
BLUETT Richard Douglas	27-Mar-2010
BODELIER André	09-Nov-1989
BODEWES Kees	20-Oct-1973
BOFFA Mario	16-Nov-2017
BOGARD Albert	17-Dec-2013
BOHN Joseph	05-May-1997
BOILLON Michel	05-Mar-1942
BOILY Thomas-Léon	26-Oct-2020
BOIRON Louis	17-Apr-2013

BOIVIN +Jean-Baptiste	24-Apr-1970
BOLLEN Frits	07-Feb-2002
BOMMER Herman	15-Apr-2021
BONAPFEL Charles	14-Jun-1912
BOND William	19-Jul-1926
BOND Wim	05-Aug-1975
BONHOMME Émile	28-Aug-1928
BONNANT Joseph	24-Jun-1971
BONNEFOY Gustave	14-Sep-1949
BONNET Auguste	30-Mar-1955
BONNET Pierre	04-Jan-2012
BONY Pierre	08-Apr-1997
BORDES Pierre	03-Oct-1972
BORGHERO Francesco	16-Oct-1892
BORNE Joseph	16-Oct-1940
BOSETTI Ugo	19-May-2008
BOTHUA René	22-Jul-1966
BOTTARLINI Gerardo	02-May-2021
BOUCHARD Benoît	01-Jun-2013
BOUCHE Pierre-Bertrand	10-Sep-1903
BOUCHEIX + Noël	07-May-1985
BOUCHEIX Germain	30-Apr-1981
BOUCHER Charles-Henri	27-Nov-2011
BOUCHIER Antoon	23-Dec-1979
BOUÉ François	25-Dec-1880
BOUHELIER André	29-Jan-2002
BOUHELIER Jean	19-Apr-2016
BOUIX Henri	26-Jan-1986
BOULAIRE Joseph	17-Jan-1975
BOULANGER Théophile	01-Apr-1956
BOULO Ange	24-Jul-1987
BOUMANS Jochem	12-Nov-1967
BOUMANS W. Gauthier	02-Dec-1933
BOURASSEAU Armand	12-Mar-1965
BOURGET Michel	14-Oct-1940
BOURGUET Joseph	15-Oct-1872
BOURSIN Théophile	07-Nov-1974
BOUTRY Louis	05-Jul-1893
BOUVET Gustave	10-Apr-1884
BOUVIER Louis	26-Jul-1976
BOVENMARS Jan	06-Mar-1993
BOYLE Michael	17-Feb-2021
BOYLE Vincent E	29-Jan-1999
BOZON Hippolyte	10-Mar-1886
BRACHET Frédéric	23-Aug-1933

BRADY Michael	17-Feb-2019
BRAKEL Johan van	27-Dec-2020
BRANIFF Patrick	03-Sep-1994
BRANTJES Joannes	28-Mar-1980
BRAUD Léon	21-Aug-1905
BRÉDIGER Georges	20-Feb-1947
BRÉGAINT François	17-Aug-1977
BREHENY John	22-Apr-2006
BRÉHIER Jean-Louis	26-Feb-1991
BREITEL Lucien	28-Aug-1911
BRÉJÉ Auguste	24-Jul-1906
BREM Gilbert	11-Mar-1998
BRENNAN Joseph	01-Mar-2006
BRENNAN Michael	11-Aug-1976
BRESLIN John James	08-Aug-1991
BRESLIN William	03-May-1978
BRESSOL Antonin	28-Mar-1938
BRESSOL Jean	15-Oct-1912
BRESSON Jean-Baptiste	05-Jun-1859
BRÉTÉCHÉ Pierre	08-Feb-1969
BRETILLOT Gérard	16-Aug-2014
BREUKEL Kees	13-Oct-1973
BREY Paul	20-Jan-1892
BRICET Hyacinthe	30-Dec-1926
BRIENS Jean	20-Sep-1995
BRIGNONE Gianfranco	25-Nov-2004
BRION Paul	28-Mar-2018
BROCHARD Jeannine	21-Nov-2003
BROCKHOFF Theodorus	27-Jun-2010
BRODERICK +Thomas	13-Oct-1933
BROEK Jan van den	26-Mar-1973
BRONK +André van de	13-May-1997
BRONK Jacques van den	02-Apr-2007
BROSSAUD Pierre	20-May-2021
BROUWER Leo	21-Nov-1976
BROWN Richard	19-Apr-1991
BROWNE John J	14-Mar-2002
BRUGGEMANS Jean	12-Mar-1978
BRUGGER Louis	08-Feb-1951
BRUHAT Auguste	21-Dec-1953
BRUINSMA Andreas	20-Oct-1993
BRUN Hugues	20-Oct-1982
BRUNET Paul	15-May-1980
BRUNGARD Antoine	13-Jan-1961
BRUNGARD Rémi	12-Mar-1984

BRUNGARD Antoine	13-Apr-2019
BRUNNER Antoine	24-May-2006
BRUYAS Antonin	22-Jul-1996
BRUYAS Jean-Baptiste	02-Jul-1977
BRUYAS Pierre	16-Oct-1963
BUCHERT Paul	15-Dec-1963
BUGNON Marcel	02-May-1915
BUMANN Charles	06-Dec-1900
BURG Antoine	28-May-1926
BURG Léon	15-Apr-1948
BURG Victor	17-Nov-1944
BURGEAT Émile	15-Mar-1893
BURGEL Jean-Baptiste	22-Feb-1947
BURGER Joseph	20-May-1917
BURKE Benedict	12-Nov-1991
BURKE Daniel	31-Mar-2021
BURKE John	19-Nov-2006
BURKE Maurice	15-Apr-1998
BURKE William	29-Oct-2013
BURLATON Justin	15-Feb-1866
BURR Charles	08-Feb-1951
BURROWS Darryl Peter	09-Jun-2021
BUTLER Anthony J	16-Oct-2014
BUTLER Joseph	26-Dec-1930
BUTLER William	30-Sep-1940
BUURMAN Gé	10-Mar-2023
BYRNE James	18-Jul-1989
BYRNE William	06-Dec-1974

C

CABELLA Andrea	15-Dec-2017
CADEL Georges	23-Jan-1997
CADIEU Clément	30-Mar-2013
CADOGAN Jeremiah	23-Nov-1988
CADOGAN Timothy	05-Feb-1984
CADOR Claude	15-Jan-1909
CAËR Jean-Louis	30-Dec-1946
CAHILL Michael	15-Feb-2012
CAHILL Patrick	12-Jul-1945
CAHILL Thomas Sexton	04-Sep-1942
CAILHOUX Antoine	17-Dec-2006
CAILLAUD Louis	03-Feb-1952
CALMET Marcel	16-Aug-1973
CALVEZ Yves	21-Jan-2003
CÁMARA Juan Maria	07-Jul-1986
CAMILLERI François	31-Dec-1942
CANAVAN Charles	02-Mar-1959
CANNON Daniel	24-May-1980

CANTILLON John	01-Jun-1997
CANTINO Secondo	15-Nov-1998
CARAMBAUD Étienne	31-Jul-1887
CARDIFF Francis	02-Dec-1972
CAREW Joseph	25-May-1973
CARMINATI Carmine	25-Apr-2017
CARNEY Luke	05-Jan-1990
CAROLAN Michael	04-Apr-1983
CARR Laurence	12-Sep-1976
CARRÉ André	31-Mar-1957
CARRIGAN Philip	03-Dec-1962
CARROLL +Francis	10-Oct-1980
CARROLL James	02-Sep-1990
CARROLL Kevin	12-Jan-1993
CARROLL Patrick	28-Jan-2009
CARTAL Prosper	19-Apr-1949
CARTERON Michel	30-Jul-2022
CASEY Edward	15-Feb-2017
CASEY Eugene	28-Apr-2004
CASEY Henry	06-Feb-2009
CASEY John	02-Mar-2015
CASSARD André	11-Mar-2001
CASSIDY Philip	28-May-1926
CASTANCHOA Jean-Baptiste	27-May-1970
CAVAGNERA Luigi	03-Dec-1927
CAVALLI Giuseppe, Don	26-Feb-2016
CAVANAGH Michael	01-Jan-1974
CERMENATI Berengario	23-Oct-1942
CESSOU +Jean-Marie	03-Mar-1945
CHABERT Jean-Marie	25-Mar-1933
CHAIZE Albert	14-Mar-1995
CHALOPIN Henri	22-Feb-2012
CHALUS Antoine	11-Nov-1907
CHAPEAU Bernard	30-Mar-1996
CHARRIER Camille	30-Aug-1955
CHARRIER Jean	05-Dec-2022
CHASSAIGNON André	05-Jul-1972
CHATAIGNE Paul	17-Jun-2022
CHATTOT Jean-Dominique	01-Oct-1992
CHAUSSE Jean-Baptiste	17-Jan-1894
CHAUTARD Eugène	19-Apr-1915
CHAUVET Gabriel	25-Dec-1984
CHAUVIN Andre	06-Sep-2017
CHAUVIN Arthur	19-Oct-1980

CHAUVINEAU Gérard	22-Feb-1962	COLLINS Michael	23-Jul-1973
CHAZAL Maxime	08-Feb-1970	COLOMBET Jean-André	17-Feb-1960
CHENEVIER Jean	06-May-2020	COLSON Alexandre	17-Jan-2009
CHENU Eustache	13-Apr-1946	COLSON Edmond	09-Jul-2020
CHEVAL Eugène	08-Oct-1887	COLSON Joseph	18-Feb-2006
CHEVALIER Charles	29-Jul-2022	COMBAT Louis	23-Sep-1950
CHEVALIER Mme Marie-Louise	18-Dec-1999	COMBY Eugene	12-Mar-1888
		COMBY Jean	21-May-2020
CHIFFOLEAU Amédée	13-Oct-1955	COMINO Piet	04-Nov-1955
CHIPOT Pierre	08-Jun-1976	COMMANDEUR Cornelius	26-Mar-1982
CHIROL Camille	12-Mar-1991	COMPAGNON Ernest	08-Apr-1946
CHOIMET Victor	24-Jan-1977	COMTE François	27-Dec-1949
CHOISNET Auguste	05-Mar-1904	CONBOY Joseph G	30-Apr-1990
CHOPARD Joseph	18-Jan-2006	CONBOY Martin	25-Apr-1993
Mgr CHOPARD-LALLIER Robert	21-Jul-1973	CONLAN Fergus	17-Jan-2006
		CONLON Hugh D	20-Oct-1999
CHOTARD Gabriel	11-Jan-2004	CONLON James	03-Apr-2011
CHRIST Eugene	02-Oct-1979	CONNAUGHTON William	13-Apr-1887
CHRIST Isidore	07-Jul-1916		
CHRISTAL Patrick	11-Dec-1967	CONNOLLY Donal	30-May-1989
CLAMENS Gabriel	16-Aug-1964	CONNOLLY Eugene	28-Apr-2011
CLANCY Cornelius	08-Dec-2002	CONNOLLY John	03-Mar-1969
CLANCY John	18-Apr-2020	CONVERS Michel	16-Dec-2000
CLANCY Patrick	20-Oct-1945	CONVEY Francis	02-Jan-1990
CLARISSE Jacques	17-Aug-1991	CONVEY Michael	04-Jul-1969
CLERY Nicholas	24-Sep-1939	CONWAY Michael	23-Feb-1997
CLEYET-MAREL Antoine	20-Feb-1961	COOLEN Jan	06-Aug-2001
		COQUARD Jean-Marie	27-Jun-1933
CLOBUS Robertus	17-Feb-2010	CORBEAU Joseph	07-Nov-1962
CLONAN Thomas	15-Oct-1968	CORBINEAU Jean-Baptiste	01-Jul-2006
CLOUD François	22-Jan-1879		
CLOUET Denis	20-Oct-1967	CORBINEAU Paul	07-Jun-2000
CLOUET Jean	18-Feb-1973	CORCORAN John	24-Jun-1967
COAKLEY Jeremiah	07-Apr-1993	CORISH Philip	11-Mar-1959
COBBEN Joseph	23-Oct-1951	CORVIN Daniel	26-Dec-1977
COCHET Étienne	16-Jul-1889	COSSÉ Simon-Pierre	11-Jul-1977
COCHO Elie	23-Sep-2014	COSSET Jean-Marie	20-Mar-1973
COGARD Théophile	04-Dec-2005	COTTER William	11-Aug-1949
COLEMAN Edward F	24-Sep-1993	COTTEZ Raymond	24-Jun-1983
COLEMAN John	26-Jun-1976	COUÉDEL Constant	28-Dec-1950
COLICHET Pascal	05-Nov-1973	COUENBERG Joseph	07-Jun-1966
COLIN Alfred	04-May-1971	COURDIOUX Philibert	27-Apr-1898
COLINEAUX Firmin	20-Apr-1942		
COLLERAN Michael J	16-Oct-1997	COUSSEAU Élie	27-Jul-1977
COLLIN Roger	05-Jan-1974	COUSTEIX Michel	22-Jun-1964
COLLINS +John M	03-Mar-1961	COUTIN Maurice	22-Apr-1944
COLLINS Gerald	13-Jun-1960	CRAMERS Joseph	31-Dec-2012
COLLINS John J	04-Jun-1979	CRAWFORD Joseph	20-Mar-1936
COLLINS Laurence	18-Dec-1996	CREAVEN John A	02-Dec-2008

CRESPEL Henri	17-Jul-1921
CRÉTAZ Josué	08-Feb-1892
CROHAS Jean-Marie	15-Feb-1896
CROS Mlle Philomène	24-Aug-2013
CROWE Jeremiah	09-Jun-2003
CRUTS Pierre	01-Jan-1996
CUENIN Charles	14-May-2008
CULLEN Daniel	05-Apr-2016
CULLIGAN Patrick	26-May-1971
CUMMINS Michael	08-Apr-1969
CUNNINGHAM Bernard	17-May-1971
CUP Theo	08-Jul-1940
CUQ Désiré	12-Apr-1977
CURUTCHET Bernard	05-Oct-2018
CURUTCHET Jean	16-Oct-1959
CUSACK William	04-May-2019

D

D'ARCY Paul	27-Apr-2010
DAHLENT Joseph	10-May-1920
DAHLENT Michel	22-Jul-1899
DALBIN Jacques	24-Mar-1998
DALY Fintan D	22-Feb-2023
DALY Daniel	12-Jul-2005
DANIEL Joseph	11-Jun-2002
DANIEL Pierre	10-Jun-1893
DANKERS Laurens	18-Sep-1951
DANJOU DE LA GARENNE Alfred-Marie-Alexandre	02-Feb-1929
DARCY Michael	10-May-2013
DARDENNE Arsène	30-Apr-1883
DARTOIS +Louis	03-Apr-1905
DASTILLUNG Joseph	02-Jun-1978
DAUDE Hubert	18-Mar-2017
DAUPHIN Jean	05-Aug-1972
DAUVERGNE Claude	12-May-1980
DE LANGE Sr Mamerta	05-Dec-2018
DEANE John	27-Oct-1954
DEASY Patrick	27-Jan-1952
DEELEY William	02-Jun-1974
DEELEY Thomas	20-Sep-1960
DEFOIN Joseph	20-May-1936
DEKKER Jan	02-Jan-2018
DELANNOY Ignace	02-Oct-1980
DELBAERE Louis	23-Aug-1984
DELFOSSE Victor	10-Aug-1922
DELHOMMEL Joseph	17-Dec-1978
DEMERLÉ Jean	30-Apr-1901

DÉMÉRLÉ Édouard	24-Nov-2011
DEMEYÈRE Joseph	14-Jul-2004
DENIAUD Michel	27-Sep-2008
DENNIEL Jean-Claude	12-Feb-1963
DERICKX Piet	27-Jan-1981
DEROCQ Louis	23-Oct-1969
DERVIN Bernard	15-Jan-1993
DESBOIS Andre	10-Aug-2019
DESBOIS Alexandre	22-Apr-1969
DESFONTAINES Joseph	27-Aug-1914
DESMOND John	08-Mar-1981
DESRIBES Stanislas	04-Jul-1933
DESRIBES Gaston	05-Dec-1929
DESSARCE Benoît	08-Jan-1970
DESSEILLE Ernest	13-Apr-1973
DEUN Jan van	26-Aug-1992
DEUTSCH André	04-Mar-2004
DEVANE Thomas	07-Oct-1992
DEVAUD Louis	23-Jun-1894
DEVIENNE Paul	21-Oct-1984
DEVINE Peter	23-Mar-2007
DEVINE Richard	11-Jun-2005
DEVOUCOUX François	17-Apr-1930
DHUMEAU Jean	14-Aug-2021
DI MARTINO Gennaro	24-Dec-2021
DICKRELL Paul	10-Aug-1999
DIDELOT Pierre	12-Oct-2006
DIEBOLD Albert	13-Feb-1986
DIJK Gerrit van	25-Jul-1969
DIJK Frits van	16-Nov-1965
DISS +Joseph	15-Sep-1963
DJOHOSSOU Donatien	07-Jul-2018
DODENBIER Bernard	04-Sep-2002
DOESWIJK Jan	20-May-1989
DOHERTY Terence	28-Dec-2016
DOLAN Laurence	15-Jun-1997
DOLAN Bernard	06-Aug-1993
DOLLINGER Jérôme	10-Nov-1935
DOMAS Raymond	16-Dec-2007
DOMENSINO Toon	14-Apr-1995
DONAGHY Joseph	23-Apr-1944
DONK Jan van den	25-Aug-1955
DONNELLY Cyril J	08-Jan-1994
DONNELLY Joseph	11-Jun-1992
DONNELLY John B	04-Jun-1997
DONOGHUE Thomas	16-Oct-1980
DONOHUE Dominic	07-Oct-1973

DONOHUE Brendan	12-Nov-1975
DONOVAN Edward J	04-Dec-2002
DORAN Thomas S	09-Sep-2014
DORGÈRE Alexandre	23-Feb-1900
DORNAN Andrew	17-Aug-1886
DORR Patrick	19-Aug-1971
DOUAU Noël	08-Aug-1998
DOUAUD Joseph	14-Sep-1958
DOUILLARD Pierre	09-Jul-1940
DOUMA Chris	08-Mar-2008
DOURIS Jean-Baptiste	14-Jun-1934
DOWNEY Patrick	24-Sep-1892
DOYLE Francis	11-Aug-1981
DRÉAN Alphonse	03-Aug-1940
DREW Michael	15-Jun-1973
DRIOT Jean	17-Apr-1989
DRISCOLL Charles	26-May-1895
DROUAULT Victor	15-Jul-1903
DRUMMOND Michael	26-Apr-1975
DRUMMOND Thomas	16-Sep-1997
DUBOIS Joseph	16-May-1979
DUBOSQ Edouard	29-Nov-1874
DUCASTAING Eugène	30-Nov-2009
DUFFÈS Jean-Baptiste	02-Sep-2012
DUFFY Patrick Joseph	24-Jun-1963
DUFFY John	02-Jun-1973
DUFFY Thomas	24-Feb-1979
DUFOUR Alfred	20-Jul-1985
DUHAMEL Jean	16-Sep-1943
DUHILL Darius	16-Sep-1963
DUIRAT +André	29-Dec-1998
DUJARDIN Jacques	18-Aug-1994
DUJARIER Michel	21-Jan-2023
DUKE Thomas Anthony	17-May-1997
DUMOULIN Arthur	31-Oct-1908
DUNGEN Antoon van den	12-Dec-1997
DUNLEAVY John	14-Apr-2023
DUNNE William	26-Jul-1959
DUNNE John J	21-Aug-1998
DUNNING Brendan	13-Apr-2020
DUPUIS Paul-Henri	20-Aug-2009
DUQUESNE Maurice	19-Feb-2004
DUQUESNE Roger	30-Nov-1977
DURAFOUR Alexandre	15-Jun-1928
DURAND Mgr Moïse	23-Jan-1982
DURAND Michel	20-Jan-2005
DURET +Auguste	29-Aug-1920

DURIEUX Antoine	12-Aug-1884
DURIF Michel	01-Feb-2013
DURIF Jean	12-Sep-2000
DURRHEIMER +Émile	12-Mar-1994
DUSSUD Marcel	11-Jan-2018
DUVAL Yves	17-Aug-1985
DWYER Jeremiah	05-Aug-2008

E

EDDE Louis	09-Apr-1861
EERD Louis van	05-Nov-1960
EERDEN Bernard	10-Dec-1986
EGAN Thomas	03-May-2006
EHRET Jean-Louis	12-Aug-1917
EIJK Wiel van	02-Aug-2022
ELBERS Gerard	13-Jan-1959
ELLIOTT William J	28-May-1994
ENGBERINK Herman	03-Oct-2010
ENGELEN Jan	27-Jun-1981
ERHARD Georges	06-Jan-2007
ERHART Ernest	19-Feb-1941
ERHEL Roger	11-Jan-2008
ERKENS Lambert	29-Dec-1972
ESCHENBRENNER Raymond	14-Apr-1967
ESCHLIMANN Joseph-Arthur	23-Jul-1983
ÉTRILLARD +Jean-Marie	16-May-1976
EUVRARD Gabriel	22-Apr-1998
ÉVAIN Jean	18-Dec-1986
ÉVAIN Joseph	22-Aug-1974
ÉVAIN Raymond	16-Sep-1968
EVANS Michael M	22-Feb-2020
EVERS Coen	22-Oct-1994
EVERS Joseph-Benoît	05-Aug-1957
EVRARD Jean	12-Dec-2009
EZANNO Paul	13-Sep-1971

F

FABLET Maurice	06-Apr-1943
FABRIE Kees	07-Jul-1936
FAESSLER David	10-Jun-1909
FAGA Alexis	07-Apr-1888
FAHRNER Joseph	06-Oct-1945
FAILLANT Claude	18-Mar-1958
FALCON Paul	07-Aug-1980
FALCONE Dario	20-Mar-2020
FALLON Francis	28-Oct-1976
FAROUD +François	05-Sep-1963

FARRINGTON Martin	05-Dec-1962
FAURITE René	02-Mar-2002
FAUVEL Louis	01-Dec-1907
FAVIER Bernard	10-Sep-2020
FAVIER Jean-Marie	20-Jun-1981
FAVIER Jean-Marie	18-Jul-1963
FAVREAU Joachim	31-Dec-1916
FECHTER Albert	02-Aug-1942
FEDERSPIEL Joseph	03-May-1986
FEELEY Bridget Agatha	10-Oct-2014
FEELEY John A	27-Feb-2002
FEELEY Michael J	11-Jul-2001
FEENEY John	02-Nov-2010
FEGAN James C	09-Nov-2020
FEGAN William	27-Mar-1972
FEIJEN Piet	23-Mar-1992
FELDER Jean-Paul	01-Jul-2013
FELLMANN Théodore	08-Oct-1974
FER Ferdinand	09-Jun-1946
FÉRA Jean-Marie	04-Mar-1991
FERGUS Gerard	14-Mar-1994
FERLANDIN Paul	23-Mar-1952
FERNANDEZ Francisco	30-Nov-1863
FERNANDEZ DE TROCONIZ Jesús	08-Feb-2020
FERNÁNDEZ GARCÍA María Auxiliadora	11-Mar-2020
FERRERIO Giuseppe	13-Nov-1911
FERRERO Paolo	16-Jun-1907
FERRIEUX Joseph	27-Apr-1911
FÈVRE Martin	01-Oct-1957
FIELD +William R	03-Feb-1988
FILIPPINI Chris	14-Feb-1987
FINN Richard	04-Jan-1989
FINNEGAN Vincent	22-Aug-1962
FINOTTI Luigi	08-Aug-2006
FIORENTINI Filippo	25-Oct-1885
FISCHER Georges	17-May-1955
FISCHER Jacques	12-Feb-1987
FISCHER Joseph	24-Jun-1965
FISCHER Piet	07-Aug-1975
FITZGERALD Richard	15-Apr-1976
FITZGERALD Thomas (Bro)	01-Feb-2018
FITZSIMONS Patrick	02-Mar-1966
FIX Georges	19-Dec-1982
FLAGEUL Paul	07-Aug-2007
FLANAGAN James	04-Feb-2004
FLEITH Paul	08-Sep-1944
FLEMING Patrick	31-May-1984
FLESCH Robert	03-May-1941
FLOCH François-Marie	16-Feb-2006
FLORACK Denis	07-Aug-1963
FLORACK Jeu	29-Aug-1997
FLOURET Germain	18-May-1995
FLYNN John	22-Jun-2022
FLYNN John F	19-Oct-1999
FOLEY Anthony J	07-Apr-1997
FOLEY Michael	31-May-1967
FOLEY William	30-Jul-2014
FOLMER Jean Baptiste	18-Aug-2020
FOLMER Joseph	05-Apr-2016
FONTENEAU Georges	06-Oct-2023
FONTVIEILLE Simon	18-Sep-1953
FORTIN Bernard	23-Jun-1992
FOUQUET Henri	31-Dec-1909
FOURAGE Pierre	13-Mar-1909
FRANCIS Jean	15-Jul-1939
FRANCK Joseph	24-May-1971
FRANÇOIS Albert	19-Apr-1971
FRANÇOIS Justin	28-May-1895
FRANKENHUIJSEN Johannes	22-Dec-2012
FRANKENHUIJSEN Wilhelmus van	02-Jan-2014
FRÉNEAU Henri	27-Oct-2004
FRÉRING Aloyse	11-Dec-1969
FRÉRING Paul	14-Jun-1984
FRÉRY Paul	23-Aug-1912
FREYBURGER Joseph	25-Apr-1954
FREYBURGER Louis	19-Apr-1949
FRIEDRICH Martin	21-Oct-1916
FRIESS Louis	22-Apr-1927
FRIGERIO Giovanni Battista	07-Apr-1928
FRITSCH Pierre	04-Jan-2006
FRITSCH Théodore	29-Dec-1997
FUCHS André	09-Oct-2017
FUCHS Jean	06-Mar-1940
FUCHS Joseph	03-May-1992
FUCHS Louis	19-Apr-1955
FUGIER Joseph	27-Jul-1942
FUREY Francis E	30-Jan-2020
FURLONG Thomas	06-Oct-2014
FURODET Alphonse	10-Jan-1934
FURST Joseph	27-Apr-1965
FUST Peter	15-Jan-1950

G

GACHET Paul	11-Mar-1998
GAGNAIRE Joseph	03-May-1947
GAIGNOUX Alexandre	30-Mar-1972
GAILLARD Julien	08-Apr-2005
GALL Adolph	24-Jan-1991
GALLAGHER Michael N	27-Dec-1991
GALLAUD Victorin	23-Sep-1903
GALLIOU François	07-Jul-1982
GALVIN John	04-Jul-1980
GALVIN Mrs Ellen	26-Jul-2012
GALVIN Thomas J	07-Aug-1985
GANDON Arsène	09-Dec-1985
GANDT de Germain	30-Nov-1940
GANTIN +Bernardin	13-May-2008
GANTLY Patrick	06-Jan-2002
GARCIA Masimino	20-Jul-1923
GARCIA Pierre	18-Oct-1921
GARNIER Joseph	22-Nov-1995
GARRETT James	13-Feb-1984
GARVEY John	18-Apr-1896
GASS Joseph	19-Apr-2003
GASSER Auguste	09-Aug-1963
GASSER Edmond	25-Jun-1968
GASSER Eugène	06-Dec-1976
GASTEL Hubert van	30-Nov-1983
GASTEL Leonardus van	22-Oct-2004
GATELY Malachy	08-Sep-1979
GAUDEUL Ange	23-May-1887
GAUDEUL Émile	10-Jun-1918
GAUDIN Emile	29-Aug-1938
GAULÉ Auguste	27-Feb-1924
GAUME Maxime	28-Sep-1995
GAUTHIER René	08-Jul-2003
GAUTIER Antonin	25-Aug-1966
GAUTIER Jean-Marie	04-Nov-1998
GAUTRAIS Pierre	01-Jul-1970
GAUTRET Paul	29-May-2012
GAUZIC Alexandre	31-Jan-1902
GAVARD Claude	26-Aug-2020
GAVILLET Raymond	16-Mar-1979
GAYMARD Albert	19-Aug-1962
GEELEN Martin	11-Jul-1999
GEELS Joseph	04-Apr-1925
GEIER Franz	25-Jan-1979
GEISSER Eugène	28-Apr-1989
GENEVAUX Louis	04-Jul-2022

GENNIP Kees van	26-Apr-1982
GERAGHTY Andrew	16-Apr-1940
GESLINIER Jules	15-Jul-1912
GESTER Eugène	18-May-1983
GESTER Louis	15-Jun-1987
GEURTS Jacques	30-May-1987
GEUSKENS Johannes Mattheus	31-Jul-1991
GEX André	15-Apr-1923
GHALI Michel	08-Nov-1954
GIEBELS Piet	27-Jan-1996
GIESEN Sjef	23-Aug-1988
GIJSELAERS Hubert	10-Oct-1996
GILFETHER Francis Thomas	05-Jun-2006
GILLIS Francis	30-Dec-2003
GILMORE Matthew	10-Jan-2004
GILORY Jean	13-Sep-1939
GILOTEAU Henri	20-Jul-1918
GILROY Mlle Elise	03-Jul-2015
GILROY Peter	18-Mar-1972
GIRARD +Jules	23-Mar-1950
GIRARD Henri	13-Mar-1969
GIRARD Michel	19-Oct-2015
GIRE Louis	29-Jan-1955
GIRERD Joseph	07-Dec-1924
GLENNON Vincent	25-Jun-2017
GLYNN Alfred	07-Jul-1961
GLYNN Michael Anthony	24-Jun-1981
GLYNN Patrick J	29-Jul-2002
GNANAPRAGASAM Aarokiasamy	20-Sep-2012
GOASDUFF Jean	27-Mar-1946
GOELLER Pierre	26-May-1953
GOETHEM René van	04-Sep-1939
GOETZ Antoine	30-Aug-2009
GOFFINET Charles	10-Jan-1931
GOMMEAUX Louis	12-Aug-1983
GONON Louis	22-Mar-2009
GOOREN Jan	20-Sep-1992
GOOTZEN Bernard	02-Aug-1981
GORJU Joseph	19-May-1924
GORMAN Thomas	04-Feb-2016
GÖRTZ Theo	02-Feb-2003
GOTTE Paul	24-Jan-2014
GOUGEON Jean	17-Jul-1953
GOURNAY Jean-Paul	08-Jan-2017
GOYHENETCHE Félix	22-Oct-1983

GOYHENETCHE Ignace	21-Jul-1970
GRAAS Edouard	19-Jan-1995
GRACE Michael	07-Jan-1989
GRANDO Jean	28-Jan-1944
GRANGEON André	21-Jul-1937
GRANIER Ernest	26-Jun-1891
GRANT John Patrick	24-Aug-1963
GRASS Alphonse	15-Mar-1915
GRASSER Jean-Paul	11-Nov-2014
GREENE Thomas M	28-Feb-1986
GRENOT Maurice	01-Jul-1994
GRETER Jean	16-Mar-1985
GRIENEISEN Hubert	10-Jun-2002
GRIFFIN Cornelius	19-Nov-2007
GRIFFIN James	25-Dec-1992
GRIFFIOEN Wim	02-Dec-1996
GRIMLEY +Nicholas	09-Jun-1995
GRIVEL Mme Colette	02-Aug-2014
GROEBLI Josef	15-Jan-1891
GROS Georges	20-Mar-2000
GROSJACQUES Maurizio	12-Aug-1902
GROSSEAU René	15-Sep-1931
GROSSEAU Rene	22-Jan-2017
GRUNDLER Léon	28-Dec-1958
GRUNENWALD Henri	28-Apr-1993
GUBBINS John	12-May-1995
GUCWA Robert	15-Nov-1994
GUÉGADEN Pierre	15-Aug-1987
GUÉGUEN Jean-Marie	24-May-1913
GUÉNO Joseph	15-Mar-1943
GUÉNOLÉ Jean-Louis	18-Sep-2004
GUERET Andre	10-Apr-2022
GUÉRIN Alphonse	11-Jul-1983
GUÉRIN Joseph	29-Jul-1981
GUICHARD Bernard	28-Jun-2021
GUILBAUD Jean-Luc	29-Jun-2001
GUILCHER René-François	14-Nov-1948
GUILFOYLE John	09-Dec-1976
GUILLARD André	04-Apr-2012
GUILLARD Bernard	01-Jan-2020
GUILLARD Jean-Paul	10-Mar-2004
GUILLEMIN Ernest	05-May-1916
GUILLET Pierre	03-Oct-1858
GUILLIEN Bernard	20-Jun-1963
GUILLO André	27-Apr-1971
GUILLON Clément	29-Sep-1886
GUILLOU Yves	04-May-2006

GUINAN Patrick	21-Apr-1979
GUINARD Paul	16-Jul-1905
GUINEY John	09-May-2014
GUINOISEAU René	15-Nov-1987
GUITTENY Jean	18-Dec-2007
GUMY Joseph	05-May-1898
GUNN Terence	10-Feb-2020
GUTHMANN Mlle Germaine	15-May-1950
GUTKNECHT Armand	14-Apr-1958
GUYOMAR Jean-Louis	09-Sep-1881
GUYOT François	26-Dec-1916
GUYOT Julien	08-Jul-1938

H

HAAS Albert	21-Dec-1969
HAAS Albert	02-May-2005
HAAS Benjamin	01-Mar-1899
HABITS Wilhelmus	19-Oct-2003
HACKETT Gerard	31-Mar-2011
HACKETT John	26-Dec-1993
HADDAD Gabriel	19-Jun-1982
HAEFFNER Charles	15-Mar-1984
HAENGGI Jules	20-Dec-1965
HAEUSSLER Alphonse	28-May-1996
HAGENBACH Joseph	23-Feb-1950
HAINES Laurier W	05-Sep-1991
HAKENS Alfons	24-Jan-1940
HALES Robert	31-Oct-2004
HALGAN Joachim	04-Mar-1867
HAMARD +Alexandre	30-Nov-1909
HAMERS Joseph	24-Dec-1902
HANNIFFY Brendan	06-Nov-1994
HANNON John F	25-Nov-2004
HARING Antoon	29-Dec-1956
HARMON Patrick	20-Aug-1973
HARRINGTON Edward	17-Feb-2001
HARRINGTON John	13-Jul-1983
HARRINGTON Peter	02-Dec-1956
HARRINGTON Stephen	29-Jan-1970
HARRISON Michael	28-Jun-1974
HARROLD James	30-Aug-2009
HARTMANN Georges	21-Apr-1939
HARTZ Joseph	21-Feb-1948
HASSETT Thomas	04-Feb-1972
HASSING Jan	04-Oct-1990
HATTEMER Eugène	28-Aug-1910
HAUGER +Ernest	12-Oct-1948

HAUSHERR Bruno	01-Aug-1974
HAUTBOIS Joseph	04-Jun-1928
HAVE Jacques ten	21-Jun-1973
HAVERTY Johnie	08-Jul-2019
HAY Michel	31-Jan-1945
HAYDEN Thomas E	31-Aug-2014
HAYES James	28-Jul-1999
HAYES John	31-Dec-1945
HAYES Sean	15-Jul-2014
HEALY Dermot	30-Mar-2012
HEALY James	19-Mar-1997
HEALY John	03-Jan-1949
HEANEY John	31-Jan-1977
HEBBEN Frits	15-Mar-2002
HEBTING Émile	13-Sep-1966
HECK Arthur	21-Jul-1967
HEEMSKERK Johan	19-Feb-1942
HEESEWIJK John van	21-Aug-1982
HEFFERNAN Nicholas	21-Mar-1955
HEGGER Jacques	06-Feb-1953
HÉGUY Joseph	06-Jan-1953
HEIJMANS Evert	14-Oct-1990
HEILIGENSTEIN Philippe	28-Mar-1893
HEINRICH Wendelin	01-Feb-1986
HÉLIAS Jean-Marie	05-Jul-1945
HELLEUX Bertrand	12-Sep-1996
HELWEGEN Louis	31-Oct-1941
HÉNAFF Pierre	11-Aug-1975
HENDRIX Willem	08-Jun-1945
HENEBERRY John	16-Jul-1885
HER Jean	29-Feb-1996
HERAGHTY Martin	25-Oct-2002
HÉRITEAU Léon	12-Jan-1948
HERMAN +Auguste	08-Apr-1945
HÉROLD Victor	07-Aug-1944
HERSEY Peter B	21-Apr-2019
HERTSIG Frans	28-Aug-1980
HERVOUET Charles	03-Jun-1924
HERVOUET Joseph	26-Jun-1965
HÉRY Francis	05-Jan-2012
HÉRY Joseph	08-Nov-2010
HESS Pierre	01-Apr-1967
HESSION James	11-Nov-1975
HICKENBICK Antoine	11-Apr-1989
HICKEY James	26-Nov-2000
HICKEY James	07-Sep-2020
HIGGINS James J	03-Apr-2016
HIGGINS Jeremiah	26-May-1978
HIGGINS Michael A	02-Jan-2003
HIGGINS Thomas	01-Feb-2005
HILBERER Othon	24-Jul-1898
HILL James B	07-Jul-2003
HILLIARD Joseph	24-Jun-1971
HIRSCH François-Xavier	03-Oct-1951
HOC René	19-Mar-2007
HOEBEN Enricus (Harrie)	26-Oct-2015
HOEGGER Jakob	21-Oct-1900
HOEPPNER Rudolf	26-Mar-1944
HOLLAND +Joseph Gerald	14-Apr-1972
HOLLAND James	16-Jan-1964
HOLLAND William	26-Apr-1952
HOLLANDER Theo	27-Jun-1975
HOLLENDER Victor	17-Feb-1986
HOLLEY Théodore	14-Apr-1885
HOLTON Michael	19-Sep-1973
HOMBERGEN Gerard	13-Feb-1976
HOMMA André	02-Nov-1962
HOOF Harrie van	14-Dec-2016
HORAN Bernard	12-Apr-2007
HORAN John	13-Jan-1989
HORGAN Denis	18-Mar-1979
HORN Henri	02-Mar-1943
HOUÉZÉ Gabriel	16-Apr-1998
HOULIHAN Peter	04-Jun-2001
HOUSMANS Harrie	07-Apr-1951
HOUT Antoon van	21-Jun-1995
HOUT Gerard van	14-Feb-1999
HOUT Jan van den	08-Jul-1980
HOUT Wim van	19-Feb-1963
HOUTMAN Jan	14-Sep-1946
HOUTMANN Octave	10-Jul-1988
HUBERT +Amand	21-Jul-1980
HUBERT Eduard	17-Oct-2016
HUBSTER Joseph	23-Nov-1926
HUCHET André	07-Jan-1970
HUCHET Joseph	05-Mar-1981
HUET Jean Marie	15-Feb-1998
HUGHES +Thomas P	17-Apr-1957
HUGHES David	13-Jan-2007
HUGHES Francis	01-Jun-1996
HUGHES Patrick	03-Oct-1964
HUGHES Thomas F	18-Oct-1960
HUGHES Thomas J	24-Mar-1966
HUGHES Thomas W	02-Jul-1964
HUGOT Étienne	27-Oct-1995

HUISMAN Willebrordus	24-Sep-2013
HULSEN Cornelius G	16-Dec-1991
HULSHOF Antonius J	20-Feb-2013
HUMBERT François	05-Apr-1999
HUMMEL +Ignace	13-Mar-1924
HUNTZINGER Marcel	18-May-2011
HURST Patrick	12-Aug-1981
HURST Paul	08-Sep-1969
HURST Thomas	09-Jan-1964
HUSSHERR Materne	12-Jul-2021
HYNES Francis	10-Mar-2000

I

IBARRETA Benito	14-Nov-1985
IMBACH Louis	11-Mar-1977
IMHOLZ Jakob	04-Dec-1957
IMOBERDORF Adolphe	25-Sep-1942
IRIGOIN Jacques	09-Dec-1949
IRIQUIN Michel	05-Apr-2016
ISOLÉRI Jaël Joseph	31-Mar-2013

J

JACOBI Hubert	24-Nov-1996
JACOBS Sjeng	29-Jun-1995
JACOBY Jean	23-Jan-1983
JACQUET Jean-Marie	06-Apr-1888
JACQUOT Louis	23-Jan-2018
JACQUOT Pierre	17-Oct-2015
JADÉ Laurent	28-Dec-1943
JAMES Albert	11-Dec-2003
JAMET Louis	30-Jan-1904
JANSMAN Wim	28-Jan-2007
JANSSEN Hubert	15-Feb-1968
JANSSEN Koos	06-Jan-2022
JAUFFRIT Edmond	30-Nov-1970
JAY Julien	06-Nov-1889
JEANNE Adrien	15-Mar-1993
JENNINGS Anthony	02-May-1998
JENNINGS Patrick	05-Apr-2020
JESTIN Jean	03-Nov-1978
JOLANS Alphée	28-Feb-1867
JOLIF Louis	20-Apr-1968
JOLIF Toussaint	20-Mar-1937
JOLY Raymond	09-Oct-2023
JONES John Henry	10-Jun-1984
JONG Henry de	14-Jun-1925
JOOSTEN Gerard	17-Oct-1992
JORET Ernest	31-Dec-1875
JOUANNE Gabriel	03-Dec-1973

JOULORD Joseph	10-Aug-1951
JOYEAU Roger	25-Feb-1987
JUNG Antoine	17-Mar-1993
JUNG Gilbert	13-Feb-2009
JUNGMANN René	17-Jul-1980
JUYN Adriaan	05-Jan-1987

K

KALBERMATTEN Théodore	24-Feb-1976
KAPFER Joseph	09-Apr-1895
KAPFER Léon	14-Oct-1947
KAPPS Lucien	07-Nov-1977
KAPUŚCIK François	04-Aug-1990
KATUNANSA Brian	26-Apr-2020
KEARNEY Thomas	22-Nov-2021
KEARNS Dominic	07-Apr-2008
KEARY Walter	28-Aug-1930
KEAVENEY John J	06-Jun-1986
KEENAN William	16-Jul-1959
KEIJSERS Adriaan	10-Feb-1980
KEIMER Hermann	11-Aug-1942
KEINHORST Martin	16-Dec-1997
KELLEHER Maurice	10-Aug-2022
KELLEHER Richard O	17-Jun-1992
KELLER Eugène	18-Apr-1936
KELLER Xavier	04-Aug-1927
KELLY A Edward (Eamonn)	29-Nov-2018
KELLY John J (Sean)	24-Apr-2005
KELLY Maurice B	19-Mar-1975
KELLY Patrick Francis	28-Oct-1962
KELLY +Patrick J	18-Aug-1991
KELLY Patrick J. M.	14-Jan-2020
KELLY Patrick Joseph	04-Aug-1938
KELLY Patrick M	10-Feb-1988
KELLY Thomas	09-Aug-1932
KENNEDY John	20-Dec-1950
KENNEDY Michael	26-Mar-2007
KENNEDY Thomas	10-Apr-1993
KENNEDY William	18-May-2015
KENNIS Emmanuel	01-Feb-1982
KENNY Henry	21-Oct-1972
KENNY Martin	09-Feb-1979
KEOHANE Bartholomew	05-Dec-1989
KERDERRIEN Michel	09-Jan-1999
KERKHOFFS Servaas	20-May-1946
KERLÉVÉO Georges	05-Feb-1999
KERN Victor	13-Dec-1958
KERNIVINEN +Pierre	22-Feb-1929

KÉROUANTON Gervais	05-Aug-1979
KERR Patrick	06-Apr-1977
KERSTEN Stef	24-Feb-2003
KESSELS Petrus G	17-Sep-2015
KETT Patrick Joseph	05-Apr-1987
KIEFFER Charles	02-Aug-1898
KIEFFER Michel	27-Sep-1895
KILBANE John (Seán)	03-May-2020
KILBEY John	22-Sep-1977
KILLEEN Patrick	06-Feb-1969
KILLEN Jerome	05-Dec-1880
KINNANE Louis	06-Nov-1985
KIRMANN +Alphonse	25-Mar-1955
KIRSTEIN James F	23-Jan-2017
KLAM Pierre	25-Sep-1893
KLAMBER Bernard	01-May-2003
KLAUSS + Isidore	20-Nov-1905
KLAVER Kees	16-Feb-1971
KLEIN Jean	11-Dec-2017
KLERLEIN Gustave	24-Jan-1994
KNAEBEL Georges	15-Aug-1966
KNAEBEL Jacques	14-Aug-1986
KNOPS Pierre	02-Nov-1986
KOCH Alphonse	01-Oct-1954
KOCH Georges	18-May-1911
KOEK Johannes Maria	19-Sep-2012
KOELTZ Aloyse	31-Jan-1977
KOENDERS Jan	12-Aug-2009
KOK Leendert de	19-Aug-1939
KOK DE Arie de	21-Jan-1978
KONIJN Kees	30-Jun-2001
KONING Henricus	22-Jul-2011
KONINGS +Antoon	11-May-1991
KOOLEN Frits	23-Apr-1981
KOOLEN Kees	21-Nov-1968
KOOY Jan van der	23-Apr-1980
KRAEMER Guy	12-Mar-1992
KRAUSS Jules	15-Feb-1993
KRAUTH Ernest	25-Jun-1984
KRAUTH Georges	29-Aug-1938
KREMSER Robert	13-Jan-1982
KRUTT Marius	16-Jul-2010
KUENEMANN Henri	22-Mar-1999
KUHN Xavier	27-May-1925
KUIJPERS Martin	11-Oct-1954
KUNTZ Francis	30-Sep-2017
KUNTZ Louis	04-Jun-2020
KURACZ Aloyse	03-Jul-1937
KURZ Frédéric	18-Feb-1966
KYNE Stephen	30-Jan-1947

L

L'ANTHOËN Yves	20-Jun-1931
LAAK Dionysius van de	22-Mar-2009
LAAR Herman van de	03-Apr-2007
LAAR Wim van de	16-Sep-1990
LABORDE Édouard	24-Oct-1900
LABORDE-BARBANEGRE Georges	21-Jun-2023
LABROSSE Joseph	07-Apr-1992
LACEY Martin	01-Dec-1944
LACEY George	28-Dec-1921
LACROIX Léopold	12-Apr-1999
LACROIX Henri	07-May-1940
LAFITTE Irénée	09-Apr-1901
LAGOUTTE Yves	23-Dec-2010
LAHARGOU Jules	14-Dec-2016
LALANDE Jacques	06-Sep-2015
LAMANDÉ Pierre	11-May-2003
LAMOTTE Jean-Marie	02-Oct-2010
LANDAIS Louis	28-Dec-1920
LANDARRETCHE Jean	14-Dec-2006
LANDOLT Johann	27-Oct-1918
LANDRY George	13-Oct-2004
LANG Joseph	02-Jan-1912
LANG Georges	17-Sep-1938
LANG Jean	29-Apr-1899
LANOË Robert	19-May-2005
LAQUEYRIE Édouard	23-Jul-1950
LARKIN Thomas	21-Apr-1974
LAROCHE Charles	24-Jan-1941
LARVOR Paul	16-Mar-1965
LASKA Joseph	18-Jan-2010
LATARD Joseph	29-Mar-1900
LATENDRESSE Léo	10-Jun-2018
LATZ Heinrich	02-Nov-1999
LAUBÉ Alfred	27-Sep-1949
LAUBIAC Clément	07-Mar-1906
LAUGEL Georges	12-Aug-1970
LAURENS Mme Françoise Marguerite	20-Jan-1945
LAURENT Alfred	09-Jan-1949
LAURENT Bernard	24-Oct-2008
LAVAN Patrick	01-Dec-1962
LAVELLE Martin	01-Apr-1945
LAVELLE John	03-Dec-1935
LAWLESS T Vincent	05-Sep-2016
LAZINIER Claude	17-Oct-1973

LE BERRE Athanase	27-Jan-2021
LE CORRE Ambroise	26-Jan-1943
Le GALLEN Léandre	04-Aug-1913
LE GLOAHEC Julien	14-Feb-1962
LE GOFF Paul	30-Jun-2017
LE GOFF Jean	13-May-1976
LE GUEN Pierre	29-Mar-1990
LE MIGNON Yves	20-Feb-2009
LE PORT François	02-Jan-1970
LE ROCH Roger	02-Apr-2020
Le ROCH Joseph	01-May-1983
LEAUTÉ Eugène	12-Dec-1984
LEBERT François	04-Mar-1956
LEBOUVIER Auguste	07-Mar-1922
LEBRUN Léon	07-Sep-1874
LEBRUN Jean-Baptiste	19-Jun-2013
LEBUS Alphonse	24-Sep-1931
LECAER François	06-Sep-1870
LECOMTE Alexandre	13-Sep-1923
LECORNO Jean	10-Mar-1963
LECRON +Joseph	22-Jun-1895
LEDIS Alphonse	20-Jun-1922
LEE John G	12-Jan-1992
LEE Patrick	23-Jun-1944
LEE James G	20-Feb-2006
LEEUW Gerrit van der	14-May-1965
LEEUWEN Wim van	25-Jun-1998
LEEUWEN Bernard van	05-Nov-1934
LEEUWEN Ferdinand van	20-Nov-1997
LEFERINK Jo	10-Aug-1990
LEFEUVRE Mme Georgette	08-May-1990
LEFORT Marcel	25-Dec-1991
LEGAL Henri	15-Oct-1915
LEGEARD Albert	10-Sep-1914
LEGEAY Pierre	07-Nov-1883
LEGENDRE Pierre	08-Nov-2022
LEGGE Edward	17-Sep-1938
LEGRAND Alfred	13-May-1968
LEGRAND Georges	02-Aug-2009
LEGRAND Joseph	23-Sep-1968
LEHAEN Hubert	22-Sep-1990
LEIBENGUTH Joseph	16-Jun-1969
LEICHTNAM Alfred	28-Mar-1964
LEJEUNE Jean	20-Jul-1985
LEJEUNE Adolphe	09-Dec-1986
LEJEUNE Willy	08-Oct-2003
LEJEUNE Georges	20-Jan-2010
LELIÈVRE Gabriel	26-Sep-1968
LEMAIRE Émile	17-Aug-1923
LEMARIÉ Joseph	02-Mar-1994
LEMASSON René	25-Jul-2007
LEMMENS Sjeng	27-Jul-1958
LEMMERLING Huub	19-Jan-1999
LENNERTZ Sjef	23-Sep-2001
LENNON Thomas	18-Jun-2000
LEPOULTEL Alphonse	04-Jul-1879
LERDOU Victor	26-Apr-1999
LEROUX Louis	24-Oct-1916
LEROY Albert Georges	24-Jul-2001
LEUVEN Jacques van	06-Jan-1958
LEVEQUE Jean	09-Nov-2018
LÉVÊQUE Pierre	02-Jun-1997
LEVINS John	02-Feb-1969
LIBS Jean-Baptiste	29-Jul-1914
LICHTENAUER Jean	24-Jul-1906
LICKEL Marcel	23-Jan-1995
LIEB Jules	11-Aug-1954
LIENHARDT Désiré	01-Jul-1968
LIESHOUT Wim van	01-Jul-1972
LIESHOUT Mattheus van	07-Oct-1967
LIEUTAUD Eugène	12-Nov-1949
LIGTVOET Kees	05-Aug-1982
LINDEN Jan ter	28-Oct-1976
LINDON Thomas	25-Dec-2004
LINGENHEIM +Jérôme	03-May-1985
LIROT Albert	23-Feb-2017
LISSNER Charles	31-May-1934
LISSNER Ignace	07-Aug-1948
LITTLE Mgr William	20-Oct-1964
LOCHTMAN Joseph	22-Jul-1997
LOHIER Isidore-Marie	19-Nov-1911
LOIRET Michel	26-Sep-2014
LOISEAU Firmin	21-Jan-1947
LOMBARDET André	04-Jan-1973
LOMELET Paul	11-Aug-1982
LOONEY Daniel	06-Apr-1989
LOOZEN Pierre	05-Nov-1963
LORTIE Raymond	19-May-2014
LOTZ Charles	11-Jun-2003
LOUBIER Mme Anne-Marie	09-Jan-2009
LOUXEN Charles	09-Nov-1945
LOVE Alfred	24-Feb-1975
LUBBERS Herman	13-Oct-1995
LUKASSEN Gerard	07-Oct-2017
LUMLEY +William	22-Sep-1962

LUPTON John	23-Apr-1969
LUSSON Alexandre	12-Dec-1965
LUTZ Félix	05-Oct-2013
LYNCH Daniel	20-Dec-2019
LYNCH Alexander	26-Dec-1994
LYNN Patrick	08-Feb-1946
LYNOTT John	12-Sep-1971
LYONS John	28-Apr-1964

M

MAASSEN Piet	02-Jun-1961
MABON Ange	06-Mar-2010
MACCARTHY Sean	23-Dec-2011
MACKLE John J	17-Feb-1996
MACKLE T Patrick	13-Jun-2019
MAESSEN Theo	19-Apr-1994
MAGEE Ernest	01-Jul-1997
MAGINN Owen	03-Dec-2006
MAGUIRE Denis	18-Mar-1975
MAGUIRE Joseph	21-Nov-2016
MAGUIRE Maurice	02-Mar-1993
MAHON John	12-Jul-1980
MAHON Philip	11-Jun-1952
MAHONY +William	15-Nov-1994
MAHONY Michael	20-Dec-1966
MAHY Louis	07-Jul-2011
MAHY Marcel	11-Apr-2011
MAISONNEUVE Jean-Marie	08-Feb-1979
MALASSENET Émile	19-Feb-1953
MALEN Cyprien	14-Jan-1885
MALGOIRE Camille	22-May-1911
MALLET Louis-Pierre	29-Jul-1960
MALO Prosper	23-Aug-1977
MALO Raymond	25-Jan-1974
MALVAL Joseph	20-Jun-2000
MANDONNET Victor	30-Sep-1884
MANNING Denis	06-Jul-1992
MANSHANDEN Antonius	17-Feb-2003
MANSHANDEN Cornelius	27-Dec-1991
MANSOUR Auguste	27-Mar-1878
MANSUY Claude	20-Dec-1955
MANZANZA Faustin	19-May-1995
MARCARIE Xalbat	24-Nov-2006
MARCHAIS Frédéric	18-Oct-1920
MARCHANT Louis	03-Jan-1986
MARGERIT François	05-Feb-2019
MARGREITHER Joseph	02-Mar-1945

MARGUERIE Alphonse	23-Oct-1989
MARIANSKI Bernard	29-Nov-2009
MARIN Pascal	25-Feb-2003
MARION BRÉSILLAC +Melchior Marie Joseph de	25-Jun-1859
MARREN John	28-Sep-1937
MARSTEAU Jacques	27-Mar-1983
MARTEL Jean-François	24-Jun-1989
MARTEL Jean-Guy	13-Jul-2015
MARTIN André	20-May-2012
MARTINET Rogatien	09-Dec-1988
MARZIN René	25-Nov-1966
MASSIOT Adrien	30-Dec-1967
MASSON Claude	06-Jul-2014
MASSON Eugène	25-Aug-1964
MATHIEU Albert	14-Jun-2006
MATHIVET Alphonse	05-May-1934
MATHON Laurent	20-Aug-1863
MATTHEWS Alexander	28-Nov-1961
MAUGARD Dominique	19-Jul-1994
MAUGHAN Michael	02-Jul-2001
MAURER Jean	21-Aug-1989
MAURIKS Piet	27-Aug-1958
MAYS Johannes	20-Dec-1961
Mc CORMACK John	24-Mar-2020
McAFEE James A	07-Jan-1985
McANALLY Patrick	29-Jun-2001
McANDREW Anthony	20-Jan-1973
McANDREW John	06-Aug-1987
McANDREW Joseph	31-Jan-2007
McARDLE Francis	09-Jul-2002
McAULEY William	21-Jul-1981
McCABE Francis	04-Sep-2007
McCABE Joseph	10-Apr-1956
McCAFFREY Michael	03-Aug-1940
McCARTHY +John	11-Jun-1975
McCARTHY Bartholomew	17-Jun-2000
McCARTHY Florence	01-Feb-1985
McCARTHY James	13-Oct-2008
McCARTHY James B	21-May-1962
McCARTHY Justin	29-Jul-1976
McCARTHY Maurice	28-Jan-1983
McCARTHY Patrick	22-Jul-1975
McCAULEY Daniel J	19-Oct-1990
McCORMACK George	19-Jun-1965
McCOY Michael	13-Sep-1996

215

McCREANOR John	27-Feb-2007
McCROREY Edward	31-May-1978
McDONAGH Anthony	23-Jan-1994
MCDONAGH Mary (Sadie)	30-Jan-2012
McDONNELL James	23-Aug-1944
McDONNELL Martin	20-Apr-1990
McDONNELL Matthew	03-Jul-1938
McEGAN Michael	18-Jun-2014
McELGUNN John	22-Jul-1966
McENIRY Michael	12-Jul-1961
McEVOY James	19-Jul-1972
McFADDEN Michael	28-Aug-1997
McGAHAN Gerard A	13-Jun-1984
McGETTIGAN James	16-Sep-1932
McGIRR Patrick	20-Dec-1962
McGLINCHEY Michael	11-Dec-2004
McGOVERN Francis J	30-Mar-1922
McGOVERN Francis P	26-Feb-1999
McGOVERN Gregory	27-Dec-2010
McGOVERN Patrick	04-Jun-2015
McGUINNESS John	06-May-1981
McGUIRK James	15-Feb-1966
McHUGH Patrick	05-Apr-1956
McKAY Patrick	03-Apr-1972
McKENNA Michael	16-Feb-1942
MCKENNA Owen	02-May-2022
McKENNA Patrick	28-May-1972
McKENNA Patrick Francis	04-Nov-1962
McKEOGH Christopher	02-Jun-2011
McKEOWN Hugh	08-Oct-2011
McKEOWN Kevin	10-Feb-1981
McLAUGHLIN Hugh	13-May-2013
McLAUGHLIN Hugh A	14-Sep-1992
McLOUGHLIN Michael	28-Jul-1983
McMAHON Margaret	23-Apr-2019
McNAMARA Francis	26-Jan-1959
MCNEELY Martin	22-Sep-2010
McNEILL Leo P	03-Oct-1986
McNICHOLAS James	01-Jan-1939
McPARTLAND Michael	06-Apr-2017
McSWEENEY Eugene	19-Nov-1966
MEDER Ignace	10-Aug-1920
MEEHAN Francis	18-Aug-2017
MEELBERG Willem	27-Aug-1960
MEERTENS Laurent	06-Nov-1966
MEEUWENOORD Piet	26-Mar-1989
MEEUWSEN Antoon	17-Mar-1962
MÉHEUST Jean-Louis	18-Aug-1911
MÉNAGER +Ernest-Marie	30-Sep-1912
MÉNAGER Aristide	25-Jun-1906
MÉNAGER Jean	13-May-1905
MÉNARD Frédéric	24-Sep-1988
MÉNARD René	14-Oct-2008
MENSINK Johan	19-May-1992
MÉRAUD Pierre	20-Oct-1958
MERCIER Victor	11-Feb-2004
MERLAUD Eugène	24-Dec-1944
MERLINI Ferdinando	27-Dec-1889
MESSNER Pierre	15-Nov-2010
MESTER Théodore	25-Nov-1902
MÉTAYER Marcel	20-Oct-1948
MEULEPAS Jan	02-Apr-1997
MEURDERS Lambert	21-Nov-2014
MEY Albert	26-May-1981
MEYER Georges	26-Dec-1900
MEYER Joseph	07-Nov-1995
MEYER Jules	28-Aug-1973
MEYNIER Jean	10-Oct-1992
MEYRANX Denis	01-Jul-1871
MICHAŁEK Jean	16-Aug-1944
MICHAUD Jean-Pierre	28-Mar-2023
MICHAUD Joseph	07-Feb-2001
MICHON +Jean-Marie	24-Apr-1895
MICOUD Marius	16-Jun-1967
MIESSEN Peter	10-Jun-1883
MIET Joseph	07-Feb-1972
MINIHANE Denis	12-Feb-1990
MINKER Georges	01-Mar-1966
MITTAINE Joseph	23-Mar-2003
MOCKERS René	24-Jun-1983
MOISON Victor	08-Jan-1933
MOLENAARS Kees	16-May-1908
MOLLIER François	06-Apr-1916
MOLLIER Louis	22-May-1899
MOLLIER Pierre	28-May-1902
MOLLOY Robert J	08-Apr-2005
MOLY Léon	30-Dec-1935
MONAHAN John Michael	02-Nov-1962
MONDÉ Henricus P	26-Dec-1985
MONKEL Ate	11-Nov-1961
MONNEY Joseph	27-Sep-1947

MONNEY Pierre	12-Nov-1939
MONNOYEUR Gratien	13-Jun-1859
MONPOINT Célestin	16-Jan-1941
MONTAGUT Jacques	09-May-1977
MONTANARO + Guido	27-Oct-2009
MONTEL Barthélemy	08-Oct-1966
MONTICONE Giuseppe	21-Aug-1972
MOONEN Louis	20-Jan-1989
MOONEN Sef	06-Oct-1990
MOONEY John P	08-Aug-1959
MOORE John	20-Jan-2010
MOORE Peter	23-Jun-1976
MOORE Vincent	28-Oct-1940
MOORHEAD John	13-Mar-1988
MOORHEAD Michael	13-Aug-1992
MORAN Jeremiah	07-Aug-1887
MORAN John	29-Sep-1974
MORAN Thomas	24-Nov-1989
MOREAU Auguste	21-Mar-1886
MOREAU Auguste-Joseph	12-Jul-1912
MOREAU Louis-Marie	30-Sep-2016
MORILLON Pierre	25-Jul-2014
MORISSEAU Claude	09-Jun-1975
MORITZ Roger	29-Jun-2019
MORON Séraphin	01-Jun-1950
MORRIS Malachy	11-Apr-1974
MORRISON James	30-Aug-1994
MORTON John	20-Nov-1960
MORY Joseph	14-Aug-1896
MOSSER Emile	03-Apr-1895
MOUESCA Gabriel	28-May-2020
MOUËZY Henri	03-Mar-1963
MOULIAN Joseph	30-Apr-2019
MOULIN Ernest	08-Jun-2019
MOUNIER Jean	12-Dec-1903
MOUREN Joseph	29-Jan-1975
MOURY +Jules	29-Mar-1935
MOUTERDE Nicolas	19-Nov-2013
MOYLAN Patrick	18-May-1945
MUCKENSTURM Joseph	27-Nov-1974
MULCAHY David	13-Sep-1991
MULDERS Joseph	26-Apr-1962
MULLAHY Thomas	05-Dec-2013
MULLER Joseph	18-Jul-1931
MULLER Nicolas	07-May-1962
MULLINS Joseph	30-Nov-1992

MULVEY John Vincent	06-May-1993
MUNCH Emile	07-Jan-1908
MUNTZINGER Philippe	08-Aug-1927
MURAT Eugène	05-Aug-1880
MURPHY Anthony L	02-Apr-1999
MURPHY Christopher	30-Jan-2007
MURPHY Cornelius D	02-Mar-1982
MURPHY Daniel	19-Oct-2014
MURPHY Edward	04-Dec-1937
MURPHY Francis	19-Aug-2002
MURPHY James	17-Apr-1981
MURPHY John M	24-Apr-1977
MURPHY John P	20-Aug-1964
MURPHY Patrick J	15-Jan-1991
MURPHY Patrick J	08-Jul-1997
MURPHY Stephen	29-Mar-1985
MURPHY William	06-Oct-1971
MURRAY Brendan	07-Mar-1996
MURRAY John F	09-Jul-2015
MURRAY Sylvester John	17-May-1996
MURRAY Thomas	22-Feb-1971
MURTAGH John	02-Jun-1980
MUTSCHLER Edmond	20-Jan-1943
MUYSER Jacob	16-Apr-1956
MYARD Jean	18-Dec-1955

N

NADORP Martin	17-Apr-1970
NADORP Koos	21-Oct-1975
NAEGEL Eugène	12-Feb-1949
NAMDEGANAMNA Barthélémy	16-Sep-2014
NASSER Louis	31-Jan-1997
NAUS Harrie	13-Dec-1985
NAYAGAM Peter Pandi	23-Jan-2017
NEAU Henri	04-Nov-2007
NÉDÉLEC Jean-Paul	18-Jan-1979
NEEFJES Piet	07-Sep-1992
NELLY Fintan P	19-Jan-1999
NETH André	27-Jun-2005
NEU Jules	27-Nov-1937
NEYME Joseph	10-Apr-1998
NGAÏZOURE Amos	03-Oct-2015
NICOLAÏ Aloyse	19-Oct-1915
NIEL Clovis	02-Jul-1996
NOCHÉ Hector	01-Jul-1864
NOËL Louis	19-Mar-1978
NOËL François	24-Sep-1990

NOHILLY Michael	27-Sep-2022
NOLAN Martin	29-Jan-2013
NOLAN Benedict	20-Jun-1997
NOLAN Alphonse	17-Oct-1880
NONNENMACHER Joseph	13-Jan-1993
NOURY Lucien	13-Oct-1990
NOUVEL Jules	08-Apr-1908
NULAND Harry van	09-Apr-1994
NUSS Philippe	10-Jul-1992

O

O'BRIEN Daniel J	07-Apr-2020
O'BRIEN John V	25-Jun-1998
O'CALLAGHAN Liam	05-Apr-2014
O'CARROLL Michael	22-Feb-1881
O'CONNELL Daniel	04-Jan-1978
O'CONNELL James	04-Aug-2009
O'CONNELL Jeremiah P	17-Aug-2016
O'CONNELL Patrick	19-Jun-1964
O'CONNELL Peter J	17-Jan-1984
O'CONNELL Seán	26-Nov-2003
O'CONNOR Daniel J	28-Aug-2002
O'CONNOR Denis	20-May-1957
O'CONNOR Donal Michael	31-May-2013
O'CONNOR Thomas	03-Mar-1986
O'DOHERTY John	22-Mar-1970
O'DONNELL Anthony	20-Dec-2010
O'DONNELL Michael	30-Mar-1893
O'DONNELL Thomas	16-Jan-1980
O'DONOGHUE Patrick	09-Apr-1987
O'DONOHUE Michael	05-Nov-1935
O'DONOVAN Denis J	03-Nov-2000
O'DRISCOLL Cornelius	20-Nov-2005
O'DRISCOLL Florence	07-Nov-1935
O'DRISCOLL Timothy	15-Jul-1983
O'DWYER Anthony	05-Oct-1937
O'FLAHERTY John	12-Jul-1959
O'FLYNN Michael	31-Jan-1953
O'HAIRE Ambrose	03-Jun-1976
O'HARA Denis	01-Sep-1921
O'HARA John	25-Jul-1968
O'HARA Patrick	15-Jul-1962
O'HEA Eugène	14-Aug-1934
O'HEA James	17-Mar-2020
O'HERLIHY Patrick	25-Jan-1945
O'KEEFFE Michael	03-Aug-1989

O'LEARY Cornelius	26-Aug-2018
O'LEARY Patrick	20-May-1961
O'LEARY Robert	12-Mar-1972
O'MAHONY Francis	04-May-1995
O'MAHONY John	12-Nov-2008
O'MAHONY Seán	07-Aug-2001
O'MALLEY John	20-Sep-1981
O'MEARA Martin	27-Apr-1992
O'NEILL Daniel J	27-Aug-2016
O'NEILL John	29-Sep-1963
O'NEILL John G	26-Feb-1975
O'NEILL Patrick	31-Jan-2000
O'NEILL Vincent	06-Jun-1996
O'REGAN Robert	21-Aug-2012
O'REILLY James	05-Feb-1981
O'RIORDAN Florence	12-Mar-1976
O'ROURKE +Francis	28-Oct-1938
O'ROURKE Andrew	08-Jan-1967
O'ROURKE-HUGHES Thomas	01-Sep-1987
O'SHAUGHNESSY Thomas	19-Jun-1992
O'SHEA Alphonsus	16-Nov-1979
O'SHEA Elisha	19-Nov-1994
O'SHEA Francis	11-Mar-1970
O'SHEA John	11-May-1971
O'SHEA Kevin	12-Oct-1978
O'SHEA Michael J	29-Jan-1984
O'SHEA Philip	17-Jan-1984
O'SULLIVAN Billy	25-Mar-2013
O'SULLIVAN Christopher (Christy)	01-Feb-2010
O'SULLIVAN Daniel	13-Jul-1930
O'SULLIVAN Denis	02-Apr-1942
O'SULLIVAN James	19-Dec-1996
O'SULLIVAN Owen	03-Jun-1990
O'SULLIVAN Richard	19-Jun-1923
OBDAM Jaap	08-Nov-2004
OBRECHT Gustave	01-Oct-1951
OBRO Robert	23-Apr-2020
OERS Cor van	02-Mar-1993
OGBOGU Sylvester	28-Mar-2018
OGÉ +Jean	16-Nov-1931
OLCZAK Józef	03-Dec-2021
OLIVAIN Eugène	03-Sep-1983
OLIVE Clovis	18-Apr-1952
OLIVONI Alberto	17-Apr-2019
OLLIER Georges	10-Jan-1923
OLLIER Georges	12-Sep-1963
OLLIVAUD Guy	18-Jan-2013

ONGOMA Lawrence N.	31-Aug-2022
ONIMUS Charles	19-Nov-1959
ONUSI Mary Candy	17-Nov-2022
OOIJEN Rudolf van	28-Apr-1975
OOSTENBACH Jan	11-Apr-1978
OP't HOOG Leo	01-Nov-1986
OTTING Beth	29-Jan-2016
OUDHEUSDEN James van	21-Sep-2007

P

PAGÉS Alexandre	19-Jan-1958
PAGÉS Liguori	07-Jul-1880
PAGNON Claude	07-Jul-1893
PAICHOUX Célestin	05-Feb-1958
PALLARÈS Jean	06-Jun-1987
PANIS Louis	29-Sep-1997
PANNETIER Jean-Marie	21-Sep-1913
PAPETARD Adolphe	06-May-1877
PAPIN Jean-Marie	24-Dec-1914
PARAGE Louis	25-Feb-1941
PARIS Maurice	01-Jun-1940
PARISEAU Jean-Paul	22-Mar-2012
PARISOT +Louis	21-Apr-1960
PARRIAUX Joseph	10-Jun-2000
PARTARRIEU Albert	25-Feb-1943
PAS Frans	11-Aug-1975
PASCAL Raymond	17-Feb-2012
PASCH Gerard van de	15-Apr-1980
PASQUEREAU Jacques	30-Jun-1889
PASQUERON DE FOMMERVAULT Henry	14-Jun-1940
PAUGAM Jean	03-Jun-2022
PAULISSEN +HUBERT	12-Aug-1966
PAULUS Robert	25-Nov-1962
PAVAGEAU Maurice	22-May-2005
PAVOORDT Cor van de	20-Sep-1891
PAY Jean	25-Sep-1925
PEETERS Antoon	26-Jul-1970
PEIRSEGAELE Dominique	22-Nov-2016
PELLAT Joseph	17-Nov-1898
PELLET +Paul	11-Mar-1914
PELLET Étienne	24-May-1899
PELLETIER Yves	23-Jan-2012

PÉLOFY Isidore	02-Aug-1953
PELTIER François	28-May-1977
PENKALA Władysław	01-May-2023
PÉRÉS André	10-Aug-1960
PÉREZ GÓMEZ José	06-Apr-2017
PERNOT Henri	18-Jul-1982
PERRAUD Armand	12-Mar-1921
PERRAUD Jean	22-Oct-1902
PERRIN André	17-Oct-2020
PERRIN Jean	06-Nov-2016
PERRIN Paul	28-Dec-1966
PERROCHAUD Louis	06-Feb-2017
PERRONE James	15-Jul-2010
PERSON +François	08-Jul-1938
PESSOZ Joseph	21-Oct-1891
PETER Eugène	30-Nov-1935
PETER Joseph	13-Jul-1985
PETIT André	30-Nov-1870
PETITJEAN Pierre	21-Jan-1988
PEYLE Raymond	21-Dec-2006
PEYVEL François	06-Jul-1968
PFISTER Joseph	14-Mar-1992
PFLEGER Martin	06-Aug-1950
PHILIPPE Joseph	15-Jul-1942
PHILLIPS Gerard	11-Sep-1980
PICHAT Jean	25-Aug-2020
PICHAUD Pierre	09-Mar-1902
PICHON Henri	08-Dec-1976
PIED Joseph	13-May-1899
PIÉDALOS Ferdinand	06-Sep-1914
PIERGENTILI Giovanni	30-Jan-1952
PILLARD Mme Dominique	30-Mar-2016
PINEAU Jean	30-Jul-1879
PIOLAT Pierre	27-May-1886
PIOTIN Pierre	22-Mar-1924
PIRANDA Gilbert	01-Dec-2019
PIREYRE Louis	05-Feb-1947
PIRIOU Yves	29-Jun-1988
PLANQUE Augustin	21-Aug-1907
PLANQUE Joseph	26-Jul-1929
PLAS Cor van der	11-Oct-1973
PLUMELET Francis	02-Feb-2007
POIDEVINEAU Henri	06-Jun-1973
POIRIER Jules	10-Jan-1933
POLOCE Josée	08-Jul-2016
POLYCARPE Louis	06-Aug-1886
PONCET Henri	19-Nov-1896
PORCHEROT Joseph	08-Aug-1974
PORTE Pierre	21-May-1952

PORTER +William	16-Jun-1966
PORTIER Harrie	03-Mar-1992
PORTIER Marie-Marthe	14-Aug-2006
POT Gerard	11-Jan-1982
POTIRON Jean	08-Feb-1972
POTTERS Cornelius	05-Feb-2001
POTTIER Emile	15-Jul-2022
POUPLIN Aimé	01-Apr-1948
POURET Jean-Paul	20-Jan-1883
POUSSIN Alphonse	11-May-1878
POWER John	27-Jun-1992
POWER William	13-Mar-2003
PRADA Marco	05-Jun-2023
PRAT Maurice	29-Dec-2018
PRAUD Ferdinand	07-Oct-1960
PRAUD Julien	22-Feb-1953
PRENDERGAST John	04-Apr-1945
PRIEMS Cornelis Z	19-Jan-2013
PRIGENT Jean	16-Mar-1975
PRINCÉE Theodorus	31-Dec-1981
PRIOUL Ambroise	07-Feb-1945
PRONK Nico	20-Jan-2000
PROU Joseph	08-May-1943
PROVENCHÈRE Antoine	06-Jul-1899
PRUAL François	08-May-1997
PUAUT Joseph	15-Jun-1997
PUECH Barthélemy	04-Mar-1867

Q

QUICKERT Joseph	16-Sep-1941
QUIGNON Jean	04-Nov-1993
QUINLAN John	16-Jul-2020

R

RABILLAT Guy	01-Apr-1964
RADAELLI Natale	29-May-1928
RAESS Eugène-Bernard	28-Apr-1903
RAFFERTY James	28-Apr-1955
RAFFERTY Seaghan	16-Jul-2009
RAINGEARD Joseph	09-Feb-1980
RAJAREEGAM Anthony	18-Apr-2009
RAMAKERS Frans	15-Dec-1995
RAMESH Joseph	27-Jul-2006
RAMIN Jean-Charles	10-Sep-2015
RAMSTEIN Aloysius	06-May-1991
RANCHIN Edouard	26-Apr-1916
RANCHIN Marcel	16-Jun-2014
RAPION Alphonse	12-Jun-2021

RASSER François-Xavier	03-May-1991
RASSER Xavier	08-Jun-1961
RASSINOUX Jean	21-Aug-2023
RAST Louis	13-Apr-1958
RAUNER Aloyse	27-Apr-2012
RAUSCHER Louis	29-Mar-1903
RAVOUX Victor	04-Jun-1932
RAY +Matthieu	13-May-1899
RAY Jean-Baptiste	03-Dec-1943
RAYMOND Bernard	19-Sep-2011
RAYMOND Bernard	25-Jun-2021
RECKMANN Wim	19-Aug-1993
REDDINGTON +John	03-Oct-1994
REDMOND James	25-Feb-2012
REDOIS +Patient	07-Jun-1993
REEKERS Anno	21-Mar-1963
RÉGNIER Félix	22-Dec-2016
RÉGUILLON Pierre	24-Mar-1903
REIBEL Lucien	21-May-1988
REIFF Albert	08-Feb-1992
REIMERT Gerard	02-Jan-1942
REINHARDT Jérôme	02-Aug-1910
REMIRO Zacharias	22-Apr-1976
RÉNIER François	11-Nov-1926
RENOU Jean-Marie	08-Dec-1953
REVEL Bernard	15-Jun-1969
REY Paul	02-Jul-1981
REYMANN Joseph	09-Apr-1926
REYMOND Louis	28-Jun-1859
REYNARD Petrus	23-Sep-2012
REYSER Lucien	25-Aug-2000
RIBAUD Jean-Baptiste	03-Apr-1895
RIBER Alphonse	29-May-1941
RICARD Jacques	12-Jul-1989
RICE Edward	05-Aug-1972
RICHARD Antoine	24-Feb-1980
RICHARD Eugène	10-Jun-1934
RICHARDSON Edward	26-Apr-2008
RICHE Alexandre	30-Apr-1895
RIEBSTEIN Emile	28-Feb-1974
RIEDEL Ernst	25-Oct-1976
RIEDLIN Camille	06-Mar-1963
RIEFFEL Joseph	20-Nov-1910
RIEGERT Aloyse	27-Nov-1968
RIEMER Jérôme	05-Nov-1967
RIJPKEMA Arjen	25-Aug-2017
RIMLÉ Johann Baptist	08-Jul-1962
RING Jeremiah	30-Jul-1976

RIOCREUX Louis 02-Jun-1859
RIORDAN Eugene 17-Jul-2016
RIVAL Paul 13-Jun-1995
ROBERT Michel 16-Aug-2001
ROBERT René 13-Aug-1984
ROCHE Michael 29-Oct-1946
ROCHER Yves 22-Jun-2003
ROCHERY Jean-Marie 18-Jul-1985
RODGERS John 08-Aug-2001
ROELOFS Albert 12-Jul-1955
ROESCH Albert 05-Oct-1951
ROGERS Peter 01-Mar-1947
ROLLAND Louis 24-Jun-2014
ROLT Thomas 26-Mar-1938
ROMAGON Louis 26-Apr-1968
ROMANIAK Pierre 26-Jan-1996
ROMEO Vincenzo 17-May-1891
ROOIJ Gerardus van 26-Nov-1960
ROONEY Michael J 01-Nov-2001
ROOY Johannes de 30-Aug-1980
ROOY Theodorus de 24-Jul-1991
ROOY Wilhelmus de 05-Nov-1986
ROPELEWSKI Alfred 19-Nov-1997
ROSIER Jean-Baptiste 30-Jun-2004
ROSTOUCHER Paul 07-Aug-2011
ROTH Joseph 21-Aug-1985
ROTH Rolph 12-Dec-2007
ROTHOFF Frans 29-Nov-1976
ROTHOFF Henri 11-Nov-1942
ROTHOFF Johannes 08-Mar-1969
ROUANET +Pierre 04-Feb-2012
ROUÉ Louis 14-Jul-1973
ROUFFIAC Paul 21-May-1914
ROUGER Mélaine 25-Mar-1969
ROULIN Marcel 02-Jul-2000
ROUMIER Jean-Louis 07-Nov-1986
ROUSSEAU Jean- 12-Jul-1926
   Baptiste
ROUSSEL Claudius 07-Jan-1965
ROUSSELET Adolphe 18-May-1936
ROUX André 09-Jun-1997
ROUX Joseph 30-Jun-1992
ROWAN Michael 08-Apr-1939
ROY Cornelius de 31-Jan-1966
ROY Joël 02-Jul-1996
ROZE Michel 13-Dec-1990
RUAULT Édouard 02-Jun-1876
RUBIE Hendrik 18-Mar-1982
RUBLON Victor 17-Dec-1986
RUIKES Wim 08-Nov-1996
RUSSELL Henry P J 30-Mar-1992

RUYLING Wynand 22-Sep-2001
RYAN Desmond 02-Feb-1926
RYAN Sean 22-Feb-2014

S

SABOT Barthélemy 22-Sep-1930
SADELER Pierre 07-Sep-1887
SAECKINGER Louis 25-Jul-1930
SAGNI René 20-Apr-1997
SAHAYARAJ 04-Apr-1999
SALAÜN Jean-Marie 14-Feb-1980
SAMUELS Wout 13-Jan-1985
SANDERS Charles 01-Oct-2017
SANDERS Henricus 27-Dec-1983
SANDERS Petrus 10-Dec-1994
SANDS Francis 19-Oct-1949
SANTOS Bembolio de 07-Jul-2011
   los
SAPET François 25-Dec-1958
SARRÁ Bartolomé 09-Nov-1912
SAUBAN Adolphe 23-Nov-1972
SAUER Ernest 27-Dec-1973
SAUL James 07-Mar-1978
SAVÉAN Jules 30-Aug-1978
SCANLAN Kevin 14-Apr-2001
SCANLAN P Gerard 05-Sep-2002
SCHAEFFER Eugène 26-Nov-1959
SCHAHL Alphonse 16-Dec-1969
SCHEIER Nicolas 14-Mar-1906
SCHELCHER Donat 19-Sep-1919
SCHELTINGA 27-May-2003
   Cornelius
SCHENKEL Peter 24-May-1897
SCHERRER Michel 27-May-1940
SCHIMPFF Casimir 20-Jan-1920
SCHLECHT Edmond 09-Sep-1942
SCHMIDT Joseph 15-Aug-1953
SCHMITT Bernard 22-Oct-1935
SCHMITT Émile 10-Oct-1940
   Joseph
SCHMITT Émile 11-Oct-1941
   Nicolas
SCHMITT Pierre 18-Apr-2003
SCHNEIDER Claude 23-Aug-1994
SCHNEIDER Henri 07-Oct-1996
SCHNEIDER Marcel 15-May-2022
SCHNEIDER Marie 30-Jul-2017
   Reine
SCHOEN Henri 02-Sep-1945
SCHOONEN Adrien 05-Dec-1958
SCHROD Alois 24-Sep-1900

SCHUH Michel	02-Jun-1944
SCHUMACHER Charles	24-Mar-1909
SCHUR Jean-Paul	27-Apr-1989
SCIAMMA Gabriel	10-Oct-1990
SCIAVI Emile	13-Aug-1951
SCULLY Michael	13-May-1959
SÉBILO Jean-Marie	13-May-2013
SÉCHER Alexis	25-Sep-1915
SÉDANT Pierre	02-Feb-1895
SEGUROLA Basilio	10-May-1989
SEILER Pie	04-Apr-1992
SELZER Georges	20-Oct-2022
SENISE Zadio	15-Dec-2017
SERENNE Emmanuel	17-May-1924
SEVRIENS Harrie	30-Apr-1968
SEVRIENS Jan	24-Aug-1964
SHEEHAN Jerome	03-Jul-1981
SHEEHAN John	06-Jul-1965
SHEEHAN John J	05-Oct-2006
SHEEHAN Patrick	27-Nov-1906
SHEEHAN William	11-May-1990
SHEEHY John	22-Sep-1966
SHEPPARD Henry	21-Oct-1981
SHINE Patrick	22-Aug-1975
SHINE William	09-May-1914
SICARD Jacques	26-Sep-2022
SILKE Leo E	16-Apr-2021
SIMON Aimé	25-Oct-1961
SIMON Auguste	05-Oct-1906
SIMON Paul	20-Dec-2020
SIMON Robert	03-May-1968
SIMPLEX Joseph	29-Nov-1900
SINGER Marcel	01-Dec-2002
SIRLINGER Eugène	10-Apr-1978
SIRONI Celso	17-May-1928
SITTLER Alphonse	17-Feb-1973
SITZMANN François-Xavier	09-Jul-1959
SKELLY Laurence	20-Jan-2005
SLATTERY Denis	07-Jul-2003
SLATTERY Maurice	11-May-1957
SLOOTS Theo	23-Jun-1982
SMEELE Henk	08-Apr-1986
SMEELE Jacobus	13-Nov-2013
SMETS Henk	20-Jun-1984
SMETZERS Antoon	22-Aug-1933
SMITH Oliver	06-Apr-2005
SMITS Harrie	18-Nov-1989
SMITS Johannes	08-May-2011
SOULÉ Bernard	25-Sep-1970

SOUTBERG Henk	21-Jan-1986
SPAMPINATI Joseph	17-May-1980
SPEITEL Joseph	01-May-2003
SPIESER Charles	09-Jan-1902
SPRONCK Frans	14-Jun-2006
SPRUNCK Jean-Pierre	21-Jun-1969
STADELWIESER Émile	29-Oct-1981
STAMM Joseph	17-Apr-1945
STANLEY James	27-May-1970
STAUFF Camille	28-Oct-1997
STAUFFER Joseph	21-Oct-1952
STEBER Ernest	07-May-1898
STECK Alphonse	04-Jan-1972
STEEMERS Nico	11-Feb-1981
STEFANACHI Mme Tina	12-Jan-2008
STEINER Frédéric	11-May-1993
STEINMETZ +François	29-Mar-1952
STEINMETZ Justin	26-May-1944
STÉPHAN Roger	09-May-2003
STEPHENS Joseph	05-Feb-1989
STITT Robert	13-Jan-1960
STOFFELS André	05-Apr-2004
STOLZ Valentin	13-Jul-1915
STREBLER +Joseph	12-Mar-1984
STRIEN Piet van	11-Jan-1967
STRUB Eugène	28-Dec-1939
STUDER Joseph	24-Mar-1904
STYLES S Joseph	22-Jul-1992
SUIJKERBUIJK Adrie	27-Sep-1974
SULLIVAN James Harold	15-Sep-2008
SULTZBERGER Ernst	22-Mar-1900
SWEENEY Owen F	12-Oct-2003
SWEENEY Seán	09-Dec-1999
SWIERKOWSKI Czesław	17-Mar-1989
SZMANIA Bolesław	23-Apr-1984

T

TACCHINI Luigi	12-Sep-1937
TAVERNIER Léon	10-Jan-1987
TAYLOR + Leo	27-Oct-1965
TAYLOR Claude	08-Apr-1958
TEILLET Gaston	02-Apr-1957
TEKRY KOKORA Noël	09-Aug-2001
TEMPLE Claude	30-Jul-2014
TERRIEN +Ferdinand	03-Aug-1929

TERRIEN Ferdinand	07-Nov-1907
TETTAMANTI Antonio	11-Mar-1885
TEVOEDJIRE Albert	06-Nov-2019
TEYSSIER Louis	18-May-1899
THÉBAULT Jean	14-Jan-2022
THEIZEN Henri	17-Feb-2008
THÉPAUT Jean	01-Nov-1980
THÊTE Eugène	03-Feb-1951
THIBAUD Henri	04-Feb-1939
THIBAUD Robert	30-Aug-1996
THILLIER Joseph	28-Dec-1875
THOLLON Gonzague	06-Mar-1871
THOMAS Henri	16-Jan-1983
THOMAS M. Antoine	21-Jan-2016
THUET Jean-Baptiste	25-Jun-1936
TIGEOT Jules	27-Feb-1947
TILLEMAN Julien	27-Jan-1961
TILLIE Alfons	13-Dec-1941
TILLIE Jan	23-Feb-2005
TIMOTHY Mlle Anne	28-Jun-2001
TOBIN James	28-Nov-1968
TOBIN Richard	15-Dec-1977
TOLAN Patrick	30-Nov-1971
TONER Gerald A J	21-Apr-2022
TONER Michael	02-Jun-1994
TOURILLON Jean-Marie	30-Dec-1969
TOUSSAINT Jacques	01-Aug-2000
TOUSSAINT Jean	02-Mar-1982
TRANCHANT Louis	19-May-1915
TRANCHANT Théodore	12-Jun-1958
TRAVERS John A	02-Oct-2017
TREACY Thomas J	11-Dec-2021
TRICHET Pierre	19-Oct-2006
TRICHET Pierre	13-Sep-2016
TRIEPELS James	26-May-1990
TRIGT Frits van	03-May-1978
TROCONIZ Candido	26-Apr-1986
TRUHAND Jean-Baptiste	27-May-1939
TUKKER Kees	08-Jan-1973
TULASNE Auguste	23-May-1881
TURCOTTE Albert	10-Jan-1982
TYNAN Claire	20-Jun-2009

U

UBBIALI Giacomo	02-Apr-2008
ULRICH Georges	06-Feb-1892
URVOY Jean Baptiste	26-Jan-1998
UUM Joseph van	14-Jan-2017

V

VACHER Pierre	23-Apr-1873
VACHERET Charles	30-Jan-1923
VACHON Antoine	19-Feb-1915
VAES Jan	22-Apr-1974
VALENTIN Josephus Petrus	19-Aug-2014
VALÉRO Antoine	08-Aug-2006
VALLÉE Emile	22-Jun-1927
VALLÉE Joseph	02-Mar-1963
VANDAELE Charles	01-May-1968
VANLEKE Henri	09-Apr-1912
VAROQUI Jacques	18-Feb-2013
VAUTHIER Gabriel	04-Feb-1979
VEASEY Richard D	08-Nov-1993
VEEN Jacques van	31-Jul-2000
VEIJFEIJKEN Frits van	21-Oct-2000
VEILLARD Ambroise	10-Feb-2003
VELDBOER Theodorus	21-May-2003
VELZEN Han van	18-Nov-2005
VEN Hans van de	06-Mar-1985
VEN Harrie van de	25-Dec-1964
VENESSY Benoît	22-May-1886
VENGEANT Eugène Louis	05-Nov-1980
VENHOVENS Theo	17-Mar-1983
VERDELET Jean	29-Apr-1869
VERGER Francis	20-Sep-1979
VERHAGEN Franciscus	15-Jul-1974
VERHAGEN Jan	27-Nov-1965
VERHEUGD Jacques	26-Feb-1979
VERHILLE Daniel	03-May-1983
VÉRICEL Roger	10-Aug-2020
VERMOREL Claude	20-Apr-1869
VERMOREL Émile	10-Apr-1896
VERMULST Henri	28-Mar-1924
VERMULST Laurens	27-Jan-1970
VÉROT Paul	24-Dec-2012
VERREUSSEL Hubertus	03-May-2015
VERSPEEK Hein	13-Sep-1996
VERSPEEK Johan	04-Nov-2008
VERT Jean	29-Oct-1952
VEST Jean-Baptiste	01-Mar-1954
VEYRET Alexis	14-Oct-1871
VIALLE Théodore	21-Feb-1898

VIAUD Gérard	24-Jul-2008
VIAUD Louis	15-Nov-1996
VIGNA Albert	17-May-1899
VILLAÇA Théophile	27-Jan-2014
VILLEVAUD Francis	29-Nov-1942
VINET Séraphin	18-Jul-1981
VINSONNEAU Jean	28-Mar-1950
VION Étienne	29-Jun-1938
VISSER Jacobus	02-Dec-1988
VIVIER Max	17-Jan-2020
VOGEL Jean-Paul	12-Aug-1942
VOGEL Joseph	06-Jul-1942
VOGEL Joseph	03-Aug-1981
VOGT Georges	07-Dec-1934
VOIT Jean-Baptiste	14-Aug-1901
VOLARD Gérard	29-Jun-2010
VOLTZ Joseph	22-Dec-1894
VONAU Alphonse	14-Jun-1901
VONDERSCHER Bernard	28-Oct-2017
VONVILLE Auguste	30-May-1901
VONWYL Edouard	26-Dec-1999
VOUILLON Louis	16-Apr-1958
VREEZE Rinke de	27-Jul-2021
VRIES Petrus de	22-Jul-2004
VUGTS Harrie	06-Nov-1936

W

WACH +Louis	09-Apr-1983
WACHT René	27-Aug-1995
WACK Michel	06-Jul-2008
WADE Michael	15-Apr-1898
WAGEMAKERS Johannes Th	16-Mar-2015
WALKER Leonard	26-Feb-2001
WALKER Michael	02-Sep-1970
WALKOWIAK Konrad	15-Apr-1997
WALLER +Oswald	06-Jul-1939
WALLON Joseph	26-Oct-1961
WALSH Martin J	29-Jul-2014
WALSH Martin John	24-May-1946
WALSH Matthew	30-Oct-1995
WALSH Maurice	21-May-1969
WALSH Michael A	15-Nov-1990
WALSH Michael J	30-Apr-2000
WALTER Freda M	30-Aug-1993
WARD Edward	22-Apr-1942
WARD James	02-Dec-1946
WATERREUS Johannes	12-Dec-1987
WATSON Daniel	07-Oct-1961

WEBER Albert	10-Dec-2010
WEBER Nicolas	23-Sep-1990
WEIJDEN Gerard van de	14-Jan-1998
WEISS Francis	01-Feb-1946
WELLINGER Henri	16-Sep-1930
WELSCH Paul	04-Jul-1966
WELTERLIN Xavier	07-Apr-1976
WENDERS Piet	20-Nov-2017
WERLÉ Joseph	20-Jan-1944
WERLÉ Victor	14-Dec-1986
WERLY Jacques	12-Jun-1900
WERNERT Joseph	26-Oct-1966
WESSELING Maarten	05-Feb-2011
WEST Charles	30-Aug-1969
WESTENBROEK Thijs	29-Mar-1979
WEVER Tamis	19-Mar-2004
WHELAN Patrick	10-Feb-2012
WHITE Eric	14-Aug-1973
WHITTAKER James	04-Feb-1995
WHYTE Martin	21-Jun-1989
WICKY Eugène	23-Jun-1978
WIDLOECHER André	29-Apr-1987
WIEDER Antoine	20-Oct-1960
WIEGGERS Bernard	22-Dec-1999
WIJNANS Hubert	28-Jan-1991
WILHELM Gilbert	01-Jun-2007
WINDEN Paulus van	22-Aug-2011
WINGERTSZAHN Joseph	08-Apr-1952
WISEMAN Robert V	29-Jan-2003
WOELFFEL Eugène	12-Sep-1992
WOERTH Joseph	30-Mar-1904
WOISSELIN Charles	23-Mar-1977
WOLFF +Edmond	04-Aug-1939
WOLFF Alphonse	21-Jun-1935
WOLFF Benno	15-Aug-1996
WOLFF Joseph	23-May-1953
WOOD John	17-Mar-1964
WOODLEY Stephen	30-Apr-1936
WOUTERS Mathieu	13-Mar-1962
WOUTERS Piet	21-Aug-1982
WURTH Victor	08-Sep-1923
WYNNE Eugene	13-Feb-1937

Y

YATES Clark	03-Jan-2013
YÈCHE Georges	17-Jul-2007
YOUNG Francis	17-Jan-1932
YOUNG James V	27-Mar-1984

Z

ZANCHI Jean-Baptiste	06-Mar-2020
ZAPPA Carlo	30-Jan-1917
ZERR Kilien	02-Feb-1939
ZERRINGER Pierre	02-Jul-1968
ZIELIŃSKI Joseph	03-Jan-1985
ZIJLSTRA Rudolf	25-Apr-1969
ZIJLSTRA Willy	28-Jan-2023
ZIMMERMANN Édouard	16-Jan-1929
ZIMMERMANN Joseph	19-Jul-1921
ZOSSO Pierre Canisius	26-Apr-2010
ZUCCARINO +Pietro	24-Aug-1973
ZUIDWIJK Louis	27-Oct-1988

Printed in Great Britain
by Amazon

31769193R00126